DATE DUE

DE 6'00			
DE 20'00			
JE 11'01			
AG 8'02			
OC 14'03			

DEMCO 38-296

THE MYTH OF THE GLOBAL CORPORATION

THE MYTH OF THE
GLOBAL CORPORATION

PAUL N. DOREMUS
WILLIAM W. KELLER
LOUIS W. PAULY
SIMON REICH

PRINCETON UNIVERSITY PRESS

PRINCETON, NEW JERSEY

Copyright © 1998 by Princeton University Press

41 William Street,

rsity Press,

ʍ Data

The myth of the global corporation / Paul N. Doremus . . . [et al.]
p.   cm.
Includes bibliographical references and index.
ISBN 0-691-03636-5 (alk. paper)
1. International business enterprises.   2. Competition,
International.   I. Doremus, Paul N., 1960–
HD2755.5.M96 1998
338.8'8—dc21   97-18349   CIP

This book has been composed in Palatino Typeface

Princeton University Press books are printed
on acid-free paper and meet the guidelines for
permanence and durability of the Committee on
Production Guidelines for Book Longevity
of the Council on Library Resources

http://pup.princeton.edu

Printed in the United States of America

10   9   8   7   6   5   4   3   2

CONTENTS

TABLES AND FIGURES

TABLES

FIGURES

PREFACE

IS THE WORLD coming apart or pulling together? In their own ways, and with a heightened sense of urgency, many business executives, policymakers, and scholars are once again asking themselves this question. When the forces of economic liberalization and the spread of democracy coexist with the resurgence of an ideology of exclusive nationalism in many corners of the world, the answer in political terms is not obvious.

Scholars who study the complex interaction between the political and economic forces reshaping the environment in which we live recognize that the answer is far from clear. In country after country, politics seems to be reshaping itself in response to both centripetal and centrifugal pressures. Rising demands for cultural and social autonomy coincide with movements toward larger-scale institutions for regional or international economic governance. The interaction of such contrary phenomena has become the focal point for much research and debate. Central to that debate is the assertion that economic policy and policymaking are indeed being pushed by deep technological, industrial, and financial forces inexorably beyond the geographic and psychological borders of the traditional nation-state. The image that best crystallizes those forces for policymakers, citizens, and scholars alike is that of the multinational corporation, massive commercial hierarchies whose far-flung activities appear to constitute the very sinews of a global economy.

Both the assertion of deep change in national policies in an era of globalization and the image of the truly global corporation revolve around the idea of structural convergence, which is defined mainly in economic terms. This book confronts that idea by taking a fresh look at the operations of multinational corporations at a time when political power in the world is dispersing and international economic competition is intensifying. Our exploration casts doubt on conventional views of the nature of contemporary change in the international economic system and uncovers sources of resistance to globalization in some surprising places.

This book is very much a collaborative effort among the four of us. Keller originally pulled us together and led us through thick and thin. Pauly focused our attention in the end and took on the task of editing, reworking, and integrating the final text. In between, we worked as a team. At the conclusion of a long journey that actually began for us all at Cornell many years ago—and after too many drafts, too many

E-mail conversations, and too many mainly friendly arguments—we claim collective ownership of the text. Individual contributions are now buried under layers of joint effort, a fact reflected in the alphabetical listing of our names. That said, of course, we each reserve the right privately to take credit for anything that is good in the book and to blame one another for any errors of fact or judgment.

Much of the empirical evidence presented below is drawn from governmental databases, some of which we assembled ourselves while in government service. For this book, we have updated those sources to the extent feasible with data available as of early 1997. Other material was systematically culled from extant research in comparative business studies. All of the evidence is assessed in light of inferences drawn from an extensive series of confidential interviews we undertook with senior executives from multinational corporations and with government officials in Japan, Europe, and the United States from 1992 through 1994. More selectively, and in the context of subsequent research carried out individually by the authors in 1995 and 1996, those inferences were refined through interviews with business leaders in the United States, Canada, Germany, Belgium, Japan, Taiwan, South Korea, and China. Wherever possible, we have preferred to cite publicly available and accessible corroborative evidence.

The genesis of this book lies in two extensive reports completed by the Office of Technology Assessment (OTA) of the United States Congress in 1993 and 1994.* The authors were members of the OTA project team. The OTA had provided balanced, nonpartisan policy analysis to congressional committees for over twenty years. It was internationally acclaimed for its ability to evaluate the impact of technological change on the economy, society, environment, and polity. We are proud to have been associated with it.

Nevertheless, in the highly charged ideological fervor that swept Capitol Hill in 1995, Congress decided to eliminate the OTA. It did so at a time when barriers to trade and investment were falling or subtly changing in many countries, and when competition among firms and nations increasingly focused on the race for technological advantage in

---

* U.S. Congress, Office of Technology Assessment, *Multinationals and the National Interest: Playing by Different Rules*, OTA-ITE-569, Washington, D.C.: U.S. Government Printing Office, September 1993; and U.S. Congress, Office of Technology Assessment, *Multinationals and the U.S. Technology Base*, OTA-ITE-612 (Washington, D.C.: U.S. Government Printing Office, September 1994). Pauly and Reich built on part of this work in "National Structures and Multinational Corporate Behavior: Enduring Differences in the Age of Globalization," *International Organization*, vol. 51, no. 1 (Winter 1997) pp. 1–30. © 1997 by the IO Foundation and the Massachusetts Institute of Technology. We are grateful to the journal for permission to adapt and reprint some of that material in this book.

a wide range of multinational industries. As we continued to conduct research for this book from 1995 through 1997, we were often greeted by foreign observers with incredulity that Congress would destroy its capacity to assess the impact of technological change when such change is accelerating and rendering the task of governance ever more complicated.

We thank the many business executives, government officials, and scholars who commented, often critically, on the original OTA reports and several drafts of this book. Special efforts were made by Jonathan Aronson, Audrey Buyrn, Alfred Chandler, Benjamin J. Cohen, Jonathan Crystal, Michael Donnelly, Carol V. Evans, Kenneth Freeman, Lawrence Friedman, Robert Gilpin, William Greider, Richard Heimlich, Robert Hermann, Lionel S. Johns, Peter Katzenstein, Carl Kester, Stephen Krasner, Theodore Lowi, Bud Marx, Michael Mastanduno, Helen Milner, William Mulholland, John Odell, William Reinsch, John D. Rockefeller IV, Richard Samuels, Harley Shaiken, Ulrike Schaede, Susan Strange, Raymond Vernon, Andrew Wyckoff, John Zysman, and several anonymous reviewers. None of these individuals, however, bears the slightest responsibility for this book. Moreover, the endorsement of no agency of the United States government is intended or implied.

At various stages, much-appreciated research assistance came from Jo-Anne Gestrin, Yoshiko Koda, Viktoria Murphy, Thomas Nevins, and Arik Preis. Throughout the later stages of the project, Pauly benefited from interdisciplinary debates with his colleagues at the Center for International Studies at the University of Toronto as well as from a research grant from the Social Sciences and Humanities Research Council of Canada, and Reich was assisted by a fellowship from the Council on Foreign Relations and a grant from the Sloan Foundation.

Walter Lippincott and Malcolm Litchfield of Princeton University Press should get an award both for their enthusiasm and their patience. Finally, we are all deeply grateful to Colleen, Lonna, Caryl, Linda, and our children. With grace and more understanding than we deserve, they endured our travels and our recurrent deadlines. Even more importantly, they gave us a reason.

The Authors
Cambridge, Massachusetts

THE MYTH OF THE GLOBAL CORPORATION

Chapter 1

NATIONAL FIRMS IN GLOBAL COMMERCE

W ITHOUT stable political foundations, markets collapse. Following years of depression and world war earlier in this century, the United States and its allies rebuilt an international economy around such an insight. Fifty years later, however, multinational business is often viewed, by proponents and critics alike, as providing a more solid foundation for a truly global economy than governments ever could. The increasingly common view today is that political authorities are relegated to the role of adapting themselves, as well as the societies over which they have receding control, to the convergent logic of an integrated, worldwide technology base crafted in significant part by corporations that owe allegiance to no state.

This book presents a very different view. In contrast to expectations now common both inside and outside the academy, the book finds evidence of the enduring influence of national structures within the home states of the world's leading corporations. Those structures continue to account for striking diversity in the character of core operations undertaken by those corporations.

Spreading the benefits of economic development and technological innovation may indeed be required to achieve and maintain peace and prosperity. But the proliferation of multinational corporations (MNCs) does not guarantee such an outcome. Despite intensifying international competition, MNCs are not promoting the ineluctable convergence and integration of national systems of innovation, trade, and investment, nor are they forcing deep convergence in the national economies in which they are embedded. They cannot do so because they themselves are not converging toward global behavioral norms.

Surface similarities in the behavior of MNCs abound. Companies selling goods or services in the same markets do have much in common, and the range of cross-border mergers and acquisitions has broadened significantly in recent decades. At root, however, the most strategically significant operations of MNCs continue to vary systematically along national lines. The global corporation, adrift from its national political moorings and roaming an increasingly borderless world market, is a myth. States charter MNCs and shape the operating environment in which they flourish. States retain the political authority to steer their activities.

Variance in the application of actual governmental power in that process of steering is particularly apparent in comparisons among the United States, Germany, and Japan. In the contemporary era, these three home states remain the territorial bases for the vast majority of the world's leading multinational firms. In each case, enduring national political structures continue to shape the operations that most decisively determine the futures of those corporations—their internal governance and long-term financing operations, their research and development (R&D) programs, and their direct investment and intrafirm trading strategies. At the core of the world's leading multinationals, in short, there is no such thing as globalization; indeed, the empirical evidence suggests durable sources of resistance.[1] This has profound implications for the way policymakers, business leaders, scholars, and citizens should think about the changing world economy. At a time when critics are seeking points of resistance to pressures associated with the word *globalization*, we find systematic national differentation inside the very corporations that many believe to be the progenitors of a new global economic infrastructure.

THE APPEARANCE OF CONVERGENCE

The nature and extent of structural convergence in the economic realm should be highly sensitive to the global operations of MNCs. If national economies are pulling together and not coming apart, support should be found among the business vehicles that most prominently appear to be weaving tightening webs of interdependence. Multinational corporate executives certainly speak in this way. From them, we hear constantly about the emergence of global markets, the globalization of industrial sectors, the potential of unimpeded electronic commerce, all leading to the obsolescence of national economic borders.[2] Ironically, their most severe critics from the political left agree with their basic analysis. The difference between them is not descriptive but interpretive. The end—one world market—is agreed upon. Where the executives promise spreading prosperity and hope, however, their critics see catastrophic competition and social disintegration.[3]

It is intuitively plausible that a global system of business is being created as increasingly autonomous business enterprises seek the ever greater economies of scale and product definition required to finance, develop, and exploit new technologies. There can be no doubt that both capital and technology harnessed by MNCs are flowing much more freely across national borders. An apparently seamless web of global financial markets is taken by many observers to be a harbinger of things to come. Even more plausible is the notion that deep regional integration is driven by the expansion of financial and industrial corporations. As MNCs extend their operations across national borders, intuition suggests that locally minded citizens and policymakers would be pushed to adapt their own thinking to a corresponding regional or global logic.

The idea that cosmopolitan big business is inexorably creating a new worldwide political order has in recent years gained considerable currency. A leading explanation traces the process to a technological revolution focused on information-based industries. As one enthusiast puts it:

> Global commerce will force through the construction of multi-media highways, and anyone by-passed by these highways faces ruin. [This] is changing the whole nature of political governance and its relationship to commerce. ... The commercial enterprise of the future will be truly global, it will relocate (physically and electronically) to where the profit is greatest and the regulation easy.[4]

Another prominent observer puts the point more poetically when he takes the multinational corporation to be the defining metaphor for a new age: "Multinationals are like the idea of God during the Renaissance. Their center is everywhere and their periphery nowhere."[5] In more passionate terms, a leading social critic depicts such firms as the observable face of "the manic logic of global capitalism."[6]

Indeed, an emerging consensus seems in view: MNCs are ever more widely understood to be the most visible elements in a vast process of economic and political transformation akin to the industrial revolution that first spawned modern capitalism. The term *globalization* is, again, commonly invoked to capture the sometimes contradictory elements involved in that process. As one political economist explains it, globalization is moving "the world economy to an even larger structural scale." At the same time, it entails a more fundamental shift toward "the privatization and marketization" of politics. The result, he contends, is the creation of new centers of power that are "more sovereign than the state."[7]

The evidence presented in this book, which focuses on the actual activities of multinational firms in technology and capital-intensive sectors, suggests something quite different.

INNOVATION AND THE STATE

In theory, technological innovation and the economies of scale it increasingly demands could undermine political order. For much of the postwar period, analysts and policymakers alike did indeed expect the day-to-day work of corporations in ever-more-open markets to promote a gradual convergence of technological capability across national borders. In this sense, they anticipated a broad movement of effective decision making on future technological development increasingly to transcend the borders of states.

Dominant models of technological change and economic growth, in short, led to the expectation that expanding demand, market liberalization, and open trade would increase the speed and scope of technology diffusion. This process was eventually expected to level the technological playing field, both among corporations and national governments. International trade and attendant flows of information, largely conducted through corporate channels, would spread the benefits of technological innovation ever more widely. This could take the form of direct knowledge embedded in industrial designs, of technologically intensive goods and services, and of production experience. As a result, many economies could eventually be expected to approach or even reach technological parity with the dominant economic powers. After a lag reflecting their delayed start, even developing countries could follow if their political authorities pursued policies that converged in the direction of openness and efficient markets.

The actual record of technological convergence and growth in recent decades has been far less than expected. Certainly the technology gap between the United States and other large industrialized nations has narrowed considerably in many industrial sectors, although at present it appears to be widening with respect to the states of the former Soviet Union. Moreover, as the twentieth century comes to a close, various developing nations appear to have found a path to rapid economic and technological advancement, even if that path has yet to become a smooth one. Certainly, the rate and extent of technological leveling has varied widely across regions and across sectors. A deep integration of national systems of innovation has, however, not occurred. New technology, and the information embedded within it, does not flow as easily or smoothly across national borders as the model of global convergence would predict.[8]

The ability to develop, adapt, and use new knowledge is not a simple by-product of production. Technological innovation also requires concentrated capital investments in human and organizational resources.

Our research indicates that the character of corporate and government sponsorship of technology innovation varies markedly, even among the most advanced nations.

Some governments commit substantial portions of national income to scientific and technological development, particularly in the military arena. Others favor investments in broad national technology missions, or investments in the acquisition and diffusion of new commercial technologies. Some promote research directly and aggressively, while others leave the majority of such activity to the private sector. Some governments regulate competition in ways that inhibit centralization and structured collaboration, while others encourage concentration and combination in the name of production efficiency.

At base, the persistent divergence in corporate strategy and structure surveyed in this book points directly to the longevity of national systems of innovation and investment.[9] Different ways of organizing the institutions and underlying ideologies that frame the modern state continue to shape decisively the organization of the MNCs whose activities often create and sustain national technological competencies. Different ways of organizing the relationship between states and their societies are mirrored directly in the relationships that constitute fundamental corporate operations. In a world where the lion's share of actual technological innovation takes place within corporate networks, the nature of those relationships continues to vary along national lines. This book explores the causes and consequences of those fundamental differences among the world's most prominent MNCs.

DOMESTIC STRUCTURES, MULTINATIONAL CORPORATE STRATEGIES

Through an empirical examination of the most basic strategic operations of MNCs across their core industrial markets, this book probes the phenomena of cross-national economic integration, technological innovation, and structural convergence. The analysis draws on a wide variety of sources, and it deliberately focuses on leading MNCs from leading states.

Despite constant references in the popular media to firms originally chartered in smaller states as harbingers of the truly global economy, we have emphasized American, Japanese, and larger European (mainly German) firms in this study. Firms from small home markets were long ago forced to adapt as they sought growth in external markets. If the term *globalization* is used simply to characterize the struggle for survival of such firms, then it refers to nothing new. Even so, among the ranks of the world's largest public firms, the number of firms like Nestle and ABB Asea Brown Boveri remains tiny.[10] In terms of market valuation in 1995, the top 100 corporations in the world included 43 from the United States, 27 from Japan, 11 from Britain, and 5 from Germany. No other country accounted for more than five. Countries as diverse and sizable as Russia, China, India, Canada, Spain, Indonesia, Australia, and Brazil could claim none.[11]

Moreover, although some of the analysis draws on the larger industrial base of the European Union, we view the German base as distinctive enough and regionally dominant enough to be the central analog to the American and Japanese cases.[12] Of Europe's top 100 firms, 27 are German. In the 1990s, they accounted for approximately 25 percent of all sales by Europe's largest firms (as compared to 21.1 percent for France and 20.8 percent for Britain).

Germany has also consistently accounted for the largest share of the internal industrial production of the European Union (23 percent for Germany, 19 percent for France, 16 percent for Britain).[13] Finally, across key technologically intensive sectors, German firms hold a much larger—and rising—share of world production than firms based in any other European country.[14] In short, if technologically driven structural convergence at the level of the multinational firm is happening, and if it is an important phenomenon capable of reshaping the contours of the global political economy, then it should be evident among American, Japanese, and German firms.

Once established, of course, the technologies developed by multinational firms tend to spread, largely through licensing agreements, joint ventures, and alliances, even though they are most often confined within networks of affiliated firms. This is important because a key determinant of the world's future political organization concerns precisely where technologies will be created, controlled, and deployed. This book seeks to shed light on just that issue as it presents a wide array of evidence on the research and development operations of MNCs, their investment and trading strategies, and their internal governance and core financing. In these fundamental areas of corporate activity, the evidence shows that convergence can be demonstrated only on the surface.

Certainly MNCs change. Indeed, continuous adaptation to dynamic markets is critical to firm survival. If firms from different regions of the world want to sell similar goods or services in the same markets, their day-to-day behavior in those markets will often be quite similar. For those firms that dominate international markets today, however, nationality continues to matter in much more fundamental ways. That nationality is not necessarily given by the location of corporate headquarters or the addresses of principal shareholders, although it usually still is. More fundamentally, it is given by history.

The core strategic behavior of multinational firms varies widely. Three main explanations have been advanced to account for that variance. The first sees firm behavior as most heavily influenced by the nature of the industrial sector. A second explanation emphasizes the importance of internal influences such as the maturity of main product lines. The third explanation underlines the essential malleability of the MNC and the determinative influence of the specific environment in which a firm operates; for example, MNCs are frequently depicted as fluidly adapting themselves to local laws and local tastes in host markets. We have doubts about all three explanations. The behavioral differences we observe do not correlate with industrial sectors. They also do not correlate with industrial maturity. Moreover, they remain observable even within identical host environments.

It would obviously be simpleminded to argue that one explanation captures the essential reality of life for all firms all of the time. The chemical industry, for example, is clearly subject to high transportation costs and particular hazards, which cannot help but influence some aspects of the behavior of all chemical companies regardless of nationality. Similarly, firms committed to a particular host market obviously must adapt themselves to that market, to one degree or another. As the following analysis illustrates, however, in the most fundamental areas of corporate strategy, most of the time, striking differences of an aggregate nature remain. The domestic institutions and ideologies within which companies are most firmly embedded offer the most plausible explanations.

The empirical evidence, upon which this book is based, suggests that distinctive national histories have left legacies that continue to affect the behavior of leading MNCs. The scope for corporate interdependencies across national markets has unquestionably expanded in recent decades. But history and culture continue to shape both the internal structures of MNCs and the core strategies articulated through them. Such a view best accounts for the patterns in the data explored in the analysis that follows.

Political scientists have focused extensively in the last decade on linkages between institutional and ideological structures and state policy. The novelty of this book lies in extending the analysis to the behavior of private actors. Using a different terminology in his magisterial *Scale and Scope*, Alfred Chandler, the dean of American business historians, suggested something similar when he sketched the rise before the 1940s of three fundamentally different kinds of industrial enterprise in the United States, Germany, and Britain.[15] In his conclusion, he asked whether such patterns endure. The central argument of this book and its supporting empirical analysis are aimed at answering just such a question. If such patterns endure, and if the argument is plausible, the implications are significant.

OVERVIEW OF THE BOOK

The next chapter examines important linkages between politics, both domestic and international, and multinational corporate activity. Focusing on the United States, Japan, and Germany, the chapter sketches the chain of reasoning that organizes the empirical analysis at the center of this book. Idiosyncratic national histories lying behind durable domestic institutions and ideologies have shaped distinctive internal structures of governance and long-term corporate financing in the world's leading MNCs. Those histories and their structural legacies have also constructed distinctive national systems of innovation and corporate investment, systems which persist to the present day. Those internal corporate structures and distinctively national systems, in turn, are associated with continuing diversity in patterns of corporate R&D and of the most fundamental investment and trading strategies of the world's leading MNCs.

The third chapter sets out the systems of corporate governance and long-term financing that shape the basic context for multinational corporate strategies. The fourth traces the distinct and structured differences in national approaches to technological innovation and to corporate investment. In such a context, the fifth chapter presents a comparative empirical analysis of corporate R&D and interlinked corporate investment and trading strategies across our three main cases. These operations were not chosen randomly; they provide a window on the strategic core of the contemporary MNC. They also provide insight into the fundamental nature of the international economic system. The concluding chapter summarizes our findings and draws out the implications for policy and further research.

Chapter 2

STATES AND FIRMS: CONVENTIONAL IMAGES,
COMPLEX REALITIES

THE NATURE OF MNCs

THE IDEA of the global corporation is not new. There has long been a tendency in popular commentary to exaggerate the rootlessness of MNCs. Nevertheless, even close observers of business today refer to them as transnational corporations or multinational enterprises, as though the intimate connections between such firms and the states originally chartering them is now fundamentally altered.

In the 1960s, George Ball predicted the imminent emergence of "cosmocorp," the progenitor of a liberal global economy where economic nationalism would be a thing of the past.[1] Others took the evocative title, if not the more subtle underlying argument, of Raymond Vernon's path-breaking book, *Sovereignty at Bay*, and painted a picture of a world economy where national frontiers gradually ceased to have meaning.[2] Within the significant body of international political and economic theory organized since then under the rubric of interdependence, MNCs came to be viewed as the embodiment of markets that spilled ever more fluidly across traditional political borders.[3] Within the United States, that work was often linked to explorations of the underpinnings of American foreign economic policy after World War II.

In principle, according to the dominant view, that policy sought to bind certain national economies more deeply together, initially to counteract the kinds of internal social and political forces that were widely seen as leading the world from the Great War of 1914–1918 directly to global war three decades later. With the emergence of the cold war, both mainstream and revisionist scholars pointed in their own ways to outward corporate investment from the United States as an effective tool for building bulwarks against the spread of communism, especially in Europe and East Asia. Disagreements concerning the ultimate political and normative implications notwithstanding, by the late 1970s many analysts as well as policymakers were convinced that a threshold had been crossed. The conceptual line between national firms with international operations and truly global firms was now so obscure as to be invisible.

But national borders were soon to make a comeback. In the aftermath of oil, exchange rate, and debt crises, states returned to center stage as they appeared to save corporations from the unintended consequences of interdependence. Bailouts, nationalization, implicit subsidies, and sectoral protectionism were the visible manifestations of state assistance. The idea that stateless corporations were emerging, which had in any case been something of an American obsession, began to fade.

At the same time, students of international business devoted increasing attention to the emergence of MNCs outside the United States. Years after J.J. Servan-Schreiber published his famous Gaullist analysis of economic domination by American firms, a substantial empirical literature began to develop.[4] Lawrence Franko, for example, wrote about the gradual evolution of MNCs in continental Europe and concluded that systematic differences existed between them and their American and British analogs in the nature of their linkages with their home states.[5] He suggested, however, that like the United States and Britain, continental European states might in the future face increasing difficulty in equating the interests of their own MNCs with clearly definable national or regional interests. Although Franko's methods and results were controversial, his core argument provided the seed for much more research on European models of multinational business.[6] By the 1990s, this research provided an array of evidence documenting striking differences between the behavior of most continentally based firms and their counterparts in Great Britain.

In Great Britain itself, an upsurge in research on MNCs also occurred in the 1980s. The research was partly driven by related policy questions concerning both inward corporate investment and potential linkages between outward investment and national economic decline. Building on the foundational work of John Dunning dating from the late 1950s, John Stopford and Louis Turner, for example, completed an extensive study of British MNCs and their competitors at home and abroad.[7] Favorably assessing the net contribution of MNCs to the British economy, they concluded that MNCs had become "the agents through which national interdependence is played out."[8] In the future, therefore, important policy issues raised by their activities must inevitably be addressed at the international level.

Obviously influenced by such research, work also began to be done on the emergence and evolution of MNCs in Japan.[9] In addition, a significant literature grew up on "third world" MNCs. Although it developed out of a tradition of research focused on the possible consequences of multinational corporate activities for host states, this new literature tended to buttress the idea that "different home environments produce different sorts of multinational corporations."[10]

Louis Wells pioneered such research with studies of the outward expansion of firms from Southeast Asian countries.[11] In general, the research documented a wide variety of reasons for the growth of indigenous MNCs in developing countries, and, most importantly for present purposes, a wide variety of incentives and reactions from home states. It did not simply establish the fact that governmental policies differed on such technical matters as the licensing of outward investments. It also demonstrated how firms sought to exploit or ameliorate the effects of basic political-economic structures in their home environments. Boxed in by tight regulation and an anti-big-business ideology at home, for example, Indian MNCs tended to seek more than production efficiencies abroad. In contrast, Hong Kong-based firms looked for competitive advantages in long-standing trading relationships and sought to compensate for rising land and labor costs in their home market.

In the 1990s, similar research focusing on the industrialized world began to hint at significant behavioral discrepancies between firms from different countries. One study noted, in particular, important differences between German firms and others based on the Continent. Where, for example, firms from France and the Scandinavian and Benelux countries invested at home between 10 and 35 times the amount they invested abroad, German firms maintained a ratio in excess of 80:1 in favor of domestic investments.[12] In the face of such differences as well as an increase in cross-border mergers and acquisitions, European business analysts were starting to speculate on the possible emergence of regional, as opposed to national or Anglo-Saxon, corporate entities outside of Germany. By the mid-1990s, European MNCs had become the subject of intense scrutiny in the context of a larger discussion on the future of the European Union in a changing world economy.[13]

The internal European debate on such matters occurred just as Americans once again argued among themselves about whether the era of the global corporation, prematurely announced in the 1960s, had finally arrived.[14] In the aftermath of the cold war, dramatic shifts were underway as formerly socialist countries turned toward market models in the reconstruction of their economies. This matched a heightening movement in many developing countries toward economic openness, including openness to foreign direct investment. An array of acronyms—from NAFTA to APEC to WTO—began to suggest that this movement had solid political roots.

At the same time, intrafirm trade was accelerating and cross-border direct and portfolio investments were mushrooming. In certain industrial sectors, especially pharmaceuticals and telecommunications, a rise in cross-border mergers and acquisitions, strategic alliances, and trumpeted international redeployments of corporate resources suggested a qualitative change in the nature of multinational corporate operations.[15] Careful comparative business studies suggested that receding national divergence might still be important in industries characterized by regulated competition.[16] But in many industrial sectors, the global corporation seemed a caricature no more.

GLOBAL-LOCAL POLITICS

Within the contemporary field of international relations, systematic study of connections between international political order at the broadest conceptual level and multinational firms began some twenty years ago. It was then that Robert Gilpin related the global spread of American firms after 1945 to the international political position of the United States. As Gilpin summarized his view:

> The necessary condition for the rapid growth of multinational corporations over the past several decades has been the steady emergence of the United States as the world's dominant power. This process began in the latter part of the nineteenth century, when American industry began to supersede its European rivals. As American power grew, the United States created an increasingly large sphere of influence. This expansionism reached its zenith in the decades after World War II: Following its victory in war and in response to the Soviet challenge, the United States created in its own security interests the pattern of relations among the non-Communist countries within which American multinational corporations have flourished.[17]

Gilpin's argument provided a provocative riposte to the then-common assertion that a new era of international economic interdependence—beyond the nation-state—had dawned. But the world has changed a great deal in the past two decades. At the very least, the relative decline of American power, the rise of Japan and Germany, and other changes in the international distribution of power demand a recalibration of Gilpin's original formulation.[18] More fundamentally, it is necessary to move beyond what scholars of international relations would label a straightforward realist analysis that conceptualizes states as central decision-making organizations and emphasizes their competition for power at the system level. An analytical framework is needed that can take central insights from system-level arrangements of power and combine them with political forces at the domestic level that can in principle exert vitally important influences on multinational businesses.[19] The key variables and their interrelationship are more subtle than realists often allow or expect. Stephen Krasner recently captured some of that subtlety as follows:

> If states are understood ... as institutional structures or polities, then the basic institutional structure of transnationals will be influenced or even determined by the institutional characteristics of states.[20]

Although this perspective helps to inform the analysis of MNCs, we believe that it does not go far enough. The core institutions worth emphasizing in such a conceptualization embody distinctive and durable ideologies or, as some analysts now prefer to call them, belief-systems. We see corporations internalizing both the basic political institutions and underlying ideological frameworks within which they remain most firmly embedded. And unlike other scholars who acknowledge such effects but assume that they will inevitably recede over time, we see them as "hard-wired" into core corporate structures.[21]

In reshaping the foundations of the international political economy, multinational corporations are clearly much more important now than they were in the early decades after World War II.[22] Intrafirm trade and foreign direct investment, for example, are powerful features of the international economy, and the activities of multinational firms are central in both regards. Moreover, an increasing number of firms cannot simply be described as national firms with international operations.[23] But states—especially home states—remain decisive. They do not just matter. In analytical terms, our approach remains open to the possibility that states retain their priority with respect to other factors influencing the operating environment of the modern corporation.

The domestic political structures within which a firm initially develops and from which it then expands may leave a permanent imprint on its strategic behavior. Adapting a term from electromagnetics, economists label such a process of marking *hysteresis*. Seen as a lagging effect after a causal force has been removed, the process carries with it the implication that the impact of unique histories will inevitably diminish over time.[24] Business analysts refer in the same way and with the same implication to "corporate inertia," "path dependence," "the legacy of past choices," and "administrative heritage."[25] Our argument and evidence raise strong doubts about the inevitable erosion of the effects of history on the core structures and strategies of multinational firms.

Although such an institutional approach is rarely applied in a systematic and comparative fashion to core elements of multinational corporate behavior, its forerunner became prominent in the field of international relations in the late 1970s, when Peter Katzenstein and a group of colleagues hypothesized a relationship between what they called "domestic structures" and the foreign economic policies of states.[26] We adapt the term to include not only basic national institutions of economic and political governance, but also dominant national ideologies—the collective understandings that channel the way individuals in particular societies relate to one another.[27] We believe such collective understandings, which remain distinguishable on national lines, continue to inform decision making at the most fundamental levels of corporate life.

Since the late 1970s, an enormous body of research has coalesced around the concept of domestic structures and their analogs in the fields of comparative politics and comparative business studies. The reader may find it useful to have an indication of the kinds of domestic structures that are associated with observable variances in the operations of MNCs surveyed in the next three chapters. Drawn from the comparative political economy literature, Table 2.1 (National Structures and Corporate Foundations) provides a schematic outline.

These structures, both substantive and ideological, can each be unpacked. Indeed, the precise character of each at specific historical junctures is much debated by academic specialists. A reasonable analytical consensus exists on most, however, and we are not the first to note that such distinctions themselves reflect deep differences in the way American, German, and Japanese societies have related economic functions to social and political purposes. Indeed, an extensive and sophisticated literature in comparative politics and comparative political economy is devoted to the exploration of such distinctions. Much contemporary work along this line rests upon the foundation of earlier historical and sociological studies of democratic capitalism and industrial development.[28] An important component of that literature takes distinctive national institutions and ideologies and relates them to a variety of governmental policy outcomes.[29] The challenge is to relate such factors in a systematic fashion to corporate behavior.

As continuing debates among scholars of comparative politics remind us, however, national structures are not static; hard and fast demarcation lines are difficult to draw. Nevertheless, a critical mass of research now associates these labels with recognizably different and relatively enduring patterns of social organization. That research also provides a basis for the central inference guiding our own research. Such factors, we believe, decisively influence significant and observable behavioral differences at the level of the firm, some of which are quite evident in aggregate national data. The weight of the evidence presented below strongly suggests that the relationship is not spurious.

TABLE 2.1
National Structures and Corporate Foundations

	United States	*Germany*	*Japan*
Dominant ideology:	Free enterprise liberalism	Social partnership	Technonationalism
Political institutions:	Liberal democracy/ divided government/interest group liberalism	Social democracy/ weak bureaucracy/corporatist legacy	Developmental democracy/strong bureaucracy/reciprocity between state and firms
Economic institutions:	Decentralized, open markets/unconcentrated, fluid capital markets/ antitrust tradition	Organized markets/ tiers of firms/ dedicated, bank-centered capital markets/certain cartelized markets	Guided, closed, bifurcated markets/ bank-centered capital markets/ tight business networks/cartels in sunset industries

Across the areas of firm behavior and the range of industries examined, relatively durable national institutions and ideologies appear to provide a more plausible source of basic differentiation than the obvious alternatives—industrial sector, firm/product maturity, and host environments. The evidence set out below supports the view that across the United States, Germany and Japan, the distinctions briefly sketched above lie directly behind striking differences in core aspects of corporate behavior, differences that persist even as firms compete more intensively in their rivals' home markets.

This book represents a systematic effort to relate such factors to the core operations of MNCs. In our view, a robust analysis of contemporary MNCs needs to be combined not just with an appreciation of the kind of international systemic dynamism emphasized by Gilpin and other realists, but also with an ever more intricate domestic-level understanding of political and economic structures.

In the end, we see leading MNCs internalizing both the basic national institutions and underlying ideological frameworks within which they remain most firmly embedded. This analytical approach concedes that the strategies and structures of corporations can and do change as they operate internationally, but only to the extent that those underlying institutions and ideologies permit such change.[30] The process can involve dynamic feedback effects, but at least for the leading states and firms covered by our evidence, the more rigid structures are not corporate but national.

THE POLICY CONTEXT

At some point in the recent past, so observers informed by either radical or liberal worldviews now commonly contend, the business world crossed a threshold. Even if they had not done so before, in the 1990s several hundred global corporations were moving dramatically away from their national moorings to create a global information society, a global corporate culture, and a global technology base.[31] States, so the argument goes, must adapt. Seeking maximum shares of the benefits flowing from that new economy, relevant national policies and practices—which together with various formal and informal agreements comprise the rules of the international business game—are bound to converge toward global norms. Mobile corporate capital now penalizes states that cannot stay abreast of those norms.[32] The new system shatters old bonds and renders outmoded traditional approaches to politics. Just as the strategies and structures of global corporations are inevitably coming together, barring some unpredictable catastrophe, so are the associated strategies and structures of nation-states.

Similar arguments are made at the grandest level of abstraction. Perhaps the most celebrated example of these in the recent past was the position taken by Francis Fukuyama in *The End of History and the Last Man*. The end of the cold war, he contended, signaled a universal shift towards normative integration on basic questions of economic order. There would, therefore, be no further progress in the development of underlying principles and institutions, "because all of the really big questions had been settled."[33]

One of those big questions involved the proper relationship between state power and personal freedom, a relationship now more extensively mediated by free enterprise and open markets. In short, the common expectation was that an expanding number of decisions affecting the lives of citizens would be made in those markets by ostensibly private actors. MNCs came instantly to mind when observers looked for examples of such actors capable of operating easily across national borders.

Such images complemented more rigorous scholarly analyses of the changing role of multinational business in national political arenas. Students of the subject have linked the degree to which firms sell and produce goods abroad with the ever more obvious preferences of governments around the world for market openness and liberalization.[34] Similarly, related theoretical work on the political impact of international capital mobility suggests quite powerfully that multinational corporate networks, through which capital actually or potentially moves, will be at the forefront of basic transformations within governing coalitions in the years ahead.[35]

The best work in this vein is careful not to assert that technological change and global corporate expansion necessarily imply convergence in governing coalitions, political institutions, or policy outcomes.[36] It does suggest, however, that internationally mobile capital, aided by and embodied in the technology linked to expanding multinational corporate and financial networks, is politically ascendant in the contemporary era. It suggests, further, that this ascendancy matters decisively in tangible political terms.[37] Effective decision making authority in this new world is shifting outside formally constituted political arenas.

But not all are convinced. Pragmatic liberals have understood throughout modern history that societies have tended to respond in somewhat different ways to common exogenous pressures. Where such differential responses threaten to have a negative impact on other societies, liberal institutionalists see the need to negotiate basic rules to guide their international interaction.[38]

For different reasons, the voices of historically minded realists are also not yet silenced. The vision of globalism, in either its liberal or radical guises, is not yet self-evident. Skeptics remind us that today's most successful MNCs do not come close to wielding the clout of companies like the great Dutch and English trading companies, to say nothing of once-dominant financiers like the Rothschilds and the Morgans. And observe carefully what happened to them, they argue, when their corporate interests came into conflict with the states in which they were ultimately based.[39] Despite breathtaking technological developments, the proliferation of cross-national corporate alliances, and the porosity of once-formidable territorial barriers, to the skeptics nothing fundamental has changed. MNCs, at base, remain national firms with international operations. International politics determine the overarching contours of international markets.

The growth of American MNCs in the wake of World War II, in the view of such skeptics, reflected both the competitive advantages inherent in American society as well as the concomitant disadvantages of devastated European and East Asian societies. During the 1980s, according to this logic, the spectacular expansion of many European and, especially, Japanese firms reflected a distinct recalibration in the balance of national advantages, mainly but not exclusively shaped by internal factors.[40] The end of the cold war and the emergence of new markets in developing and formerly communist countries signaled another rebalancing, a rebalancing that would ultimately be determined by the interaction of national competitive advantages. The deregulation of foreign direct investment, the attendant spread of production facilities across borders, the privatization of state assets, and the liberalization of financial markets—all comprise a process of profound but indeterminate policy change.

The realist challenge to liberal and radical characterizations of the nature of contemporary MNCs is closely related to debates on the putative homogeneity of the global capitalist system. The most common distinctions made by antagonists are between Anglo-American capitalism, Continental European capitalism, and East Asian capitalism. Depending on the value under discussion, credible arguments are made all the time that one system is better than another.

During the 1980s, for example, it was common to hear enthusiasts extol the virtues of the East Asian and Continental systems: long-term focus, continuous improvement in technologies, efficient diffusion of the fruits of research and development, loyalty among corporate stakeholders. In the 1990s, it was just as common to hear about how the Anglo-American model had reasserted its superiority: rough but rapid restructuring, flexibility, technological innovativeness, financial efficiency, and entrepreneurialism.

This book does not aim to resolve such arguments, but it is obviously influenced by them. Moreover, it does not deny that multinational firms adapt themselves as necessary to compete as fully as possible across diverse systems. But its focus is on those firms themselves. And contrary to the argument that intensifying multinational competition is breaking down the institutional and ideological roots of diversity, it aims to demonstrate that the reverse is the case in the three states widely acknowledged as the international pacesetters.

This book, moreover, does not offer a full account of the dynamics of global capitalism. Its primary concern is more limited, although we believe our work sheds light on much larger issues. At base, our emphasis is on the conditional nature of MNC behavior, and we contend that the most enduring of those conditions arise out of unique national institutions and ideologies.

The evidence gathered and analyzed in this book may be read as an initial test of a set of linked propositions that can readily be derived from the broad range of research surveyed in this chapter. Unique national histories gave rise to highly differentiated domestic institutional and ideological structures in leading states. In the world's leading MNCs, those structures decisively shaped distinctive and enduring relationships among key corporate stakeholders. Despite common systemic pressures associated with the globalization / internationalization phenomenon, and despite changes at the margins, those relationships continue to influence the most fundamental strategies of leading multinational firms. The observable consequences of those strategies therefore exhibit a striking lack of convergence. Before turning to an examination of those consequences in the core strategic operations of MNCs, the next two chapters set out the most fundamental contexts within which they need to be compared and assessed.

Chapter 3

NATIONAL FOUNDATIONS OF MULTINATIONAL

CORPORATE ACTIVITY (I)

BEFORE a corporation develops global aspirations and multinational strategies, it must establish itself in some legal context. Its owners must then set in place the financial foundations necessary to sustain its existence as a going concern, and its owners and financiers must devise arrangements to guide and constrain corporate managers as they go about the business of earning and distributing returns on investment and otherwise seeking to sustain the firm in perpetuity. These arrangements must be consistent with the laws of the jurisdiction within which establishment took place.

Corporate governance and long-term financing arrangements thus provide the canvass upon which the corporation then paints its strategies and operations. Reflecting distinctive national laws and distinctively structured national financial markets, that canvass has traditionally been comprised of different material, differently woven, across the United States, Germany, and Japan.[1] This chapter introduces basic patterns of corporate governance and long-term financing in those three countries and assesses the degree to which those patterns have converged in recent years. Against this background, as well as the background provided in the next chapter on differences in national innovation systems and investment regimes, we will be in a position to examine recent evidence on the core strategic behavior of leading MNCs.

CORPORATE GOVERNANCE AND FINANCE

In its narrowest sense, the term *corporate governance* refers to the measures the owners of a firm (the principals) take to ensure that the managers of that firm (the agents) return their investment to them with a reward commensurate to the risks undertaken.[2] In the real world, the term refers more broadly to the rules and norms that guide the internal relationships among the various stakeholders in a business enterprise. These typically include owners, directors, managers, creditors, suppliers, employees, and customers. For comparative purposes, one of the two main points of emphasis in this chapter concerns the central relationships between the managers of a corporation and the owners of voting shares, whose interests are in principle mediated by boards of directors. Those relationships center on respective rights and obligations that are either specified in law or legitimated by long-standing custom and practice. Since MNCs span a number of legal jurisdictions, their internal governance is more complicated than it is for local firms. The core governance structures of almost all MNCs are nevertheless still clearly associated with prevailing norms in the jurisdiction within which their head offices are incorporated.[3] At times, however, MNCs must find ways to cope with the disruptions that occur when separate subsidiaries and affiliates operate in conformity with the not necessarily consistent laws of host countries.[4]

The second point of emphasis in this chapter, intimately related to the first, concerns the ways MNCs finance themselves over the long term. We hear a great deal these days about how short-term liquid capital moves ever more rapidly around the world. While important national financial markets are still not wholly integrated with one another, cross-border linkages have indeed tightened recently as explicit and implicit controls on capital movements have been abandoned.[5] But the mechanisms that channel long-term capital to corporations are different matters. The reliance of corporations on decentralized equity markets or banks, for example, have long differed quite strikingly across countries. Such differences entail distinctive financial monitoring and security arrangements—once again, arrangements at the heart of corporate governance. Closely related to such arrangements, accounting and tax rules that influence the decisions of corporations to retain earnings, often the cheapest form of long-term corporate financing, have been notably distinctive across countries.

The evidence presented in this chapter suggests that governance and financing structures combine to form patterns of industrial organization that continue to differ markedly across the United States, Germany, and Japan. Historical background and contemporary adaptations are complex; the conclusion is not.[6] Leading Japanese, American, and German MNCs continue to differ systematically in the relative priority they assign to the immediate interests of their shareholders, in the centrality of their banking relationships, in their exposure to impersonal capital markets, and in the nature of the accountability of their managers. More broadly, they also appear to differ in the clarity with which those managers see their own personal interests as coinciding with commonly perceived national interests.

COMPARATIVE ANALYSIS OF THE UNITED STATES, GERMANY, AND JAPAN

United States

Corporate governance for American-based MNCs, and publicly owned American firms in general, centers on formal legal relationships between shareholders, directors, and managers. The complex and evolving nature of American federalism is crucially important here. The foundations for those relationships are set mainly in state laws, although various national laws have an important impact. It was once conventional to refer to the overall system as "shareholder capitalism."

In theory, American corporations exist mainly to create wealth for their owners, whose interests are overseen by increasingly specialized managers. In practice, the links between owners and managers have tended to become more attenuated over time. Founder-owners have historically used American capital markets to cash out. Contemporary ownership stakes in large American corporations have therefore tended to be fragmented, held either separately or collectively as relatively passive investments by individuals. Few individuals or institutions hold large blocks of shares in major American companies.

Like citizens in a democratic republic electing individuals to represent and govern them, fragmented owners technically delegate their right to oversee the corporation to a board of directors. Directors, in turn, empower increasingly specialized managers to run the corporation. In principle, owners retain a stake in the long-term success of the corporation. Moreover, they can replace directors, and through them managers, if they perceive the actions of either group to be compromising that success.

The actual voice of individual shareholders in the United States, however, has generally declined over time. Increasingly, individuals have pooled their resources and acquired corporate shares collectively through mutual funds, pension funds, and other investment vehicles. With the rise of such institutional investors, and the increasing turnover of ownership stakes, links of accountability between owners and managers have in practice weakened considerably in recent decades, with a few notable exceptions. Moreover, boards of directors are now often in practice closer to the managers they are supposed to oversee than to the shareholders they are supposed to represent.

The phenomenon began to be recognized as early as the 1930s, when Adolph Berle and Gardiner Means drew their paradigmatic picture of corporate America.[7] As Berle and Means pointed out, the modern American corporation reflected a novel separation between ownership and control. Even as their stakes became more fragmented, in this system the narrow and generally short-term financial interests of stockholders became more important than the interests of other corporate stakeholders. As long as they satisfied those interests—through stable and rising dividends and rising stock prices—managers became increasingly independent. Berle and Means worried about the social consequences of that tendency. But other observers made the case that the system accrued significant efficiency advantages. Among other things, specialized managers were freed to marshal new resources, which enabled them to reap economies of scale through merger and acquisition strategies and to develop and exploit expensive new technologies. Following Alfred Chandler's pioneering historical work, it is now generally accepted that the central drama in the development of the American corporate system involved the simultaneous fragmentation of owners and the emergence of that autonomous managerial class. As Mark Roe puts it, "Dispersed owners and concentrated management became the quintessential characteristics of the large American firm."[8]

During the 1980s, it seemed for a time that a spectacular series of hostile corporate takeovers and renewed activism by groups of shareholders and sometimes by labor unions would shift the internal power balance back a bit toward the broader interests of owners and other stakeholders. But managers soon found allies, especially in state legislatures. The result was the construction of ever higher legal hurdles for collective action by shareholders. At the same time, the inefficiencies that might have been associated with such protections appeared in many cases to have been discouraged by the size and openness of the American market as well as by a deregulatory policy movement in key industrial sectors, which continued to foster a significant degree of competition among large firms. Throughout the 1990s, therefore, Chandler's famous label for the real American system, "competitive managerial capitalism," remained apt.[9]

Again, the owners of most American MNCs tend mainly to be individual investors, whose holdings are increasingly aggregated by institutional agents. In recent years, the fastest-growing agents have been mutual funds (Table 3.1. Growth in American Mutual Funds). For the 1,000 largest corporations in the United States, estimates of the percentage of voting shares held by pension funds, mutual funds, and other investment vehicles run as high as two thirds. In the mid-1960s, large block trades represented around 3 percent of the annual volume of trading on the New York Stock Exchange. Two decades later, it exceeded 50 percent.

Except in atypical cases, the directors of American MNCs are only ratified, not actually chosen, by shareholders. Most directors on MNC

TABLE 3.1
Growth in American Mutual Funds

	1980	1985	1990	1995
Number of equity funds	267	579	1,127	2,211
Number of income and bond funds	191	492	1,235	2,253
Millions of shareholder accounts in equity funds	5.8	11.5	23.0	70.7
Millions of shareholder accounts in income and bond funds	1.5	8.3	16.6	30.9
Billions of U.S. dollars in assets owned by equity funds	135	496	1,067	2,820
Billions of U.S. dollars in assets owned by income and bond funds	14	135	323	798

Source: U.S. Department of Commerce, *Statistical Abstract of the United States,* 116th edition, 1996, table 818.

boards are tapped by, and therefore in some sense beholden to, chief executive officers. Nevertheless, prompted by shareholder suits and other pressures unleashed in the wake of the turbulent 1980s, many American corporate boards became more assertive in meeting their oversight responsibilities. In the case of several leading MNCs such as IBM, Kodak, and Westinghouse, such assertiveness even culminated in the ouster of chief executive officers. Behind these actions often lay the mounting discontent of large institutional agents. In the course of interviews undertaken for this study, several directors of American MNCs praised the heightened interest in monitoring corporate performance coming from such institutions as the California Public Employee Retirement System (CalPERS). None, however, perceived such activism to reflect a fundamental shift in norms of corporate governance in America. They expected it to be difficult to sustain and difficult to imitate.

On the whole, most shareholders in most public American corporations continue to have little voice in day-to-day management. They do, however, have the option of exit. And they continue to exercise that option with much more vigor and regularity than do their counterparts abroad. Less than 5 percent of American firms listed on national exchanges have a shareholder with more than a 50 percent stake.[10] For all the talk in business circles about the wisdom of long-term investment strategies, the prospect of exiting quickly retains its attractiveness for investment managers. This is especially true for pension and mutual fund managers whose own performance is measured on a rigorous comparative basis that tends to emphasize short-term financial performance. For pension funds in particular, that tendency has been strongly reinforced by federal law. The Employee Retirement Income Security Act, which Congress enacted in 1974, intentionally biased the system in this direction by encouraging the diversification of fund holdings. Managers were to be guided by the "prudent man" rule, which effectively meant that their portfolio strategies had to conform to prevailing patterns of risk management. Concentrated holdings, long discouraged by an array of other factors, including legal restrictions on the powers of financial intermediaries, became even less attractive. Trading shares, not holding them, continues to be the norm.

Because of their reliance on open and active stock markets, sometimes to raise new capital but more often to provide signals to creditors, competitors, employees, and others, the managers of American MNCs appear obsessed by short-term returns. Although the absence of concentrated owners in some sense frees them from personal oversight, the constant "churning" of their firms' shares reinforces one central message: keep current earnings rising on a steady track. The message is often strongly reinforced by the explicit linkage between executive compensation packages and stock prices. Two astute observers summarize the consequences:

> U.S. CEOs understand this message. When they issue their companies' quarterly earnings report and meet with security analysts, they believe they are being judged on a 90-day basis. If the verdict is not positive, many sell orders will be forthcoming with a commensurate decline in share prices. In an era when many CEOs have been seriously concerned about unfriendly takeovers, such a decline was an especially unpleasant prospect. But even in more halcyon times, CEOs feel the pressure to keep earnings up.[11]

Compounding a bias toward the short-term in managerial decision making are the vagaries of the U.S. corporate proxy voting system, which can make it difficult for shareholders to cooperate in disciplining entrenched managers. Working in the same direction are disclosure requirements, antitrust rules, and tax policies that discourage significant cross-shareholding by unrelated corporations. For example, under rules first specified in the 1934 Securities and Exchange Act, when an individual or related group seeks more than 5 percent of the shares of a corporation, public disclosure of plans, financing sources, and other information is required.[12] Securities and Exchange Commission (SEC) proxy rules may also come into play when a group seeking a controlling position is formed. Together with the effects of a long-standing tax on corporate dividends received, such rules have made it increasingly costly and risky for large blocks of stock or cross-shareholdings to be assembled. As we shall see later, such an outcome stands in sharp contrast to the Japanese and German cases. The real roots of that difference must be traced to deeper structures in the American political economy, especially differences in the nature and functioning of financial intermediaries.

Financial markets in the United States are among the world's most dynamic and most idiosyncratic. The potential size of the overall economy, together with its relative isolation, created conditions which permitted a high degree of political intervention and experimentation in those markets as industrialization occurred. The interplay between democratic politics and industrial expansion combined to build a complex and, ultimately, highly decentralized system of corporate financing.[13] Not coincidentally, it also developed the world's largest pool of venture capital.

In the nineteenth century, many banks in the United States were able, at least indirectly, to perform both commercial and investment banking functions. They could raise deposits and make loans, as well as underwrite, hold, and sell corporate securities. The overarching financial system within which they operated, however, ensured that most banks remained quite small. A unit banking system, as distinct from a branch banking system, developed from policy decisions made during the country's earliest days.

The Constitution itself created an opening for both the federal government and state governments to regulate banks. Subsequent jurisdictional battles culminated in Andrew Jackson's famous abolition of the Second Bank of the United States in 1832. National branching, the principal mechanism behind the growth of very large banks in many other countries, was effectively discouraged by restrictive state and national laws. Compounding the consequent tendency toward financial fragmentation was the absence of a national central bank, a situation which persisted until 1913, when the Federal Reserve System was created.

In 1927, the first major breach in the barriers to branching came when the federal government put the liberalizing McFadden Act into place. Provided state-chartered banks had the same rights in given jurisdictions, nationally chartered banks were henceforth permitted to set up branches in their home cities and then in their home states. In practice, powerful local lobbies often made such expansions difficult. Together with provisions in the Banking Act of 1933, however, McFadden effectively prohibited interstate branching. That ban was reinforced in 1956 and again in 1970 through the federal Bank Holding Company Act. Although commercial banks as a group long remained the most important financial intermediaries in the United States, in consequence of this constitutional and legislative history, individually they have always lacked both the scale and the scope of equivalent institutions abroad. Their collective inability to provide directly a significant share of the financing needs of a burgeoning corporate America in the late nineteenth and early twentieth centuries was reinforced by explicit legislative and regulatory constraints on their functional powers.

In the wake of a series of financial scandals and crises culminating in the Great Depression, strict rules on the mixing of commercial and investment banking operations were imposed at both federal and state levels of government. As occurred in the case of branching prohibitions, various institutional interests gradually coalesced around those separation rules. Over time, the embryonic financial-industrial combinations that existed in the late nineteenth century, complete with interlocking boards and cross-shareholding, were deliberately demolished. In truth, fear of the political and social consequences of financial concentration is a constant theme in American history, and depression era events only crystallized it. Its most common focus, throughout modern American history, has been on the role of bankers in the strategic development of big business.[14]

The first restrictions on the ability of commercial banks to own shares directly in industrial enterprises emerged between 1863 and 1892 in the National Bank Act, its revisions and regulatory interpretations, and various state laws. Using the vehicle of investment banking affiliates, however, commercial banks remained involved in the underwriting and selling of corporate shares until 1933, when the Glass-Steagall provisions of the federal Banking Act effectively forced them to divest. Bank holding companies came under analogous constraints in 1956. In 1970, the so-called Douglas amendments to the Bank Holding Company Act ensured that, even indirectly, banks could not own more than 5 percent of the shares of non-banking companies. They were also precluded from seeking to control such companies in other ways, for example, through cross-shareholding arrangements. Reinforcing such restrictions was the evolution of bankruptcy law within the United States; creditors to a bankrupt firm could find their claims subordinated if the courts hold that they also have a controlling equity stake in the firm.

The functional segmentation of the U.S. banking industry and the restriction of bank-corporate alliances evolved along a parallel track to the geographic limitation of bank branching. Both worked to discourage the emergence of large corporate-financial structures. Reinforcing that outcome have been strict regulations on the corporate financing activities of insurance companies. In Mark Roe's terms:

[F]ederalism created fragmented banks and gave them a strong voice in Congress, populism made concentrated power in or out of government unpopular, and interest groups—bankers or managers seeking to preserve their favored setting—did not have to fight strong popular opinion or the political structure. These forces, some weak, some strong, all marched in the direction of fragmented finance. Once they succeeded—and only once they succeeded—did the Berle-Means corporation become inevitable.[15]

At the ideological center of this evolution was the will to fragment power. Notoriously difficult to pin down in American history, policymakers have again and again given evidence by their actions that the national interest is best served by the avoidance of concentrations of power, financial or otherwise. Despite recent federal- and state-level moves in a liberalizing direction, fragmentation and segmentation continue to distinguish the American system. Even as Glass-Steagall and interstate banking restrictions eroded and the executive branch of the federal government took measures to widen the scope for banks to grow in size and expand their ownership stakes in industrial enterprises, interest group pressures, supervisory practices, and other legal impediments worked to ensure that market outcomes in the United States remained distinctive.

Notwithstanding the consequences of fragmented finance on the fundamental organization of American corporations, "relationship banking" characterized their short-term financing activities until the early 1980s. Unlike analogous links in Germany or Japan, in the United States it was always much easier to switch lead banks. Especially during periods of passing difficulty, however, most corporations could long rely on their lead banks for a degree of patience, special loans, and other useful services. In addition, as they expanded abroad, U.S.-based MNCs could rely on the support of the international networks of their lead banks.[16] During the period after World War II, when many of America's top corporations were transforming themselves into MNCs, this form of relationship banking provided a useful assist. In recent years, however, even this looser type of bank-corporate alliance has been undermined. As in other countries, successful corporations gradually built up substantial retained earnings and thus came to rely less and less on banks for financing. This natural trend was reinforced by technological and regulatory developments, which led to the creation of an array of new debt instruments and new competitors for the banks. In addition, heightened price competition eroded bank profit margins on traditional forms of corporate financing. Over time, the aggregate market share of the banking industry declined dramatically.

The response of banks to the heightened competition was skewed by the legal restrictions noted above. Within their confines, however, many banks sought new and often riskier clients to take the place of prime corporate borrowers. Many also expanded their foreign operations, as well as their trading and money market activities. Through such avenues, commercial banks gradually began poaching the corporate clients of investment banks. Investment banks returned the favor. All of this activity helped establish the financial conditions in the United States for the spectacular rash of corporate takeovers that occurred in the 1980s. Many formerly staid corporate banks, driven by fierce competitive pressures, even helped hostile buyers acquire their own clients. In so doing, some came richly to deserve the label "predator," widely associated with them in the popular media. By the 1990s, relationship banking had been fundamentally transformed.

The same could not be said for other countries, as would partly be indicated by the pullback of many U.S. banks from foreign markets in the early 1990s. Although German, Japanese, and other markets were in a legal and regulatory sense now more open than they had ever been, many American banks, unable to earn enough to justify the expenses involved, retreated or scaled down their operations. In the competition for high-profile corporate business, they now often found themselves up against formidable indigenous banks and an array of informal barriers. Not only could those banks match their pricing, but they also had long-standing and meaningful relationships with the leading corporations in their markets, relationships often formalized through reciprocal shareholding. As a former U.S. Treasury official put it, such bonds no longer existed "in the commoditized U.S. market where price is virtually all that matters."[17]

The stunted growth and gradual decline of banks as sources of long-run financial stability for American corporations has not been matched by the rise of other institutions that could be expected to play a role equivalent to that played by lead banks in Germany and Japan. American insurance companies have long been prohibited from assuming controlling positions in corporate shares. Mutual funds are strictly discouraged by federal regulations, and by the national tax code, from concentrating their assets in individual firms. Similarly, as noted above, pension funds are subject to formal fiduciary obligations that require them to shift out of investments if certain return-on-investment criteria are not met. Liability laws, governmental regulation, and the mandates given by most plan sponsors actively reinforce the urge to diversify. The situation remains much different in Germany and Japan.

Germany

German MNCs, which remain Europe's leaders across a range of industrial sectors, are embedded in a distinctive system of corporate governance. Despite recent measures to encourage a degree of structural convergence across the markets of the member states of the European Union, the German system remains distinguishable from that of France, and it differs quite markedly from that of Great Britain. In a number of ways, it is similar to that of Japan. The system is generally recognized to have been a critical component of the country's initial industrialization and of its miracle recovery and growth after World War II.[18] In the most basic sense, the system provides an important part of a broad normative framework within which government, corporations, and labor unions continuously negotiate their respective adjustments to changing market conditions.[19] Not known for the creation of startling innovations in new sectors, the industries organized around that system are often cited as excelling in the diffusion of new production and process technologies. The record is especially impressive in such sectors as high performance transportation systems, automotive components, inorganic chemicals, metals processing, and machine tools.[20] Currently, synergistic expansions are occurring in the aircraft, aerospace, and pharmaceutical sectors.

In the 1990s, German industry confronted the formidable twin challenges of assisting in the absorption of a backward industrial base in the states of the former East Germany and, simultaneously, of adapting the entire national technology base to a much more competitive global and regional environment.[21] German productivity levels had not advanced as quickly as they had elsewhere, unit labor costs had swollen in relative terms, and exchange rate effects were undercutting hard-won gains. Successful adaptation was increasingly recognized, not least inside Germany itself, as crucial to regaining and improving the country's position. It is possible that fundamental structural changes will be needed to achieve those goals. Our analysis suggests, however, that German industry is adjusting within constraints posed by its traditional system of corporate governance. That system may be reshaped, but it will not likely be abandoned. Negotiated and incremental reform remains probable. The principal reason has to do with perceived advantages that have flowed to corporate managers in Germany from a system of strategic design biased toward stability.

Managers of American MNCs frequently remark on the ability of their German counterparts to operate with a high degree of apparent independence from shareholder pressures for immediate returns. The view is commonplace that this independence has been crucial to the maintenance of stable levels of investment in the technologies at the core of leading German industries. There is an element of truth in this, but the ability of German industrial managers to plan with other than short-term profit-maximization goals in mind appears to be associated with the fact that the expectations of German shareholders have long been organized and expressed quite distinctively. In such a context, German managers have really not been more autonomous than American managers. They have simply been subject to different pressures, some of which can be quite severe.

German law distinguishes between two types of companies with limited liability. Joint stock companies, which are publicly owned and listed (Aktiengesellschaft [AG]) and privately held, unlisted companies (Gesellschaft mit beschraenkten Haftung [GmbH]). German MNCs come in either form. The best-known German MNC, Daimler-Benz, falls in the former category, while one of the most successful, the auto-parts MNC, Robert Bosch, falls in the latter.

Under the terms of the 1976 Co-Determination Act, in a company with more than 20,000 employees, half of its supervisory board must comprise directors chosen by the shareholders and half by employees (one of whom must be from the company's management). The chairman, elected by the shareholders' representatives, all of whom are outsiders, is empowered to break tie votes. The supervisory board appoints a management board, usually ten in number; by law, those managers are provided with a formal contract extending from one to five years.

Although they have formal responsibilities for reviewing management contracts and providing general oversight, supervisory boards are generally passive organs. The chairman, however, can often be quite actively involved in the most important strategic and financial decisions. Both the chairman and the board also play a critical disciplinary role when the company gets into trouble. Their direct intervention in management, in such an event, provides the functional equivalent of hostile takeovers in the American system. To participants and close observers, the German method of encouraging corporate restructuring when required has the notable advantage of precluding the asset-stripping, short-term planning, and social disruption characteristic of American and British corporate takeover battles.[22]

Beyond the prominent role given to employee representatives, the majority of the members of most corporate supervisory boards come from other companies with direct supplier or customer ties. But the distinguishing characteristic of the German system is the explicit role that continues to be played by banks, particularly in Germany's largest companies. The leading industrial banks—Deutsche Bank, Dresdner

Bank, and Commerzbank—are universal banks. This means they are permitted to engage in a full range of commercial and investment banking activities under one roof; they are also permitted to cross the financial-industrial divide characteristic of the U.S. system. Throughout modern German history, such powers have made them the key providers or organizers of capital for corporate Germany.

The role of the banks continues to be reflected both directly and indirectly in Germany's corporate governance system. Bankers hold nearly 10 percent of all seats on the supervisory boards of the 100 largest nonfinancial companies in Germany (Table 3.2. Composition of Supervisory Boards of the 100 Largest German Enterprises). Moreover, in the largest companies, the lead bank often provides the chairman of the supervisory board. Given the fact that there are relatively few banks involved in corporate finance in Germany at the highest level, this essentially means that supervisory boards in Germany are extensively interlocked.[23]

Underpinning such networks, as in the case of Japan, are significant cross-shareholdings among the top German financial and nonfinancial corporations. It is not uncommon for a corporation's leading creditor to hold between 10 and 20 percent of its voting shares.[24] Combined with cross-shareholdings involving suppliers, major customers, and other firms, intercorporate shareholding frequently meets or exceeds half of the voting shares in many German firms. The connection between owners, managers, and creditors is even more intimate in Germany's privately held companies, many of which now have operations on a global scale.[25]

The center of gravity in Germany's corporate governance structure is in the reciprocal and enduring relationships that exist between a typically small number of individuals representing the various groups most involved in the life of a corporation. This tends to create a deep sense of mutual trust, which is reinforced by continual interaction. That sense is backed up, however, by the certainty of severe sanctions in the event of breaches. Although similar in nature to the ties that bind intercorporate alliances in Japan, the relationships in Germany appear to be more broadly based, overlapping, and inclusive. They are also strongly reinforced by certain features of the national financial system. The workings of that system were highlighted in the case of the near bankruptcy of Metallgesellschaft, Germany's fourteenth largest industrial conglomerate.

On December 17, 1993, the entire senior management of Metallgesellschaft was abruptly dismissed by the firm's supervisory board.[26] The dismissal followed reports of massive trading losses in the firm's New York office. The chairman of the supervisory board, a senior exec-

TABLE 3.2
Composition of Supervisory Boards of the
100 Largest German Enterprises (in percent)

Private banks	7.0
Other banks	2.2
Insurance companies	1.6
Trade unions	12.4
Other employee representatives	36.3
Representatives from industry	25.8
Other shareholder representatives	10.2
Politicians and civil servants	4.5

Source: Federal Association of German Banks
data, adapted from Ellen R. Schneider-Lenné, "The
Role of German Capital Markets, the Universal
Banks' Supervisory Boards, and Interlocking Directorships," in *Capital Markets and Corporate Governance*, Nicholas Dimsdale and Martha Prevezer,
eds. (Oxford: Clarendon Press, 1994) p. 303.

utive from Deutsche Bank, which along with Dresdner Bank is one of
the company's leading shareholders, publicly criticized the managers
for inadequately supervising the New York operation. At the same
time, he announced the appointment of a new senior management
group mandated to turn the company around. It later transpired that
losses extended far beyond those of the New York office, and a massive
restructuring of the company ensued. Reports in the financial press
interpreted these events as indicative of the erosion of the traditional
German system of corporate management, particularly of the role of
the supervisory board and of banks as shareholders. It is more plausible, however, to read it the opposite way. Crisis makes visible the
fundamental principle of German corporate law: ultimate authority
over German corporations remains vested in supervisory boards. And
at the core of the supervisory boards of many of the most prominent
German MNCs are banks.

Supervisory boards typically become more assertive and intrusive
when serious troubles arise. At such times, banks can play a crucial
coordinating role. Unlike their analogs in Japan, however, they do not
generally intervene directly in management. As in the Metallgesellschaft case, they may nevertheless oversee change in a top management team. If they have confidence in a troubled firm's management or
if they are assured that new management will be effective, their most
important function is to organize the financial side of a rescue. Their
motivation does not necessarily come from the fact that they are lend-

ers as well as equity holders, especially in large firms. There is, indeed, no evidence that their loans to affiliated companies are priced to include an implicit subsidy, and bank loans in Germany are in most cases very heavily collateralized.[27] From whatever historical wellsprings it flows, however, banks do seem to have played a stabilizing role in the German corporate system.[28] Combined with the effects of shareholding patterns in the big German corporations, the end results include the virtual absence of hostile takeovers, rapid reorganizations in emergencies, and the assurance of backup resources if required. A key question engaging contemporary researchers, nevertheless, is whether (or how fast) that system is fading.

The scale and timing of Metallgesellschaft's problems led to new scrutiny of the system in the mid-1990s. As some observers read into those problems the ultimate dismantling of traditional mores, it did look likely that the functions of the supervisory board would be clarified and board activism promoted. In this context, the role of banks will continue to be analyzed, but it will not likely be diminished. The Economics Minister of Germany implied as much in the midst of Metallgesellschaft's crisis, when he publicly urged its banks to assist the company to the fullest extent necessary. German banks have done so in many other such cases before, and the historical result has been a significant bolstering of their various roles in German corporate affairs.

Those roles represent the legacy of Germany's rapid but relatively late industrial development.[29] In the absence of broad and deep capital markets, the banks performed a crucial function in organizing the financial resources required for that development. During the past couple of decades, their direct financing and ownership role has declined somewhat as corporations succeeded in building up their internal reserves. In cases where the reverse has occurred, financial distress has usually been the cause. Because it agreed to convert some of its prior loans to equity when Daimler-Benz was having difficulties, for example, Deutsche Bank wound up owning more of the firm than it probably ever wanted. For that reason, the bank has been intimately involved in Daimler's efforts over the past decade to diversify both its corporate assets and its shareholder base.

More broadly among German MNCs, however, the continuing influence of the banks becomes evident when the corporate proxy voting system is scrutinized.[30] In addition to being legally empowered to lend funds directly to firms as well as to underwrite stock and bond issues, German banks can perform these functions for firms in which they themselves have a long-term ownership interest. In addition, the banks also act as agents for individual shareholders. An individual, for example, typically signs over the voting rights assigned to his shares to a bank, which serves as custodian. When votes are to be taken, the bank must now tell the shareholder how it intends to vote those shares. Unless the shareholder specifically disagrees, a rarity, the bank then effectively controls those shares as well as any shares it holds in its own name.

After World War II, as was the case during Germany's initial industrialization in the late nineteenth century, banks managed the flow of funds from savers to companies. The German financial system today actually comprises a large variety of banks and other credit institutions. Private commercial banks, approximately 340 in number, account for about one quarter of total business financing activity. Of that amount, the Big Three—Deutsche Bank, Dresdner Bank, and Commerzbank—account for approximately one third. By the 1960s, companies gradually began to reduce their reliance on the banks as their internal reserves recovered. Over the next three decades, nevertheless, the banks' holdings of all corporate shares nearly doubled.[31] The interests of the banks, as well as of the largest insurance companies, ranged widely. They have tended, however, to be concentrated on the leading corporations of the country. Along this dimension, and especially in the extent to which founding family, labor union, and state government ownership interests remain high, the largest companies in Germany contrast markedly with their American and Japanese peers (Table 3.3. Proportion of Stock Held Directly by Largest Stockholders in Selected Large German Companies). Indeed, nonfinancial enterprises represent the largest shareholding group; the proportion held has been rising over time to a current level around 40 percent.[32] Along two dimensions, the German experience differs then from the American and Japanese experiences: concentrated share ownership and the direct ownership role of banks. By 1990, it was true that in only three of the largest German companies did banks or insurance companies directly control a majority of voting shares. In another thirteen, they held significant minority interests. But this understated their actual influence.

In terms of the actual voting of shares, one authoritative study estimated that banks controlled thirty-four of the largest German firms in 1975 and thirty-nine in 1988.[33] Another influential study tried to get a better measure of the actual role of the banks by examining voting patterns at the 1986 annual meetings of the largest German MNCs. Of the shares voted at the meetings of eight of the largest, the Big Three banks voted the following proportions: Siemens (60.6 percent); Daimler-Benz (81 percent); Volkswagen (50.1 percent); Bayer (53.2 percent); BASF (55.4 percent); Hoechst (57.7 percent); VEBA (50.2 percent); Thyssen (68.5 percent).[34]

TABLE 3.3
Proportion of Stock Held Directly by Largest Stockholders in Selected Large
German Companies (in percent)

Company	Largest Stockholders		Proportion of Shares Held
Siemens	Siemens family		about 10
Daimler-Benz	Deutsche Bank		24.4
	Government of Kuwait		14
	Stella Automobil-Beteiligungs		12.6
	(Commerzbank	12.5	
	Bayerische Landesbank	12.5	
	Robert Bosch	12.5	
	Dresdner Bank	12.5)	
Deutsche Bank	Allianz		5
Volkswagen	State of Lower Saxony		20
AEG	Daimler-Benz		80.2
Bayer	Unspecified banks and insurance companies		38
BASF	Allianz (insurance)		14.4
Hoechst	Kuwait Petroleum Corp.		about 25
VEBA	Allianz		12.1
Thyssen	Thyssen Holdings		about 25
	(Thyssen estate	63.5)	
	Allianz		20
	Fritz Thyssen Foundation		about 9
	Commerzbank		5
Robert Bosch	Robert Bosch Foundation and Robert Bosch Industrietreuhand		92
	Bosch family		8
BMW	Quandt family		about 60
	GFA		10
	(Dresdner Bank	50	
	Siemens	10	
	Stefan Quandt	10)	
Preussag	Westdeutsche Landesbank		about 28
Westdeutsche Landesbank	State of North-Rhine Westphalia		43.2
	Regional savings bank associations		56.8
Dresdner Bank	Allianz		22.5
	Vermögensverwaltung		10.5
	Frankfurter Gesellschaft für Finanzwerte		10
Allianz	Munich Re-Insurance		about 25
	Bayerische Vereinsbank		10
	Deutsche Bank		10
	Dresdner Bank		10

TABLE 3.3 *(cont.)*

Company	Largest Stockholders		Proportion of Shares Held
	Bayerische Hypotheken-und Wechsel-Bank		5
Klöckner-Humboldt-Deutz	Deutsche Bank		31.8
Linde	Allianz		14.8
	Commerzbank		10.3
	Deutsche Bank		10
Degussa	GFC		25
	(Henkel family	46	
	Dresdner Bank	27	
	Munich Re-Ins.	27)	
Bayerische Vereinsbank	Bavarian State Foundation		11.8
Bayerische Hypotheken- und Wechsel-Bank	Allianz		24.8
Metallgesellschaft	Allgemeine Verwaltungs- gesellschaft für Industrie- beteiligungen		about 25
	(Deutsche Bank	55.35	
	Allianz	44.65)	
	Kuwait Investment Authority		20
	Dresdner Bank		13
	Daimler-Benz		10
	Australian Mutual Prov. Soc.		8
	M.I.M Holdings, Australia		2.5

Sources: Commerzbank, *Wer gehört zu wem: Beteiligungsverhältnisse in Deutschland*, 18th enlarged edition (1994); and Frankfurter Algemeine Zeitung, *Germany's Top 500*, 1995 edition.

The German system was reshaped after World War II, and it continues to change. What has never taken root at the highest levels of German corporate finance, however, is a broad and deep deconcentration effort similar to that which transformed the American system in the 1930s.[35] As one senior German executive told us, "The core of the German company has been and remains in its financial structure and the associated mentality of its most senior managers."[36] In fact, a range of German executives interviewed for this study suggested that Germany's economic difficulties in the 1990s—associated mainly with the impact of reunification on one hand and technological change on the other—are reinforcing the traditional system of corporate governance rather than eroding it. Senior officials from one of Germany's leading banks, for example, were forthright in explaining that a number of client firms, which had sought to loosen their ties with the bank during the booming 1980s, had abruptly reversed course in the 1990s. Given a rising demand for capital, however, this did not mean that German MNCs would not continue to seek resources abroad. With the full support of their banks, for example, Daimler-Benz and others entered U.S. equity markets during the 1990s with precisely that goal in mind. (A 3.2 percent stake in Daimler-Benz was initially offered for sale from shares held by Deutsche Bank.) One would be hard-pressed, however, to find a German industrialist who believed that this presaged the loss of control to impersonal capital markets commonly associated with American MNCs.[37] Helping to prevent such an eventuality are other building blocks of Germany's financial structure, including corporate accounting rules and tax policies.

German accounting rules have long assisted firms in building up substantial internal reserves, typically the cheapest source of capital for expansion and growth. Daimler-Benz's foray into the U.S. stock market provided a rare opportunity to measure their effects. Daimler officials told us that the move comprised part of a larger effort to raise the firm's profile in the United States at a time when it was putting up a new plant in Tuscaloosa, Alabama. Another motivation apparently came from Deutsche Bank, which welcomed the chance to reduce its 28.1 percent equity stake. To meet SEC requirements, the firm agreed to translate its financial statements in line with generally accepted accounting principles of the United States. In December 1993, after a disastrous downturn in its core businesses, the company reported in Germany that it had lost DM 181 million ($105.4 million) during the previous nine months. Under American accounting rules, however, it had to report that loss as DM 2.05 billion (1.19 billion).[38] Among other things, the difference provided an indication of the importance of hidden reserves in German corporations. Such reserves can be created in a number of ways. German firms, for example, frequently make large provisions for possible future contingencies and pensions, taking them out of current earnings. Tax laws encourage such conservatism by making these provisions deductible. Moreover, the relatively high marginal tax rate on reported profits discourages firms from not making such provisions. Hidden reserves can also be created by the practice of carrying (appreciating) long-term investments on the balance sheet at historic book value, a practice common in Germany.[39]

A basic lack of transparency with regard to such reserves must surely be intentional. For many years after World War II, German corporate balance sheets were quite weak. Disclosing the full extent of that weakness threatened to scare off necessary financing. Over time, hidden reserves became an important tool for coping with uncertainty, for smoothing out earnings, and for bolstering the confidence of creditors and investors. Even if they provide only the illusion of strength, that illusion can easily translate into competitive advantage. For example, partners or competitors might draw comfort or discomfort, as the case may be, from the assumption that a firm has plentiful resources to call upon to support the successful implementation of strategic investment plans.[40]

Despite continuing challenges, universal banking, the main-bank system, and key aspects of German financial reporting face adaptation, not annihilation.[41] The Metallgesellschaft case and others certainly caused public soul-searching in the 1990s, and anxiety concerning the country's technological future is frequently linked in policy debates to criticisms of the financial foundations of German corporations. In light of Germany's industrial history as well as the constraints posed by circumstances prevailing in European and world markets in the 1990s, however, it seems more than reasonable to expect those foundations to be reinforced even as they are incrementally adjusted. This will not preclude successful German MNCs from attempting to constrain the influence of their main banks during good times, for example, by building tactical relationships with other banks.[42] But neither this nor the global strategies of the big German banks imply that the German system of corporate governance and financing is moving decisively away from its roots.

Japan

The effort to understand how Japanese corporate governance and financing systems differ from their American counterparts has in itself become something of a growth industry. The once common view that Japanese MNCs represent the visible face of Japan Incorporated, with the implication that government really calls the shots, is now widely dismissed as simplistic. So too is the more recent characterization of those firms as run by and for an unaccountable managerial elite. Even inside Japan, elaborate related debates are taking place about whether bureaucrats, politicians, bankers, or corporate managers deserve the lion's share of the credit—or the blame—for the success and the problems of Japanese industry. A more complex view is warranted.

The managers of Japanese MNCs do play the key role in a system of corporate governance that has evolved gradually over time. And, indeed, the system does free them from some of the pressures that their American counterparts face, especially pressures for short-term returns. Extensive institutional cross-shareholding arrangements, for example, can help explain why real earnings might be allowed to fluctuate widely in order to keep R&D budgets stable. It needs to be emphasized, however, that executives of Japanese MNCs, most of which are embedded in formal corporate networks, are intimately accountable for their overall performance to a wide array of constituencies.

The constituencies to which Japanese corporate managers do primarily attend include employees, lead banks, other long-term creditors, regulators, other corporations with which they are directly or indirectly affiliated, suppliers, and important customers. These constituencies share certain basic interests in the firm beyond simple survival. Unlike their American counterparts, however, Japanese managers find it impossible to agglomerate even a fraction of those interests under a single financial indicator, such as return on investment. One very basic interest, nevertheless, appears to have long been broadly shared by many constituencies: the need to compensate for past technological weakness and to ensure national technological parity or leadership in the future. Indeed, this theme was a common refrain throughout a long series of interviews with senior executives in Japan. Although administrative guidance from governmental officials may once have been required, a broadly shared commitment between business and government now pursues that interest.[43] Elements of the contemporary structure of Japanese corporate governance appear to have evolved in light of an overriding national vision keyed on technological advance. Two elements, both related, deserve to be highlighted in any attempt to understand the nature of contemporary change in corporate Japan as that vision is rearticulated: the main-bank system and the networks of relationships often signified by reciprocal shareholding.

During the late nineteenth century, a reformist elite developed Japan's corporate financing system on an indigenous base but with the German model clearly in mind. In economist's terms, under conditions of capital scarcity, the system was designed to funnel personal savings as rapidly as possible into production-oriented investment. Political scientists add to this an underlying strategic intent—the defensive commitment to industrialize quickly and catch up to the West. Such economic nationalism obviously had analogs in many other countries. In Japan, however, it has long had a relatively clear technological focus. It has therefore become common to depict the financial system as a component part of a "technonationalist" development and national security strategy.[44]

During the early phases of industrialization, private banks operating under the close supervision of government and combining commercial and investment banking functions provided the lion's share of external corporate financing. The high end of industry was dominated by organized networks of firms—the former *zaibatsu*—all of which had a bank at their center. After World War II, these old corporate networks reemerged, bearing names like Mitsubishi, Mitsui, and Sumitomo. Although links among affiliated companies were looser than before, banks remained the principal financial intermediaries. As Carl Kester and other analysts have noted, new bank-centered *keiretsu*, or *kigyo shudan*, also arose. These new "enterprise groups" were all widely diversified, horizontally organized (or intermarket) corporate alliances at the upper reaches of the industrial chain. As Japanese economic growth took off in the 1950s, so-called production or vertical *keiretsu* also developed around large manufacturing enterprises like Nippon Steel, Hitachi, Nissan, and Toyota. These networks of affiliated contractors and subcontractors also tended to cluster their financial relationships around a few banks.

The big change after World War II came with the imposition of a U.S.-style separation of financial functions on the system of corporate financing. In effect, Article 65 of the country's Securities and Exchange Law imposed a Glass-Steagall-type barrier between commercial banking and investment banking. Following adoption of the law, the "city" banks (the main corporate banks) were restricted mainly to traditional lending and deposit-taking functions. Long-term credit banks developed to do what their name implies, and they funded themselves mainly through the issuance of long-term debentures. A niche was carved out for trust companies. A relatively small securities sector took on the functions of bond and stock underwriting, and insurance companies gradually became more important. In this system, Japanese banks continued to be permitted to own important equity stakes in nonfinancial companies. The limit has long been 5 percent, ostensibly the same that applies to bank holding companies in the United States. As we shall see, however, the actual effect of such stakes is multiplied by other features of the system.

Despite Article 65, banks played the key corporate financing role in Japan during the period of rapid recovery and growth commencing around 1950. The city banks as a group were quite focused on their corporate lending role, but the market for retail deposits was quite decentralized. Government effectively used the banking system, as well as an intricate set of public institutions engaged in deposit-taking and policy-based lending, to steer household savings to industry. Postwar banking markets developed under the tight constraints of interest rate and foreign exchange controls.[45] Short-term commercial bank loans consistently rolled over, longer-term credits from the industrial banks, and emergency financing as needed from both—all effectively repressed the need for impersonal bond and stock markets. Contemporary Japanese MNCs collectively benefited from the system. Even into the 1970s, banks continued to provide Japanese borrowers with over 60 percent of the financial requirements they could not meet from retained earnings; securities markets remained quite underdeveloped, providing only 7 percent of the country's financing in the mid-1970s, a number which would grow only marginally until the mid-1980s.

In the late 1970s, aspects of the system began to change. The same technological and market pressures that promoted a financial deregulatory agenda elsewhere were at work in Japan. In addition, the leading Japanese MNCs had reached maturity. The corporate bond market began to expand as long-standing interest rate and residual foreign exchange controls were relaxed. As Japanese MNCs built up their own internal reserves, corporate borrowing in general fell sharply. The banks, in turn, began diversifying their operations abroad. At the same time, banks and securities companies started to "swim in one another's ponds." Foreign political pressure reinforced an overt trend toward deregulation and liberalization.[46] By the end of the 1980s, Japan's financial economy was booming, and Japanese financial institutions dominated global markets. It was not uncommon to hear market participants as well as observers speculate about the end of the mainbank system and Japan's inevitable convergence toward global norms.

By the early 1990s, the financial euphoria that had dramatically pushed up Japanese stock and real estate prices during the previous decade had long since passed. A deep recession (Japanese corporate leaders commonly referred to it as a depression) followed a tight credit squeeze. Leading Japanese MNCs, as well as their bankers, suddenly found themselves overextended, while a rapidly appreciating yen tightened the squeeze. Mergers swept the banking industry, the most dramatic of which created the world's largest financial institution by amalgamating Mitsubishi Bank and the Bank of Tokyo.

Despite the fact that they now supplied only around 20 percent of the financing needs of large corporations, the banks' role as lender of last resort once again became apparent. It was an inauspicious time for a corporation to be caught without a solid relationship to a main bank. In a series of interviews undertaken for this study, corporate executives noted without dissent that they expected the economic problems facing corporate Japan in the 1990s to be resolved in the traditional ways, that is, by concerted efforts within industrial groups to restructure with the active assistance of their bank creditors. Indeed, some expressed relief that the wild ride of the 1980s was over.[47] The widely predicted death of the main-bank system was not on the horizon, even as a banking crisis ensued. Its endurance owed much to deeper structures in corporate Japan, especially to the practice of reciprocal shareholding.

In contrast to the legalistic, arm's-length, and often antagonistic relationships at the core of American corporate governance structures, it is meaningful to depict the Japanese equivalent as networks built upon relationships of trust, the reciprocal exchange of information, technology and even management, and expectations of long-term endurance. Within a corporate network, managers often compete energetically. But they also cooperate to the fullest extent required to maintain the network. During periods of crisis, this can entail directly intervening in one another's most intimate affairs.

For most Japanese MNCs, internal network structures are linked to, and reinforced by, external relationships with other firms and financial institutions.[48] These connections tend to be stable and have traditionally been sealed by mutual cross-shareholdings. Individually, those shareholdings may be small, but their size is not as important as their existence, for they signify valued and durable business relationships.[49] Reciprocal equity ownership comprises a critical element in a weblike system of corporate interdependence, an especially obvious feature in the major bank-centered *keiretsu* (Tables 3.4 to 3.6. Major Members and Affiliates in Leading Keiretsu). On an aggregate basis, and combined with other stable shareholdings by affiliated companies, the system can have the consequence of closing the market for corporate control, not only for potential foreign investors but also for domestic rivals. In the early 1990s, over 70 percent of the outstanding shares of publicly listed Japanese corporations were held by Japanese financial institutions and other corporations.[50] With little fear that key shareholders will sell, managers can also be conservative in their dividend payouts, especially when stock prices are rising and unrealized capital gains can be recorded as assets. In addition, they can compensate their main shareholders in other ways, for example, by giving their lead banks a right of first refusal when new financing is required and by directing other types of business to related companies.

Sectoral studies indicate a much wider set of reasons for reciprocal corporate shareholding. These include the desire to solidify a relationship with a leading supplier of vital technology. Japanese automobile companies, for example, are famous for pushing key engineering and design functions down into their supplier companies. Cross-shareholding can seal the resulting relationship of technological cooperation and mutual dependence.[51] Other contractual or noncontractual business

TABLE 3.4
Major Members and Affiliates of Sumitomo Group—Percentage
of Stock Held by Other Group Members or Affiliated Companies

	1992	1993	1994
Financial Institutions			
Sumitomo Bank	19.32	19.25	18.53
Sumitomo Trust & Banking	26.64	25.27	23.47
Sumitomo Marine & Fire Insurance	26.62	27.08	26.29
Trading, Manufacturing, and Other			
Sumitomo Shoji	33.08	32.83	31.64
Sumitomo Coal Mining	38.59	34.83	32.55
Sumitomo Construction	30.44	27.04	26.28
Sumitomo Forestry	29.92	31.10	31.04
Sumitomo Chemical	23.11	23.92	24.03
Sumitomo Bakelite	47.40	48.15	47.31
Sumitomo Cement	32.34	25.55	20.75
Sumitomo Metal Industries	19.50	32.77	18.20
Sumitomo Metal Mining	29.87	19.24	28.17
Sumitomo Light Metal Industries	48.48	29.64	46.45
Sumitomo Electric Industries	20.84	48.17	21.00
Sumitomo Heavy Industries	28.38	20.60	27.80
Sumitomo Realty & Development	17.38	27.85	16.47
Sumitomo Warehouse	37.49	26.38	38.24
Nippon Sheet Glass	25.34	17.17	23.66
NEC	27.10	38.53	25.11

Source: Kigyo Keiretsu Soran (Tokyo: Toyo Keizai Shinposha, 1994,
1995, and 1996).

obligations have traditionally been sealed with an equity exchange.
Corporate interlocks can also represent the legacy of divisions spun off
as independent companies, Japan's analog to the gestation of new companies in the United States through the venture capital market. In addition, they frequently represent the purchase of "insurance policies"
from financial institutions, since such bindings yield a degree of protection in the event of a crisis, albeit at the possible price of having to allow
the financial institutions to intervene directly in management. Finally,
cross-shareholdings sometimes directly result when funding needs to
be raised in a hurry; in return for expanded equity positions, financial
institutions or affiliated companies inject necessary cash.

In light of the historical path of their firms, it is not surprising that
even when deep crises roil their markets, Japanese corporate managers
"tend to view their proximate task as being the preservation and enhancement of complex relationships rather than the immediate, direct

TABLE 3.5

Major Members and Affiliates of Mitsui Group—Percentage of
Stock Held by Other Group Members or Affiliated Companies

	1992	1993	1994
Financial Institutions			
Sakura Bank	15.98	16.60	16.52
Mitsui Trust & Banking	24.42	24.94	24.09
Mitsui Kaijo Kasai	28.90	28.62	27.93
Trading, Manufacturing, and Other			
Mitsui Bussan	20.11	20.43	20.19
Mitsui Mining	37.48	37.02	37.02
Mitsui Construction	41.96	41.85	41.16
Sanki Engineering	20.65	20.61	20.62
Nippon Flour Mills	26.32	26.45	26.13
Toray Industries	16.45	16.57	16.50
Oji Paper	12.11	12.03	11.95
Nippon Paper Industry	—	10.73	11.47
Mitsui Toatsu Chemicals	18.65	18.28	18.02
Denki Kagaku Kogyo	17.56	17.30	17.15
Mitsui Petrochemical Industries	38.39	38.83	38.76
Onoda Cement	19.94	19.71	15.08
Japan Steel Works	19.56	19.50	18.85
Mitsui Mining & Smelting	12.70	13.25	12.23
Mitsui Engineering & Shipbuilding	18.16	18.05	16.56
Mitsukoshi	14.39	14.05	13.45
Mitsui Real Estate Development	17.64	17.32	17.09
Mitsui O.S.K. Lines	21.60	21.20	19.73
Mitsui Warehouse	29.95	29.97	29.06
Toshiba	11.41	11.55	11.84
Ishikawajima Harima	10.72	10.44	10.44
Toyota Motor	10.30	12.70	12.95

Source: Kigyo Keiretsu Soran (Tokyo: Toyo Keizai Shinposha, 1994,
1995, and 1996).

pursuit of any one stakeholder's interests, such as that of exclusive equity owners."[52] Western economic orthodoxy notwithstanding, it is not
clear that such proclivities have been inefficient for Japan as a whole.
Michael Gerlach puts the point as follows:

Reliance on intercorporate networks has in many ways helped to keep
the Japanese firm smaller on average and more focused than its American
counterpart while combining many of the advantages of vertical integration. Moreover, the corporate equity holders that predominate in Japanese

TABLE 3.6

Major Members and Affiliates of Mitsubishi Group—Percentage of Stock Held by Other Group Members or Affiliated Companies

	1992	1993	1994
Financial Institutions			
Mitsubishi Bank	25.62	25.45	25.38
Mitsubishi Trust & Banking	27.35	26.43	26.06
Nihon Shintaku Ginko	13.59	14.10	72.25
Tokyo Marine & Fire Insurance	22.61	22.31	22.26
Trading, Manufacturing, and Other			
Mitsubishi Construction	—	99.81	70.69
Mitsubishi Shoji	33.22	32.72	33.10
Kirin Brewery	19.20	20.23	20.39
Mitsubishi Rayon	22.85	22.62	22.70
Mitsubishi Paper Mills	31.87	32.02	31.88
Mitsubishi Kasei[a]	22.12	21.85	—
Mitsubishi Gas Chemical	24.68	23.62	24.60
Mitsubishi Petrochemical	32.99	36.03	36.24
Mitsubishi Jushi	57.32	57.50	56.95
Mitsubishi Oil[a]	44.60	43.31	—
Mitsubishi Steel Manufacturing	37.18	37.17	37.10
Mitsubishi Materials	24.90	24.68	24.78
Mitsubishi Shindo	53.27	51.51	43.56
Mitsubishi Cable Industries	49.75	48.74	48.45
Mitsubishi Kakoki	36.68	36.24	40.29
Mitsubishi Electric	16.47	16.09	16.06
Mitsubishi Heavy Industry	19.93	19.43	18.78
Mitsubishi Motors	56.44	56.63	52.91
Mitsubishi Estate	26.46	26.38	25.36
Nippon Yusen	26.07	25.09	24.69
Mitsubishi Warehouse	42.57	42.29	42.27
Asahi Glass	28.09	28.17	28.09
Nikon	27.88	28.18	28.46
Mitsubishi Kagaku[a]	—	—	24.73

Source: *Kigyo Keiretsu Soran* (Tokyo: Toyo Keizai Shinposha, 1994, 1995, and 1996).

[a] Mitsubishi Kasei and Mitsubishi Oil were merged in 1994 to form Mitsubishi Kagaku.

stock markets have proved far more willing to take long-term investment positions in other companies than have the institutional investors common in the United States.[53]

Despite the historical record of this system, which stands up well in terms of the actual long-term enhancement of shareholder value and certainly in terms of the competitiveness of Japan's leading industries, observers frequently contend that it is breaking down. Some see this as the inevitable consequence both of corporate maturity and of global financial integration. Others see fundamental competitive problems emerging from a relatively inefficient domestic economy, the consequence of financial and corporate structures that have long siphoned high domestic savings away from internal infrastructure improvement and consumption. Despite some evidence of marginal changes in the system, however, our interviews and analysis indicate caution in the interpretation and projection of such changes.

Aggregate data suggest that there is no overall trend away from what has been called the "keiretsu-ization" of the Japanese economy. Despite the rapid growth in the number of companies in existence over the past three decades, there has been little change in the percentage of those firms embedded in *keiretsu* networks. In 1970, some 370 companies in *keiretsu* accounted for 66 percent of total corporate assets and 71 percent of total sales; twenty years later, 577 such companies accounted for 69 percent of corporate assets and 76 percent of sales.[54] To some extent, the weakening of individual equity ties between financial intermediaries and Japanese MNCs during the late 1980s and early 1990s may have reflected the unusual circumstances of Japan's infamous financial bubble. The bursting of that bubble, however, encouraged a number of firms to repair their financial relationships, despite the fact that major banks were having severe difficulties in the wake of that bursting. In that regard, the few publicized instances of firms attempting to sell off their holdings in banks represented exceptions to the rule.

Senior Japanese executives quite openly explain that such behavior risks retaliation. It is well understood that the web is only as strong as its weakest thread. This is not to say that the system is inflexible, or that equity holdings are absolutely necessary to secure solid ties between firms. Indeed, some of the turbulence experienced in the Japanese corporate equity market in the early and mid-1990s, for example, reflected the efforts of some shareholders, mainly financial institutions having problems with their own capital bases, to increase dividend flows at a time when routine capital gains could no longer be assured. For similar reasons, many companies have rationalized their cross-shareholdings and reduced their volume. Since the amount of shares held is often irrelevant to its major purposes, however, neither development necessarily implies the unraveling of the cross-share-holding system overall.[55] Certainly within the major intermarket *keiretsu*, changes in the cross-shareholdings over the past decade have been marginal (Table 3.7. Average Cross-Shareholdings within Major Japanese Keiretsu).

The importance of equity ties as sources of intragroup discipline, however, should not be exaggerated. Within leading corporate networks, managers continue to be disciplined by their bankers and affiliates for poor performance. Hopelessly weak firms tend to be quickly and quietly liquidated or merged. Informal supplier ties can be critically important in this regard. Nissan Motor, for example, effectively took over the management of Fuji Heavy Industries (Subaru) in 1990. At the time, Nissan owned only 4 percent of Fuji's shares, but the two companies collaborated intensively, shared managerial staff, and depended upon one another for crucial supplies. The "takeover" occurred without any debt being restructured or any transfers of stock between Fuji's major shareholders. The role of financial institutions, as well as the alliance structures in which that role plays out, is critical in such cases. Indeed, it is quite reasonable to suggest that the direct discipline such institutions and alliances can exercise is the functional equivalent of a U.S.-style market for corporate takeovers.[56] The argument for historical continuity, moreover, remains quite plausible. In Gerlach's terms:

> Japanese firms have long sought to stabilize their external environment in the face of dramatic shocks and restructuring. [T]he trend [toward internationalization and liberalization] could actually have the opposite effect from that predicted. In the market for corporate control, at least, firms have used new threats imposed by hostile outside interests as a rationale to strengthen alliances with selected affiliate-shareholders. The apparent chinks in what seems a formidable wall around Japan's markets for corporate control, [acquisitions of generally weak companies by foreigners], have actually proven how formidable the wall remains. . . . While specific *patterns* of relationships in Japan are evolving, there remains an important continuity in the underlying *processes* of alliance formation.[57]

In short, the Japanese system of corporate governance continues to render the managers of Japanese MNCs accountable to a wide range of stakeholders. But that same system has freed them from the need to focus their strategies rigidly on the achievement of high, direct, and near-term returns to shareholders. This has enabled them to pursue the

TABLE 3.7
Average Cross-Shareholdings within Major Japanese Keiretsu[a]

	Mitsui	Mitsubishi	Sumitomo	Fuyo	Sanwa	DKB
1980	17.62	29.26	26.74	16.26	16.78	14.12
1985	17.87	25.18	25.01	15.79	16.84	13.33
1988	17.09	26.87	24.42	15.29	16.38	12.24
1991	16.58	26.37	24.67	15.62	16.67	12.16
1992	16.58	26.33	24.65	15.62	16.72	12.19
1993	16.77	26.11	24.45	14.90	16.41	11.92
1994	16.50	27.54	23.35	14.61	15.98	11.72

Source: Calculated from *Kigyo Keiretsu Soran* (Tokyo: Toyo Keizai Shinposha, 1987–96).

[a] Average of the ratios of stocks in one member company owned by other companies within the group.

kinds of longer-term strategies needed to acquire or develop new technologies, and to emerge relatively quickly as world-class competitors in key industries. The system also provides most Japanese MNCs with implicit safety nets in the event of serious managerial mistakes or unanticipated market shocks. Among other things, the existence of such safety nets helps explain why corporate bankruptcy in Japan appears to be less frequent and less costly than in the United States. During phases of aggressive expansion overseas, it also helps account for the oft-noted ability of Japanese MNCs to downplay short-term calculations of return on investment while market shares are firmly established and defended. In addition, whether deliberately or not, the system works to discourage new entrants—both foreign and domestic—to Japanese markets, especially but not exclusively if entry is sought by way of acquisition. Finally, the system provides group members with a sense of identity that manifests itself in measurable business consequences. As one study found, for example, intermarket *keiretsu* members are on average three times more likely to trade with their affiliates than with companies in other groups and ten times as likely to raise debt and equity from affiliates.[58]

The relationships that underpin particular Japanese MNCs may shift somewhat over time, but periods of turbulence bring to light the durability, not the fragility, of traditional patterns. In contrast to the American system, the Japanese system of corporate governance well deserves the label "alliance capitalism." The system came under unusual strain in the 1990s in the midst of a general national financial crisis and in anticipation of regulatory change, but it remains more difficult to imagine its demise than its adaptation to new circumstances.

TABLE 3.8

Ownership Structure of Publicly Listed Corporations (in percent)

	United States	Japan	Germany
Banks	0.3	25.2	8.9
Insurance companies	5.2	17.3	10.6
Pension funds	24.8	3.6	
Investment companies	9.5	3.6	
Nonfinancial businesses		25.1	39.2
Households (direct or through mutual funds)	53.5	23.1	16.8
Government		0.6	6.8
Foreign	6.7	4.2	17.7

Source: Central bank and stock exchange data, early 1990s, cited in W. Carl Kester, "Industrial Groups as Systems of Corporate Governance," *Oxford Review of Economic Policy*, vol. 8, no. 3 (1993).

National Distinctions

American, German, and Japanese MNCs continue to differ systematically in the relative priorities they assign to the maximization of shareholder value, the satisfaction of customer needs, and the stabilization of employer-employee relations. Unique patterns of corporate ownership and associated differences in patterns of corporate control appear crucial (Table 3.8. Ownership Structure of Publicly Listed Corporations). Those patterns are linked with differential roles assigned to financial institutions in the three countries.

The dispersion and mobility of shareholders in the United States continue to fixate the managers of American corporations on short-term financial performance. This is not necessarily a bad thing, but it needs to be remembered that those corporations are engaged in global competition with rivals capable of longer-term thinking.[59] In fact, German and Japanese MNCs have demonstrated just such a capability in the past. After years of low profitability, for example, American car manufacturers used a lengthy cyclical upswing in the mid-1990s to rebuild their reserves by pushing through dramatic price increases in their domestic market. Their Japanese competitors did not follow suit, despite the significant extra pressure generated by a staggering rise in the value of the yen. Against all odds, the market share of Japanese cars in the United States was thus defended, and Japanese manufacturers were poised to reap new gains when the yen depreciated. Similarly, despite immense losses that might easily have sunk strong American firms, during the same period Metallgesellschaft was able to avoid bankruptcy and dismemberment.

Along with tax, accounting, and other regulatory distinctions, the concentration of corporate ownership and/or control back home helps to explain the enduring abilities of Japanese and German MNCs to absorb losses in the short term and focus their basic strategies on the long term. As two analysts recently put it:

> In contrast to the United States' primary focus on shareholder value, these other countries' corporations are seen as durable national assets that serve a broad base of constituents. Quality products, market share, and employment are just as legitimate as goals as return on shareholder investment. While some U.S. top managers and directors prefer this perspective themselves, they are swimming against the dominant national tide.[60]

In Michael Porter's suggestive terms, the U.S., German, and Japanese systems contrast along both internal and external dimensions of the capital allocation process.[61] Such differences are reflected not only in the investment decisions of particular firms, but also in the nature of the national technology bases those firms have created and exploited on global markets.

Throughout the postwar period and in various high technology sectors, most notably in electronics, transportation systems, and others involving advanced manufacturing techniques, Japanese MNCs became famous for pursuing aggressive strategies keyed on market share. Their corporate governance structures helped foster enduring relationships among their core constituencies, namely employees, managers, and institutional owners. They facilitated the sharing of information across allied firms. Most importantly, they rendered the providers of base capital "patient," while simultaneously attempting to limit the scope for managerial abuse. Occasional scandals indicate that the latter attempt sometimes fails. Japanese consumers, moreover, continue to bear significant opportunity costs associated with this "patient capital" system. Meanwhile, Japan's large trade surpluses and international investment imbalance seem fair measures of the external consequences.

The critical governance mechanism in Japan is the spreading of large volumes of minority equity claims among lenders, customers, suppliers, and affiliates. Despite some recent flux, available empirical evidence and our interviews in Japan suggested strongly that this system is not now changing in a fundamental way. Rather, the current period of painful corporate restructuring appears to represent an attempt to come to grips with several unforeseen consequences: the building of surplus capacity in sectors where growth has turned down dramatically, ill-advised diversification (especially into U.S. and Japanese commercial real estate), and poor management of cash reserves built up during the 1980s.

The managers of Japanese MNCs are aware that successfully charting their way through difficult times and recapturing technological advantages may well depend upon maintaining the essential structure of their equity bases, the confidence of their lead banks, and the loyalty of long-term employees, suppliers, and affiliated companies. This remains true even as financial factors encouraged the movement of some production facilities abroad. The possibility of retaliation for basic breaches in network solidarity is not abstract. Bankers as well as MNC managers explained to us, for example, that all firms in industrial groups understood well the fact that any firm contemplating appreciable sales of shares in related banks or companies would elicit immediate retaliation. The consequent sense of responsibility for collectively managing continuous processes of restructuring within tight traditional constraints is palpable.

Obvious parallels exist in the case of Germany. The country's overarching system of corporate governance has in the past provided German MNCs with the financial stability required to build and exploit technological advantages in key industrial sectors. It reinforced long-term relationships between stakeholders and enabled substantial reserves to be built up. Those reserves, and the knowledge that owners and creditors will not abandon them at the first sign of trouble, encouraged corporate managers to pursue long-term strategies. Cross-shareholding is a critical part of the traditional German system, but the more important influence for many of the most prominent German MNCs comes through the less obvious maintenance of share-voting control by core financial institutions. A comparison of actual voting patterns at the annual meetings of Daimler-Benz, Toyota, and General Motors, for example, reveals that the top five institutional shareholders—all themselves incorporated in the home countries of those firms—routinely account for around 70 percent in the first case, 20 percent in the second, and 5 percent in the third.[62] Interlocking supervisory boards symbolize the inbred stability of the German system, but, in a pinch, those boards are capable of more than symbolism. Especially under conditions of financial distress, they can very effectively discipline managers.

The consequences of the German system can be seen in a number of sectors, but perhaps most obviously in the chemical and automotive industries. Hoechst's purchase of Celanese, the slow and deliberate expansion of BASF in the United States, the simultaneous building of major new plants in the mid-1990s by BMW in Bavaria and South Carolina and by Mercedes Benz in Alabama and Baden-Württemberg—all require a highly developed ability to endure short-run perturbations in tough markets. Traditional corporate governance structures, among other things, have helped foster just such a capacity in the past.[63] We found little reason to assume that they will not do so again in the future.

Each of the three main systems of corporate governance compared in this chapter has its own strengths and its own weaknesses. It is important to emphasize, however, that they are all deeply rooted in the distinctive histories of national financial markets. In a 1995 survey of those markets, *The Economist* magazine depicted continuing deregulation, particularly in the United States, as inevitably melding them together, not just in terms of obviously expanding cross-border financial flows, but also in basic institutional terms. Because they are more "efficient" by standard economic measures, the survey foresaw the emergence of a mainly American "oligopoly" of financial powerhouses that will dominate the issuance and underwriting of corporate securities and challenge "long-established domestic businesses in banking and broking from Germany to Japan."[64] This chapter suggests the opposite. While there is no doubt that corporations from around the world are increasingly interested in tapping large pools of capital, no matter where they are located, core Japanese and German capital markets are not likely to be overwhelmed by American institutions.

Certainly the links between the major indigenous financial institutions in Japan and Germany and their most prominent corporate clients look sturdy. Before the financial bubble of the 1980s burst in Japan, commentators frequently noted that the centrality of banks was breaking down and Japanese MNCs were becoming more independent. In the mid-1990s, such suggestions were muted. In Germany, for its part, banks have never ceased to play their central roles. Available evidence on the role of banks in the financing of corporations, indeed, supports the continuity argument across Japan, Germany, and the United States (Table 3.9. Indicators of Relative Importance of Banks in Financing of Corporations). Similar patterns emerge when corporate debt/equity ratios are compared; since the late 1970s, German corporations have maintained consistently higher ratios than their Japanese counterparts, which in turn have maintained consistently higher ratios than U.S. firms.[65]

Our interviews in Europe and Japan underscored the importance of reliable corporate financiers to the strategic planning process of a wide range of MNCs. This appears to be one reason behind the current spread of the universal banking model within the European Union.

TABLE 3.9

Indicators of Relative Importance of Banks in Financing of Corporations (in percent)

	Ratio of Bank Deposits to Corporate Financial Assets	Ratio of Bank Loans to Corporate Liabilities
USA		
1980	17.8	33.0
1985	21.5	29.2
1990	18.8	25.4
1992	—	30.0
Japan		
1980	78.9	67.4
1985	77.8	67.4
1990	46.5	58.8
1992	—	74.0
Germany		
1980	57.7	63.1
1985	51.1	60.9
1990	43.8	61.3
1992	—	89.0

Source: Data for 1980, 1985, 1990 from IMF, *International Capital Markets: Developments, Prospects, and Policy Issues* (1992), p. 3; data for 1992 from Bank for International Settlements, *64th Annual Report* (March 31, 1994) p. 139.

Certainly the future of that model is not compromised by the steady growth of stock and bond markets in Europe. In fact, the two trends—the spread of universal banking and the growth of nonbank capital markets—seem to go together. The liberalization of capital markets at home and abroad provides German banks, for example, with new ways to retain their existing clients and seek new ones without losing their positions in the real market for corporate control at home. A similar process is underway in Japan, although a deep conflict of institutional interests between the city banks, long-term credit banks, and securities companies, together with a banking crisis, complicates the move toward regulatory reform.

The network corporate alliance structure that centers itself around concentrated banks does provide financial stability and facilitate long-run investment decision making. It can also contribute to excessively conservative management. There is little evidence, however, that it is being held responsible for the severe financial pressures that have arisen for German and Japanese MNCs during the past few years. Indeed, our analysis suggests the reverse. In the face of deep domestic and regional recessions, dramatic developments in exchange rates, and problems in key export markets, many German and Japanese MNCs were reminded in the 1990s of the wisdom of having long ago purchased the "insurance policy" of stable financing relationships.

The U.S. corporate governance and financing systems, of course, have their own strengths. From a purely economic point of view, these include the capacity to let the pendulum of adjustment to market changes swing rapidly. Periodic bouts of excessive risk taking are followed almost predictably by phases of rapid restructuring. The wild takeovers of the 1980s, for example, led to credit losses and legal liabilities for some financial institutions, and a pullback from excessive lending for leveraged buyouts subsequently occurred.[66] But this sort of "normal" turbulence is no longer occurring in a system that is isolated.[67] The swinging pendulum can in principle provide incentives for entrepreneurial innovation, but it can also compound long-term adjustment costs for American MNCs when foreign rivals are playing by different rules. In the face of such costs, American MNCs search for ways to shield themselves and stabilize their financial foundations.

Despite the difficulties confronting their Japanese and German competitors in the 1990s, American MNCs had reason to remain concerned.[68] Beyond traditional strategies of diversification, there has been little sustained movement to deal with the root causes of the corporate planning myopia so obvious in the 1980s. Cyclical upturns in key sectors helped to mask the problem in the next decade. Despite much talk, for example, about moving the financial foundations of American corporations in a direction that might compensate for the relative dearth of significant and long-term shareholding blocks, there was little action. Moreover, traditional American concerns about the risks of financial concentration, as well as traditional interest group politics conducive to fragmentation, remained observable even as mega-mergers swept through the canyons of Wall Street.

In Germany and Japan, conversely, an observer would be hard-pressed to find evidence of strategies truly aiming at financial fragmentation or deconcentration at the externally-oriented edge of the national economies. The large Japanese *keiretsu* are certainly not coming apart. Similarly, hints of capital diversification in Germany need to be interpreted cautiously. They do not likely signal a new willingness on the part of German industry to move decisively away from traditional financial and strategic relationships. Our view, indeed, is that they are typically tactical moves only. Corporate control is the key issue, and there is precious little evidence of either Japanese or German MNCs ceding it to impersonal global markets (Table 3.10. Summary Comparison of Mechanisms of Corporate Control).

TABLE 3.10
Summary Comparison of Mechanisms of Corporate Control

Mechanism	United States	Japan	Germany
Independent board oversight of management	Limited	Formally, limited; informally, can be extensive, especially in crisis	Extensive
Monitoring role of financial institutions	Weak	Strong	Moderate, but can be strong in crisis
Monitoring role of non-financial share-holders/affiliates	Weak	Moderate	Strong
Monitoring role of individual shareholders	Weak	Weak	Can be strong
Hostile takeovers	Common	Very rare	Very rare

Source: Adapted from Stephen Prowse, "Corporate Governance in International Perspective," *Bank for International Settlements Economic Papers*, no. 41 (July 1994) p. 53.

Chapter 4

NATIONAL FOUNDATIONS OF MULTINATIONAL

CORPORATE ACTIVITY (II)

C ROSS-BORDER flows of technology, these days often embedded within multinational corporate networks, represent one of the defining features of the contemporary international economy. Largely because of the rapid growth of digital communication and advanced information technologies, many forms of knowledge have in fact become far easier to create, reproduce, modify, and transmit across national borders. In the wake of their development, channels for knowledge diffusion and exchange have been reshaped. International flows of scientific and technical information among academic, governmental, business, and independent research communities have exploded. The simultaneous growth of international trade and investment has facilitated the process of technology diffusion by embedding innovations in intermediate and finished goods, in new services, and in the facilities that comprise the visible face of the MNC.

Multinational firms can indeed provide a powerful mechanism for the internationalization of technology. Implementing aggressive foreign direct investment (FDI) strategies throughout the post–World War II era, they have dramatically expanded their local presence in markets outside their home bases. With that expansion has come a rapid growth in overseas research and development facilities as well as in less tangible forms of technology transfer. Observing such trends, some analysts have concluded that technology itself has globalized so extensively that it is becoming impossible either to identify particular innovations with individual firms or even to distinguish one national technology and investment base from another.[1] On the other side of the argument, much of the research introduced in chapters 1 and 2 suggests that national institutional structures continue to shape profoundly the technological and economic trajectories of individual countries. Chapter 3 examined key structural differences in the way MNCs govern themselves and finance their operations. This chapter puts into context the apparent contradiction between the widespread perception of convergence in basic corporate behavior across the modern industrial world and the idea of enduring national systems of technological innovation and national systems of investment.[2]

The policies of home and host governments alike shape the FDI strategies of MNCs. Current policies, and the sometimes unintended consequences of past policies, affect the development of technology and the transfer of technology across national borders. Underneath those policies, however, lie characteristically different patterns of economic and political organization.

INNOVATION SYSTEMS

Neoclassical economists have not yet provided us with a robust theory of industrial development, technological change, and economic growth.[3] Any such theory, however, will ultimately be tested against the empirical evidence of national variations in the institutional arrangements behind technological innovation and diffusion.

Innovation systems in the United States, Europe, and Japan differ substantively. They differ in the style and focus of underlying national science and technology policies; in the distribution and performance of R&D funding; in the technological orientation of the industrial research base; and in the blend of corporate technology development and acquisition strategies. Although there are important interactions and interdependencies across national innovation systems, these systems endure as distinct and powerful institutional environments that shape the overseas investment and technology strategies of MNCs.

The world's leading industrial nations have all taken distinctly different paths to technological innovation. To set the stage for a comparison of the ways MNCs contribute to such innovation on a global scale, certain features of national innovation systems may be usefully arrayed on three dimensions: the style and focus of science and technology policy; the location of R&D performance and funding; and the technological orientation of the industrial research base. Table 4.1 (Typology of National Innovation Systems) summarizes how those systems look today. The following sections delve more deeply into each category and closely compare the national innovation systems of the United States, Germany, and Japan.

Style and Focus of Science and Technology Policy

Mainly by design but sometimes by accident, governments deeply affect the innovation strategies and capabilities of firms. The policy inclination is often transmitted through indirect channels, such as tax rules, laws on intellectual property rights, antitrust and competition regimes, official procurement practices, and funding for education, science,

Table 4.1
Typology of National Innovation Systems

	United States	Germany	Japan
Style and focus of science & technology policy	Mission-oriented; defense and health	Diffusion-oriented; industrial	Mission/diffusion; energy and civil space
National R&D funding and performance	Mixed: Large public sector funding of industrial and total R&D; strong university research base with good industry linkages; relatively high foreign funding	Industry-centered: Modest government funding of industrial R&D; strong interindustry linkages; low foreign funding	Industry-centered: Low government funding of industrial R&D; strong intraindustry linkages; very low foreign funding
Technological orientation of industrial research base	Science-intensive, high technology (aerospace, pharmaceuticals, instruments)	Specialized supplier & scale-intensive, medium technology (transportation, electronics, chemicals)	Specialized supplier & scale-intensive, medium technology (electronics, transportation)

transportation and communication infrastructures. Governments also use a number of policy mechanisms that directly affect the innovative capabilities of firms. They fund specific R&D programs, for example, set up public laboratories that cooperate with industry, and provide various forms of programmatic guidance associated with military and civil objectives.

The fact that national governments make very different choices along these lines can be seen in Figure 4.1 (Government R&D Support, by Country and by Socioeconomic Objective). Compared to Germany and Japan, the United States, United Kingdom, and France each devote extremely large shares of their direct governmental R&D expenditures to national defense. The United States and France, moreover, each direct approximately 10 percent of their official R&D to civilian space applications. The United States stands out from all the others, however, in the unusually large share of public R&D resources it devotes to health, and the unusually small share it devotes to industrial development. German policy, conversely, emphasizes industrial development, while energy applications account for the largest share of public R&D resources in Japan.

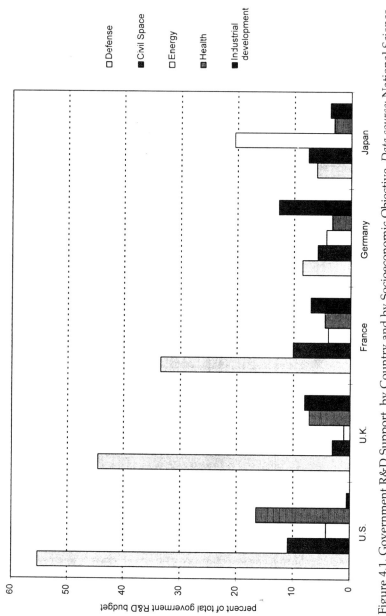

Figure 4.1. Government R&D Support, by Country and by Socioeconomic Objective. *Data source:* National Science Foundation, *Science and Engineering Indicators—1996:* appendix table 4.32.

Such national variations reflect historically rooted differences in basic approaches to technological innovation itself. In the United States, technology development in the postwar period has focused on singular, radical innovations designed to achieve prominent public goals, especially in defense, outer space exploration, and medicine.[4] This style of technology development, often referred to as mission-oriented, concentrates national innovation resources on breakthrough technologies.[5] Public sector mechanisms supporting the adoption and diffusion of new technologies are relatively weak, with partial exceptions in certain agricultural and health-related fields.[6] U.S. technology policy also tends to downplay the innovative and commercial significance of the knowledge embodied in scientists and technologists in government employ.[7]

Technological missions in the United States have generally been science-intensive, partly reflecting the nation's success with such wartime missions as the development of radar and atomic energy. More broadly, World War II and its aftermath fundamentally shaped the nation's orientation toward science and technology, legitimating certain types of governmental intervention in the cause of national security.[8] But postwar security imperatives, combined with a still dominant laissez-faire tradition outside the military arena, prevented the development of any overarching economic strategy on national science and technology development.[9]

Roughly comparable mission-oriented innovation systems emerged in the United Kingdom and France after the war, which defined local technological capacity as the sine qua non of national security. The British and French systems differed from the American one, however, in the scope and size of national technology missions, the degree of government centralization and coordination, and the existence and effectiveness of diffusion channels to other segments of the economy. The United States, largely because of its postwar security posture, was able to afford a diverse set of very large mission programs. Those programs, nevertheless, were established and implemented within a highly fragmented administrative structure with little apparent coordination from either the executive or legislative branches. The situation was quite different in France and to a certain extent the United Kingdom, where centralized strategies could be implemented.[10] The United States, however, developed more robust internal diffusion mechanisms than either the United Kingdom or France, largely because a relatively high share of research was contracted out to private firms and not undertaken in government labs. The U.S. government generally eschewed the development of national champions and worked to develop links between university research centers, private think tanks, and industry. Although such efforts reinforced a tendency to encourage technology diffusion through the indirect means of labor mobility, the American system, like the British and French systems, remains mainly mission-oriented. Both public and private sector actors continue to place big money on the next big breakthrough. Diffusion, incremental adaptation, and commercialization of existing technologies are not basic motivating forces.

In contrast, Germany's style of technology development is intensely oriented toward diffusion. Government R&D programs and related institutions aim directly at facilitating incremental adaptation to technological change and the dissemination of new knowledge throughout the German economy.[11] This orientation derives in part from Germany's well-known vocational education system, centering on formal apprenticeships, which provide a broadly skilled labor force as well as the capacity to retrain and continuously develop new skills. In addition, there exists in Germany an extensive array of institutions for cooperative R&D, focusing on specialized R&D labs that complement the in-house research capabilities of large firms and provide small- and medium-size firms with access to technological resources typically unavailable to equivalent firms in other countries. Moreover, Germany's influential industrial standards institutes provide an important element of coordination as best-practice technologies are diffused throughout the national industrial base.

Although Germany certainly has a sizable defense sector, and also has important mission-style programs for civilian technology development in energy, electronics, telecommunications, and aerospace, the country's core technological assets are oriented less toward the development of major innovations and more toward downstream adjustment processes that affect the rate and scope of technology adoption and diffusion. This system corresponds to Germany's industrial structure, with its large export-intensive industrial conglomerates and broad and dense supplier subcontracting relationships. The relatively cooperative organization of German industry also bears on public policy: governmental goals typically are defined in terms of and in conjunction with industry. This is congruent with a tradition of direct industry participation in formulating and implementing governmental policies, largely through industry associations. In this respect, Germany's innovation system displays a producer orientation analogous to that of Japan. Also like Japan, the country directs comparatively few R&D resources to the defense sector.[12] The analogy, however, should not be pushed too far.

Japan's producer-oriented innovation system is unique among the advanced industrial nations in its unusual combination of both mission-oriented and diffusion oriented innovation styles.[13] The postwar economic development imperative created by Japan's relative technological weakness and its low productivity level created incentives for government directly to stimulate innovation as well as to encourage its rapid diffusion throughout the national industrial base.

The government has long encouraged industry to upgrade its knowledge through a variety of policy mechanisms, including sectorally-targeted financial inducements (tax breaks, loans, and direct subsidies); procurement and other demand management measures (often while providing a measure of import protection); targeted export assistance; access to public sector R&D facilities; encouragement of cooperative interfirm R&D; and assistance to firms in gaining access to foreign technology through such methods as controlling license conditions and providing intellectual property rights rules that favor imitation and reverse engineering. At the same time, the government has encouraged technology diffusion by using methods similar to those in Germany: developing a skilled labor force through the national educational system, providing technical assistance to industry through cooperative R&D labs, and encouraging technical standardization.

A distinct feature of the Japanese innovation system is the government's ability to direct national resources toward private sector technology development and diffusion without entirely subordinating market signals to administrative management. In addition, Japan's technological trajectory has depended to a substantial extent on acquiring technology developed abroad. This style of technology development, emulated to a certain extent by Korea and Taiwan, is evidently related to Japan's postwar imperative to catch up to the technological level of the United States and Europe. The roots of this imperative go deeper, but the outcome has in the contemporary period tended to give the country's definition of national security a distinctively economic cast.[14]

R&D Performance and Funding

Across the advanced industrial states, most R&D is conducted and funded by a combination of industry, government, higher education, and nonprofit organizations. Countries vary significantly, however, in the relative weight given to each of these sectors, as well as in the magnitude of R&D financed from foreign sources.

In most countries, R&D is actually conducted primarily by private industry. In 1994, private enterprise in Germany, Japan, and the United Kingdom conducted two thirds of the total national R&D; the equivalent percentage in France is slightly lower (62 percent) and, in the

TABLE 4.2
Sources of R&D Funding within National Innovation Systems (1993)

	U.S.	U.K.	France	Germany	Japan
Percent of All National R&D Expenditures Funded by:					
Industry	5?	52	46	60	73
Government	36	32	44	37	20
Higher Education	3	1	(0.4)	—	6
Private Nonprofit	2	3	1	1	1
Foreign	7	12	9	2	(0.1)
Percent of All Business R&D Expenditures Funded by:					
Industry	71	72	70	88	98
Government	19	12	18	9	1
Foreign	10	15	12	3	(0.1)

Source: National Science Board, *Science & Engineering Indicators–1996* (Washington, D.C.: US GPO, 1996): appendix tables 4–35, 4–36.

United States, slightly higher (71 percent).[15] The percentage of total national R&D conducted directly by government ranges from a high of 20 in France to a low of 9 in Japan, with the German and U.K. governments in the middle (15 and 14 percent, respectively) and the U.S. government at the lower end (11 percent). In most countries, institutions of higher education conduct 20 percent or less of all national R&D, while nonprofit organizations account for 4 percent or less.

The institutional sources of R&D funds, however, vary considerably across countries. Industry and government typically fund most national R&D expenditures in the advanced industrial states (Table 4.2. Sources of R&D Funding within National Innovation Systems). Examining these sources of funds more closely in the next chapter, however, we shall see that industry plays a proportionately stronger funding role in Japan and Germany, while government plays a proportionately stronger funding role in the United States, France, and the United Kingdom. Japan marks one extreme, with industry funding nearly 75 percent of the nation's R&D expenditures. France marks the other end of the spectrum, with industry funding slightly less than half of all R&D. The relative weight of industry and government is nearly identical in the United States and the United Kingdom, and approximates the distribution in France. Germany marks the midpoint between the French and Japanese models.

Cross-national patterns in the financing of business R&D—as distinct from total national R&D—reflect similar if not sharper differences in the weight accorded each sector across national innovation systems. In Germany and Japan, business funds nearly all of the R&D it conducts. By contrast, industry funds approximately 70 percent of the R&D it conducts in the United States, United Kingdom, and France. Much of this difference reflects the relative size of government funds directed to industrial R&D: in the United States and France, the government funds nearly 20 percent of industrial R&D, while the government funds only 1 percent of industrial R&D in Japan and 9 percent in Germany.

Foreign sources of R&D funds represent an additional source of cross-national variance in business R&D funding. In the United States, United Kingdom, and France, foreign sources account for a significant percentage of business R&D expenditures (as well as total national R&D). By contrast, foreign funds account for a very small portion of both business and national R&D funding in Germany. In Japan, foreign R&D funding is virtually nonexistent.

Business-financed R&D differs across nations not only in the institutional source of funds, but also in the source and type of corporate funding devoted to R&D.[16] Differences in the corporate governance structures, banking relationships, accounting methods, and interfirm linkages outlined in the previous chapter are directly relevant in this regard. All can and do have profound effects on the sources, character, and strategic significance of the internal financing available to firms. Similarly, external financial markets differ in structure and scope, and when they are used by firms, they can profoundly affect corporate funding alternatives and development strategies more generally. For example, U.S. capital markets are among the richest and most diverse in the world; they provide a great deal of financial flexibility and opportunity to firms in a variety of growth positions. At the same time, the central role of equity finance for U.S. corporations, combined with the typically wide gulf between owners and managers, tends to create an institutional incentive for firms to weigh technology development plans and strategies in the context of market expectations of short-term equity performance. In contrast, dominant financial and governance structures in Germany and Japan have tended to lengthen the time horizons for corporate technology development strategies.

Evidence of cross-national variation in the sources of R&D funds, however, cannot fully capture the importance of each sector to the innovative capabilities of each nation. In particular, it provides us with no measure of the quality or significance of the R&D financed. Many observers have nevertheless noted that such quality in fact differs substantially across countries and sectors. For example, higher education in the United States conducts 15 percent of all R&D—-less than any other industrial nation—-but the scientific and technological quality of the research conducted in U.S. universities is widely considered to be unmatched.[17] Similarly, higher education in Japan accounts for a larger percentage of national R&D than in other advanced industrial states, but the overall quality and strategic significance of Japanese university research is regarded as comparatively weak.[18]

In addition, the straightforward distribution of R&D funding does not capture the depth and breadth of linkages across sectors, which can affect national innovative capabilities. For example, long-standing and close linkages between universities and private industry in the United States provide important sources of innovative capability and organizational flexibility that are not readily available in other economies. By many accounts, these linkages are critical to the productivity of the U.S. technology base—-especially in science-based industries such as biotechnology and scientific instruments.[19]

Finally, funding indicators do not provide information on the character of R&D conducted within particular sectors. As mentioned, over half of the governmental R&D in the United States has focused historically on defense technologies.[20] By contrast, governmental R&D in Japan and Germany is directed almost entirely toward industrial technology development and diffusion.

Despite such caveats, there is no disputing the evidence demonstrating that different national innovation systems favor particular types of technologies. The point is reinforced in the next section of the chapter, which dissects the sectoral distribution of corporate expenditures on R&D. Viewed in their entirety, however, national innovation systems provide fundamentally different institutional contexts for corporate technology development. The U.S. system retains an institutional structure that reflects the nation's postwar military-political circumstances, decentralized and short-term-oriented governance and financial structures, a long-standing liberal economic ideology, and a mission-oriented style of technology development. The government plays a prominent role in the system, but more as a funder than a performer. Universities conduct, but do not fund, a significant quantity of world-class research to which industry has easy access. Governmental and other outside sources of funds contribute more to industrial R&D than in many other countries, and the system altogether specializes in science-based, high technology industries.

The United Kingdom and France are closer to the U.S. model than to the German or Japanese ones in that they also demonstrate mission-oriented styles of technology development, a prominent role for government in funding research, and an historical orientation toward technologies that have a significant defense component (primarily in aerospace and electronics). Germany and Japan, on the other hand, have established systems that largely favor innovation in commercial technologies and that devote far more resources to technology diffusion. Japan is particularly adept at learning and adopting commercial technology generated abroad. In both nations, industry retains a considerable degree of financial and strategic independence, although in different ways and through different channels. Similarly, government in both nations plays a relatively weak role in industrial R&D, although Germany's federal political structure allows for more diversity and experimentation in public sector programs to support science and technology. Finally, as the next section of this chapter shows, both nations also have a strong orientation toward medium technology and specialized supplier industries. Germany, nevertheless, directs a larger portion of national R&D resources to medium technologies, while Japan continues to devote a comparatively large fraction of its R&D resources to low technology sectors.

Sectoral Distribution of Corporate Research and Development[21]

National innovation systems differ in the technological sectors they emphasize as well as in the degree to which they concentrate resources on particular types of technologies. In most countries, corporate expenditures on R&D have traditionally been concentrated in a relatively small set of technologically-intensive industries. As Table 4.3 (Distribution of Business R&D across Technology-Intensive Industries, by Country) indicates, eight sectors—aerospace, scientific instruments, pharmaceuticals, industrial chemicals, office machinery and computers, electrical machinery (excluding electronics), electronic equipment and components, and motor vehicles—continue to account for over 80 percent of all business R&D conducted in manufacturing industries in the United States, United Kingdom, France, and Germany.[22] Business R&D in Japan remains slightly less concentrated on these industries.

In the United States, business R&D continues to be distributed relatively evenly across technology-intensive sectors.[23] Compared to other countries, the aerospace and scientific instruments sectors account for unusually large fractions of total business R&D, while the electrical machinery sector accounts for relatively little. Since the 1970s, the electrical machinery, electronics, and office machinery and computers sectors have all declined as a percent of U.S. business R&D. The sharpest decline over time, however, has been in the aerospace industry—traditionally and still the largest R&D sector—which slid from 25 percent in 1973 to 18 percent in 1993. On the other hand, the share of business R&D in the pharmaceutical industry has nearly quadrupled

TABLE 4.3

Distribution of Business R&D across Technology-Intensive Industries, by Country, 1993 (in percent)

	U.S.	U.K.	France	Germany	Japan
Aerospace	18	12	17	8	1
Instruments	12	1	1	2	4
Pharmaceuticals	11	23	9	6	7
Industrial chemicals	11	12	10	14	11
Office machinery & computers	6	6	4	3	9
Electrical machinery (excl. electronics)	1	8	4	9	11
Electronic equipment & components	13	13	23	19	16
Motor vehicles	13	9	13	20	12
All eight sectors, percent of total R&D in manufacturing	*85*	*84*	*81*	*81*	*71*

Source: Organization for Economic Cooperation and Development, *Scoreboard Indicators* (Paris: OECD, 1996). Numbers represent percent of total R&D expenditures by businesses in all manufacturing industries in each country, 1993. According to the OECD's classification of industries by average R&D intensity levels, all but two of these sectors are "high technology" industries; the two exceptions, industrial chemicals and motor vehicles, are "medium technology" industries.

since 1973. Similarly, the share devoted to the scientific instruments sector more than doubled.

Business R&D in the United Kingdom is dominated by the pharmaceutical industry, which accounts for nearly one-quarter of the total—by far the largest share for this industry in any industrial country. Business R&D in France is similarly concentrated in electronic equipment and components. Both countries also have sizable shares of business R&D in aerospace and, to a lesser extent, industrial chemicals. In addition, as in the United States, the largest decrease in R&D share since the 1970s in both countries has been in the aerospace industry, while the share in the pharmaceutical industry has increased substantially.[24]

Relative to other countries, business R&D in Germany is highly concentrated in motor vehicles, industrial chemicals, and (like France) electronic equipment and components. The motor vehicles sector has grown substantially over time, from 12 percent of all business R&D in 1973 to 20 percent in 1993. R&D in industrial chemicals—once the largest R&D performer in Germany—has moved in the opposite direction, from 20 to 14 percent. Over the last two decades, the share of R&D in electronic equipment and components has grown slightly, while the share in electrical machinery (excluding electronics) has decreased slightly.

By comparison, business R&D in Japan is less concentrated in any single sector than other countries. Relative to other countries, a large share of business R&D in Japan is located in electrical machinery as well as office machinery and computers. Within Japan, the largest R&D performers are electronic equipment and components, motor vehicles, electrical machinery, and industrial chemicals. Over time, moreover, the distribution of business R&D across sectors has been far more constant than in other countries. The largest change has been in office machinery and computers, which increased from 3 percent of all business R&D in 1973 to 9 percent in 1993.

In most but not all cases, the sectors with the highest R&D shares within each country also represent the highest shares across countries. Viewed comparatively, moreover, business R&D in the United States is concentrated in aerospace and instruments; in the United Kingdom, it is concentrated in pharmaceuticals; in France, electronic equipment and components; in Germany, motor vehicles and industrial chemicals; and in Japan, electrical machinery and office machinery and computers. These differences in the relative share of business R&D by sector and across countries generally reflect broader differences in the orientation of national innovation systems toward particular types of technologies.

As Table 4.4 (Technological Orientation of Industrial Research, by Country) illustrates, approximately two thirds of all business R&D expenditures in the United States are directed toward high technology industries, reflecting the relative concentration of U.S. R&D in aerospace, instruments, and, to a lesser extent, pharmaceuticals.[25] Medium technology industries receive half the volume of R&D resources. The United Kingdom and France have a similar distribution of R&D across high and medium technology industries. By contrast, Germany directs the largest percentage of national R&D resources to medium technology industries, reflecting the relative concentration of Germany's R&D in industrial chemicals and motor vehicles. Japan also directs a large percentage of its R&D resources to medium technology industries, and has a comparatively large share of R&D resources in low technology industries (primarily the basic metals and stone, clay, and glass sectors).

Most of the U.S. emphasis on high technology sectors is obviously related to its comparatively greater orientation toward science-based industries.[26] Germany and Japan, by contrast, each direct far more of their R&D resources to the specialized supplier industries noted in Table 4.4. In addition, both Germany and Japan concentrate similar and

TABLE 4.4
Technological Orientation of Industrial Research, by Country, 1993
(in percent)

	U.S.	U.K.	France	Germany	Japan
High technology industries	60	63	57	47	49
Medium technology industries	31	30	34	46	38
Low technology industries	9	7	9	7	13
Science-based industries	46	42	30	19	21
Specialized supplier industries	19	28	33	38	37
Scale-intensive industries	28	23	28	37	30

Source: Organization for Economic Cooperation and Development, *Scoreboard Indicators* (Paris: OECD, 1996). Data represent average percent of R&D in each category, by country, in 1993.

comparatively large percentages of their manufacturing R&D expenditures in scale-intensive industries such as industrial chemicals, motor vehicles, and rubber and plastic products.

Distinctly national differences exist not only in the distribution of R&D resources, but also in the intensity of R&D conducted in different types of technologies. R&D intensity, which represents the ratio of R&D expenditures to either production or value added, constitutes one of the best indicators of the technological orientation of firms operating within the same sector but in different countries.[27] In each country, firms operating in those sectors that receive the highest share of R&D resources also tend to have higher R&D intensities than their foreign counterparts in the same sector.

Indeed, U.S., U.K., and French firms generally have maintained higher R&D intensity levels in high technology industries than German and Japanese firms, as is consistent with the stronger orientation of the former three countries toward high technology sectors.[28] Likewise, German and Japanese firms have maintained the highest R&D intensity levels in medium technology industries, again as is consistent with different national orientations toward these sectors.[29] In addition, the R&D intensity of U.S. firms in high technology industries is four times the level of firms in medium technology industries. Similar large differences occur in France and the United Kingdom, while in Germany and Japan the difference in R&D intensity between firms in high versus medium technology industries is much smaller.[30] Overall, across both high and medium technology industries, variation in the relative R&D

intensity of firms conforms to the technological orientation of the national innovation systems in which they are based.

In short, cross-national variations in the sectoral distribution and relative intensity of corporate R&D point more toward technological specialization than toward convergence. Alternative measures, such as those based on patent indicators, support the same conclusion.[31] Although the general level of national technological capacity across the major OECD economies has converged over time, each national industrial group continues to display distinct technological emphases and competencies. In general, U.S.-based corporations remain oriented toward science-based, high technology products and processes—particularly related to aerospace, scientific instruments, and pharmaceuticals. British and French firms emphasize similar types of technologies. By contrast, German corporations remain more oriented toward medium technology, scale-intensive industries (motor vehicles and industrial chemicals) as well as toward specialized suppliers to such sectors (principally electronic equipment and components). For their part, Japanese firms continue to behave in a fashion similar to their German counterparts, emphasizing specialized supplier industries (electrical equipment and components, electrical machinery) and, to a lesser extent, scale-intensive sectors (motor vehicles and industrial chemicals).

In sum, technology development in U.S. firms continues to rely relatively heavily on traditional pillars of the national innovation system. In fact, those U.S. industries that absorb large shares of the nation's R&D resources—science-based industries such as pharmaceuticals, instruments, and aerospace—are also those industries most reflective of the mission-oriented style of national technology development. They also reflect the strong bonds among government, business, and the universities bequeathed by World War II and its aftermath. British and French firms have long been on a similar trajectory. By contrast, technology development in German and Japanese firms is far more independent of governmental and other outside resources. The supplier and scale-intensive industries in which leading MNCs specialize remain much more oriented toward intra-industry linkages for resource sharing and knowledge diffusion. Both sets of MNCs retain a striking commitment to the incremental improvement of technological products and processes as well as to their rapid commercialization. Japanese MNCs continue to be marked as well by a propensity to acquire and quickly adapt technology generated abroad. Such differences in the structure, trajectory, and outcomes of national innovation systems are mirrored in distinct national approaches to foreign direct investment, a subject to which the next section turns.

INVESTMENT SYSTEMS

Foreign direct investment (FDI) virtually defines multinational firms. Through outward investment, firms based in one country can establish wholly-owned facilities in foreign markets, or obtain a managerial presence through partial ownership of existing foreign firms. FDI represents firms in one country establishing a potentially lasting interest in firms operating abroad.[32]

FDI has expanded dramatically over the last decade. The world's stock of FDI grew from approximately $500 billion in the early 1980s to nearly $2.0 trillion by the early 1990s, a fourfold increase.[33] More than any other single fact, this explosive growth has captured the attention of observers of MNCs. It also has led many to expect the gradual emergence of a truly global industrial and technology base: greater in number and more deeply embedded within local economies, multinational firms would channel economic growth and technological progress across borders and eventually compete as fully global corporate entities.

Direct investment has not, however, flowed evenly across countries. On a global basis, most direct investment has remained concentrated in advanced countries that are members of the Organization for Economic Cooperation and Development (OECD). And on a bilateral basis, direct investment flows between countries often vary markedly. As Figure 4.2 (Total Direct Investment Positions: U.S.–Europe and U.S.–Japan, 1984–1995) illustrates, direct investment flows between the United States and both Europe and Japan vary substantially. While direct investment in each direction has increased over time, direct investment by Japanese firms in the U.S. economy far exceeds U.S. direct investment in Japan. By contrast, direct investment between the United States and Europe, and in particular Germany, has become much closer in volume.

Many factors affect the volume and direction of direct investment flows in the world economy. In part, variation in the direct investment relationship between the United States and both Germany and Japan reflects differences in the size and structure of each nation's economy, differences in the relationship between currencies over time, and a host of additional factors. But these patterns also reflect distinctive national styles of direct investment. As portrayed in Table 4.5 (Typology of National Investment Systems) and discussed below, the United States traditionally has been more accommodating of direct investment inflows than either Japan or Germany, and of these three countries, Japan has clearly been the least accommodating.

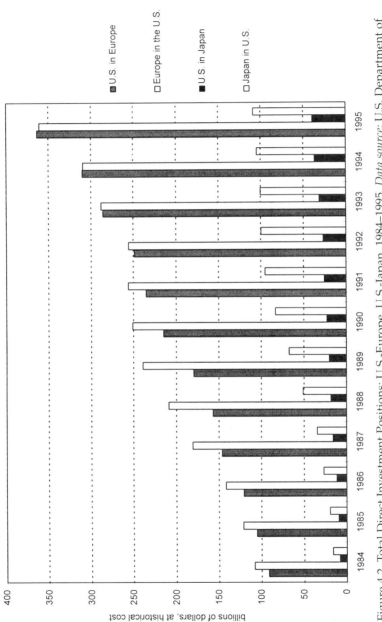

Figure 4.2. Total Direct Investment Positions: U.S.-Europe, U.S.-Japan, 1984-1995. *Data source:* U.S. Department of Commerce, Bureau of Economic Analysis (BEA), *Survey of Current Business,* "Foreign Direct Investment in the U.S.: Detail on Historical Cost Position" (annual series); BEA, *Survey of Current Business,* "U.S. Direct Investment Abroad: Detail on Historical Cost Position" (annual series).

TABLE 4.5
Typology of National Investment Systems

	United States	Germany	Japan
Inward Direct Investment	Liberal; no constraints	Liberal; tacit constraints	Resistant; formal and informal constraints
Outward Direct Investment	Broadly supportive	Neutral	Selectively supportive

Different National Approaches to Direct Investment

THE UNITED STATES

The U.S. approach to direct investment has long been grounded in the principle of national treatment. Foreign investors are generally to be treated, for regulatory, tax, and other purposes, as if they were domestic investors. However, the federal government does retain the authority to block inward investment that is deemed to be harmful to national security.

The institution directly responsible for addressing such concerns is the Committee on Foreign Investment in the United States (CFIUS). Created as an oversight body in 1975, CFIUS is an interagency body composed of officials from the Departments of State, Commerce, Defense, and Justice, the Office of the United States Trade Representative, the Office of Management and Budget, the Council of Economic Advisers, and the Treasury.

The authority of CFIUS was made explicit in the Exon-Florio provision in the *Omnibus Trade and Competitiveness Act of 1988*, which empowered the President to veto any takeover of a U.S. firm on national security grounds. CFIUS officials, however, see that mandate as consistent with a broader U.S. policy "to welcome direct investment and to support free and open foreign direct investment among all nations."[34]

CFIUS has in practice played a relatively passive role.[35] During the most active period of inward direct investment between 1988 and 1992, for example, CFIUS received 700 cases deemed worthy of review, subjected 13 of those to a 45-day extended review, and sent nine cases to the president's desk for decision. In eight of those nine cases, the president took no action.[36] In the case of the attempted purchase of General Ceramics Ltd. by the Tokuyama Soda Co. of Japan, CFIUS recommended that the acquisition be blocked because the U.S. firm was a supplier of nuclear defense technology. The sale eventually went through after the firm's nuclear operations were spun off and sold to an American company. In one other case, after CFIUS review in February 1990, the president ordered the China National Aero-Technology Import and Export Corporation to rescind its agreement to purchase Mamco Manufacturing of Seattle.

JAPAN

By contrast, Japan's approach to inward investment is far more restrictive, while it maintains a fairly supportive attitude toward outward investment. The result is the single best indicator of Japan's distinctive one-way globalization: outward investment from Japan exceeds inward investment by multiples, with ratios at times as high as 20 to 1.[37] Other indicators reflect the same picture. For instance, Japanese government statistics show foreign-owned firms employing 0.5 percent of Japan's workforce in the early 1990s, compared to the 3.8 percent of the U.S. workforce employed by foreign affiliates. Similarly, foreign firms account for only 1.2 percent of total sales in Japan (the equivalent measure in the United States is 16.5 percent), and control less than one percent of total assets (compared to 20.4 percent in the United States).[38]

In contrast to most industrial countries, mergers and acquisitions involving Japanese and foreign firms traditionally have been discouraged by both regulation and custom.[39] Over time, Japan's distinctive system of cross-shareholding, along with relatively closed business organizations and tight relations between the public and private sectors, have systematically impeded inward FDI.[40]

As a result, foreign firms rarely merge with or acquire Japanese firms. Of the 584 mergers and acquisitions reported in 1992, for example, 387 involved Japanese firms acquiring other Japanese firms, 165 involved Japanese firms acquiring foreign firms, and only 32 involved foreign firms acquiring Japanese firms.[41]

Since mergers and/or acquisitions are so difficult, inward FDI in Japan usually occurs through greenfield establishments and/or joint ventures. Yet formal and informal impediments hinder this form of investment as well. For instance, the high cost of land can be a serious disincentive to greenfield investment.[42] In addition, foreign investors face complex and inefficient distribution systems, weak intellectual property protection, and frequently onerous regulatory burdens.[43] And despite an increasingly liberal policy environment, administrative guidance and opaque regulatory requirements remain commonplace.[44]

Furthermore, Japan's legal system often favors domestic conglomerates. Japan's Anti-Monopoly Law, for instance, is weak, rarely enforced, and quick to recognize exemption cartels.[45] Nor does the Japan

Fair Trade Commission (FTC) aggressively enforce competition policy.[46] Through such legal and regulatory mechanisms, the Japanese government can restrict competition in the name of national security or public order.[47] These practices can discourage foreign firms from entering markets where Japanese firms often are least competitive, such as aircraft, space development, agriculture, fishing and forestry, oil and gas, mining, leather and leather product manufacturing, nuclear power, weapons and ordnance manufacturing, and tobacco.[48]

GERMANY

Germany's approach to inward direct investment is less accommodating than that of the United States, but hardly as restrictive as Japan. With the exception of legislation introduced in the mid-1970s to protect specific national assets (such as Daimler-Benz) from foreign takeover, German law imposes few direct restrictions upon inward investment.

Germany's policy environment is essentially liberal, similar to the United States in its attention to national treatment. At the same time, the direct investment environment in practice is also shaped by the policies of the Länder states as well of the European Union (EU). Some policies, such as EU domestic content and/or voluntary export rules, can constrain inward FDI. Other practices, such as Länder investment incentives, can actually encourage inward FDI—although perhaps with market-distorting effects.

Arguably, the most powerful domestic factor that affects inward FDI is Germany's distinctive corporate governance structures. Germany's strong, bank-centered corporate networks often can effectively impede unwanted corporate takeover attempts.[49] As a result, much of Germany's industrial base remains comparatively insulated from foreign incursions.[50] As noted in a Coopers and Lybrand study, many contested takeovers do not take place "for the simple reason that nobody really believes that they can happen; indeed, German companies may be impregnable as long as they have the support of big German banks."[51]

Combined, the constellation of tacit constraints on inward direct investment in Germany may effectively encourage informal market-sharing arrangements. In this regard, it is noteworthy that Japanese automobile manufacturers have never come close to penetrating the market in Germany to the same extent that they have in the United States.[52]

As they do in other countries, these different approaches to inward direct investment reflect unique national economic histories and ideological orientations.

Historical Foundations

The European colonial powers, especially Britain, generated the first major wave of direct investment in the modern world economy. Before 1914, Britain alone accounted for over one third of global FDI.[53] The earliest British MNCs focused on trade (East India or Hudson's Bay Companies) and on basic manufacturing (Lever Brothers, J. & P. Coats, and Dunlop).[54] After World War I, American firms began coming to the fore as a second wave of FDI gathered speed. One group specialized in the extraction of minerals, oil, and other natural resources, especially in the developing world. A second group concentrated on manufacturing activities and food processing. This group included the major U.S. automobile firms (notably Ford and General Motors) as well as others with familiar names (Coca-Cola, Gillette, Heinz, and Singer).[55] A third wave of FDI followed World War II. It was marked especially by capital-intensive, high technology firms (for example, IBM, Motorola, and Texas Instruments).

A key structural feature of this third wave carried over from the second: a categorical difference between those governments that encouraged foreign investment (mainly Britain and the United States) and those that discriminated against foreign investors (Germany, Japan, Italy, and sometimes France). This structural difference emerged in the context of Europe's experience with fascism. Prior to the establishment of antidemocratic regimes in Germany in 1933 and Japan in 1931, foreign investors had received comparable treatment to their domestic counterparts. American automobile manufacturers dominated local production in Japan. Similarly, Opel, a subsidiary of General Motors, was by far the largest producer of automobiles in Germany. The gradual shift to a war footing changed all that during the 1930s.

Policy in Japan was reoriented around a developmentalist ideology that differentiated sharply between foreign and domestic firms, and even among domestic ones.[56] In the key automobile sector, government measures stimulated the growth of Isuzu, and also Nissan and Toyota in the context of a clear commitment to national security, both broadly and narrowly defined. From the mid-1930s onwards, measures designed to expel American automobile companies were sponsored by the military and supervised by the Ministry of Commerce and Industry (MCI). The critical measure was the Automobile Manufacturing Enterprise Law of May 1936, which required firms producing more than 3,000 cars per year to be licensed by the state and to have most of their shares held by Japanese nationals. Licensees were given five-year exemptions from income taxes, local and business revenue taxes, and import duties on machinery, equipment and materials purchased abroad.

In addition, licensees were exempted from restrictive aspects of the commercial code relating to the issuance of new stocks and bonds to raise capital. In exchange, they granted the government supervisory rights over their mergers and acquisitions and over their production of military vehicles or equipment.

Three further measures were more explicitly aimed at curtailing the operations of the American car companies. First, their production was capped at 1934–1935 levels. Second, import duties on finished vehicles and components were raised to 50 percent. Third, Japan's foreign exchange regulations were revised in order to make it difficult for the American subsidiaries to pay for any parts they imported.[57] By 1939, all of these measures had the effect of creating an oligopoly for the three licensed domestic producers and driving Ford and GM out of the country.[58]

In less draconian fashion, the same basic policy line followed the war. Although the United States, in particular, objected, its economic agenda was long subordinated to the security concerns attending the Korean War and the cold war in East Asia more generally.[59] The ideology guiding later purveyors of "administrative guidance" in modern Japan would not be entirely dissimilar to that guiding their predecessors in the 1930s. Discrimination against foreign investors continued in all sectors deemed strategic, including automobiles, electrical machinery, machine tools, and eventually semiconductors.[60] At the core of the motivating ideology was the belief that Japanese security could only be achieved through the development of an indigenous technology and manufacturing base. In this context, fierce domestic competition would be encouraged, at least in higher technology industries, and foreign competition would be restrained. Where required, new technologies would be imported, often by way of licensing arrangements and sometimes by way of joint ventures that promised limited access to the Japanese market in exchange for technology.[61] Such orientations were built into the very fiber of the Japanese business networks that replaced the prewar *zaibatsu* and dominated all industries at the interface of the Japanese economy and the international economy. In retrospect, it seems clear their job was selectively to integrate those economies, but to do so in a way that built up national strength in high technology. As one senior Japanese industrialist asked the authors of this book, "What would you have done if two atomic bombs were dropped on your country?"

The experience of Germany in the formative period of the 1930s in many ways paralleled that of Japan, but significantly departed from the Japanese experience in the postwar period. Like Japan, the shift away from democracy was accompanied by a corresponding shift towards a discriminatory state apparatus. While foreign firms were driven out of Japan completely, however, they were often allowed to retain their manufacturing facilities in Germany if they adhered to new national production requirements and postponed the repatriation of profits.

Indigenous German firms benefited from the new discriminatory order, and there exists much evidence concerning their efforts to push the policy line further.[62] The German government, like its Japanese counterpart, was concerned to establish an autonomous economic base. Out of this coincidence of interests grew a network of economic relations; between the German government, the major German banks, a select group of dominant national producers, and (in part, at least) the German labor movement. The orienting ideology had deeper roots, but in the years leading up to World War II it is aptly termed "an ideology of social partnership." In Peter Katzenstein's words, such an ideology "mitigates class conflict between business and unions, . . . integrates differing conceptions of group interest with vaguely but firmly held notions of the public interest, and [builds political arrangements around a] 'culture of compromise'. . . that manage to couple narrowly conceived group interests with shared interpretations of the collective good."[63] Such an ideology survived the war, albeit in a much less totalistic and exclusionary form, and in that form it underpinned the rise of Germany's new social market economy.

It is clear that the Federal Republic of Germany and Japan took very different roads to industrial reconstruction and development in the 1950s and 1960s.[64] Deeper administrative and political reform after the war, the process of European economic integration, active membership in NATO and other postwar international organizations—all had contributed to that difference. For their part, foreign investors also had a role to play. Many remained after the occupation period ended, and their infusions of capital remained important to the continued reconstruction of the German economy. In light of the progress of European integration, their exports helped Germany build up hefty export surplus; in turn, they benefited from an increasingly liberal approach to the regulation of foreign investment in Germany. Foreign investors, however, were not permitted to dominate German markets or purchase the country's most valued corporate assets. Through a mix of tacit constraints embedded in predominantly private industrial structures, and sometimes by legislation or administrative action, the interests of dominant German producers were effectively protected in such industries as automobiles, chemicals, telecommunications, and machine tools.

Couched as they were in the context of a generally liberalizing trade policy, such constraints did not compromise the opportunities for German firms abroad. In contrast to their Japanese counterparts, they proved to be aggressive outward investors from an early date. Even in the 1950s, German MNCs positioned themselves in diverse markets in Latin America, Eastern Europe and the United States. In a manner consistent with both an emphasis on an "ideology of social partnership" and a strategic conception of trading relationships, however, German investment abroad tended to stimulate exports from Germany and therefore to maintain domestic employment.[65]

In both their intent and their consequences, British and American policies and practices with respect to overseas investment and trade contrasted markedly with those of Japan and Germany throughout the postwar period. Accounting as they did for the overwhelming proportion of the world's MNCs, both countries had a strong vested interest in market liberalization. National treatment regimes—treating foreign firms operating in the domestic market as if they were domestic firms for regulatory and other purposes—seemed a logical tool for encouraging openness abroad.

Such a stance was easier to implement in the United States, which remained relatively isolated from inward direct investment inflows until the early 1980s. Geographically separated from all developed markets except Canada's, the size and level of competition within many American markets, as well as the high value of the dollar, served to keep incursions from foreign investors at a relatively low level.[66] Acceptance of the principle of national treatment came easily. As American firms grew during the postwar period, often by exploiting the economies of scale made possible by mass production techniques in their vastly expanding home market, aspiring foreign competitors faced a major challenge. With few formal barriers to entry and no public debate, American policy was liberal by default. Over time, it was reinforced by the fact that the operations of the affiliates of American MNCs abroad were highly successful, with repatriated profits consistently yielding a surplus on the national direct investment account, especially in the early postwar period.[67]

Britain, for its part, confronted the issue of inward direct investment directly as early as 1915, when the McKenna tariffs were introduced with the partial objective of encouraging the investment inflows that could create new jobs in Britain. The vast majority of these flows came from the United States. In later years, a national regime was formalized around the principle of national treatment. In certain cases, British governments even favored foreign affiliates over domestic investors, since foreigners could more easily exercise the option of exit.[68] Neither the depression, nor the onset of fascism abroad, would shake the foundations of this British policy. Outward and inward investment policy continued to be subject to a broadly liberal regime after the war. The policy line reinforced the position of the affiliates of British MNCs abroad and infused the British economy with new capital at home. Victory over the Axis powers, and the prominent role of American business in that regard, only served to strengthen the dominant national sense of the appropriateness of the policy.[69] In later years, the affiliates of foreign MNCs would become major beneficiaries.

STRUCTURAL CONTEXT AND MULTINATIONAL CORPORATE BEHAVIOR

Distinct national histories and attitudes toward foreign direct investment represent one element of a complex set of structural factors that condition the behavior of multinational firms. Multinational firms based in the United States, Germany, and Japan have fundamentally different internal governing structures, different approaches to finance, different types of linkages with nationally specific science and technology resources, different degrees of exposure to competition from inward investment, and different degrees of access to technological and market opportunities within national economies.

Undoubtedly, the rapid rise in foreign direct investment over the last fifteen years signals a far more pervasive presence of MNCs in the domestic markets of advanced industrial states. As the overseas operations of MNCs expand, and as the channels for international technology development and diffusion widen, multinational firms have become ever more significant actors in an increasingly complex and interdependent international economy.

However, MNCs have been responding to this increased economic and technological complexity in dissimilar ways. Their actual behavior reflects distinct styles of pursuing technology development abroad, investing in foreign markets, trading within or outside affiliated networks, and producing in local markets. Ultimately, these behavioral styles mirror the structure and character of the political and economic systems in which they remain based, systems with deep historical roots.

Chapter 5

THE STRATEGIC BEHAVIOR OF MNCs

HAVING SURVEYED the national systems of internal governance, financing, innovation, and investment within which the majority of the world's leading MNCs were originally grounded, we return to the questions that opened this volume. In the midst of markets now widely perceived to be fundamentally global, we ask in this chapter whether multinational firms are now truly losing their national moorings. More precisely, in their most crucial strategies and operations, we ask whether patterns of convergence are now emerging, patterns that herald the emergence of a global corporate economy. This chapter seeks answers in the two strategic areas at the core of the multinational corporation: strategies for creating and managing technological innovation, and the intimately linked strategies of foreign direct investment and intrafirm trade.

Technology and Commerce

Many observers have noted that MNCs have in recent years increased the cross-border development and transfer of technical knowledge and technological assets.[1] The term *globalization*, in this sense, is often used to suggest that national technology bases are by virtue of that expansion becoming more integrated and interdependent.[2] Generally speaking, and certainly in sectors like pharmaceuticals, that integration is obvious. But it is also neither new nor particularly profound. As long as MNCs have been able to establish themselves in diverse markets, a degree of technological integration has always occurred. The key questions concern the relative magnitude and significance of any recent changes in this process. Has a threshold been crossed in the fundamental integration of national systems of innovation? Is a global technology base emerging?

The evidence presented below suggests not. The recent rapid growth in FDI has certainly expanded the local presence of foreign corporations, and with that has come growth in overseas R&D and increasingly dense channels for technology transfer across national borders. Yet the magnitude of this trend remains quite small relative to the national innovative activities of the world's leading MNCs. Those firms, moreover, continue to innovate as well as acquire and transfer new knowledge in distinct ways. Across the world's leading MNCs, and especially across American, German, and Japanese MNCs, distinctly national patterns can be seen in the three principal mechanisms through which MNCs extend technology across national borders: first, through overseas R&D activities; second, through the direct sale of technology in the form of intellectual property (in exchange for royalties and license fees); and third, through strategic technology alliances between firms.[3]

The Location and Intensity of Corporate Research and Development

Historically, R&D has been the last aspect of corporate activity to take on a multinational dimension. The economies of scale associated with research activities naturally tend to favor centralization, but that is not the end of the story. As firms establish foreign production capabilities, they in fact often decentralize selective elements of their R&D. In addition to supporting local production facilities, firms will move R&D abroad for a variety of reasons: to acquire foreign technology; to customize products for local markets; to stay abreast of technological developments; to gain access to foreign R&D resources, such as universities, public and private laboratory facilities, and scientists and engineers; to assist the parent company in meeting foreign regulations and product standards; and to gain cost efficiencies. Consequently, as production and commerce increasingly cross national borders, R&D might likewise be expected to exhibit a more global character.

Close observers of this process differ, however, in their diagnoses of its extent and nature. Some note that major MNCs are expanding their core R&D activities across national borders at unprecedented rates.[4] Foreign acquisitions often are aimed at gaining access to technology and other R&D resources that already are established in particular markets, such as biotechnology in the United States. In the United States, Germany, and the United Kingdom, foreign firms "are spending substantial sums on R&D, mainly for local markets though increasingly for global ones, reflecting new strategies in R&D intensive industries."[5] Other studies note that while R&D has indeed become more mobile, MNCs move R&D abroad far more slowly than production, sourcing, marketing, and other business activities.[6] Others contend that firms are responding to global competition by watching R&D activities closely and striving to retain centralized control.[7] Still others agree that MNCs conduct relatively little R&D outside the home country, but note that the strategies and policies of MNCs affect the way R&D is owned, organized, and located.[8]

Our own analysis notes the recent growth in the overseas R&D activities of foreign affiliates. Beneath that observation, however, it focuses on the distribution of R&D within multinational firms and shows that corporate R&D remains highly centralized in home markets. It also demonstrates that both the level and intensity of R&D conducted by MNCs outside their home markets varies markedly along national lines.[9] We suspect, moreover, that more than economic factors are needed to explain this variance.

R&D WITHIN MULTINATIONAL FIRMS

Although the aggregate volume of overseas R&D by corporate affiliates has increased substantially in recent years, it is still a relatively small fraction of total corporate R&D. The domestic and overseas R&D conducted by U.S.-based MNCs since the early 1980s illustrates both of these points (Figure 5.1. Distribution of R&D Expenditures within U.S.-based MNCs). Between 1982 and 1994, total R&D expenditures by U.S. multinational corporate parents increased an average of 12 percent per year, from $38.2 billion to $91.1 billion. During the same period, R&D spending by affiliates of U.S. MNCs grew at a faster rate of 18 percent per year, rising from $3.6 billion to $12.1 billion.[10] The accelerating growth of R&D by affiliates indicates that R&D has become more international in scope. At the same time, however, the proportion of total multinational corporate R&D conducted by affiliates remains relatively small—in 1994, the R&D conducted by majority-owned affiliates comprised 12 percent of the total R&D expenditures of U.S. MNCs, up slightly from 9 percent in 1982.[11] By comparison, in 1994 majority-owned foreign affiliates of U.S. MNCs accounted for 30 percent of net income, 24 percent of total MNC capital expenditures, and 23 percent of all employment.[12] Although no comparable data exists for European and Japanese MNCs, our interviews suggest that they conduct overseas similar if not smaller percentages of their R&D than do U.S. firms.[13]

Like the aggregate level of R&D spending, the R&D intensity of foreign affiliates tends to be substantially lower than that of parent groups.[14] For example, the R&D intensity of U.S. multinational corporate parent groups in 1994 was 2.3 percent, compared with 0.8 percent for their majority-owned foreign affiliates.[15] With the exception of foreign affiliates in the United States, the R&D intensity of foreign affiliates in most countries tends to be lower than or at best equivalent to the average for all manufacturing firms in the host country.[16] However, as with the volume of R&D spending, the R&D intensity of foreign affiliates has been increasing at a faster rate than that of MNC parent

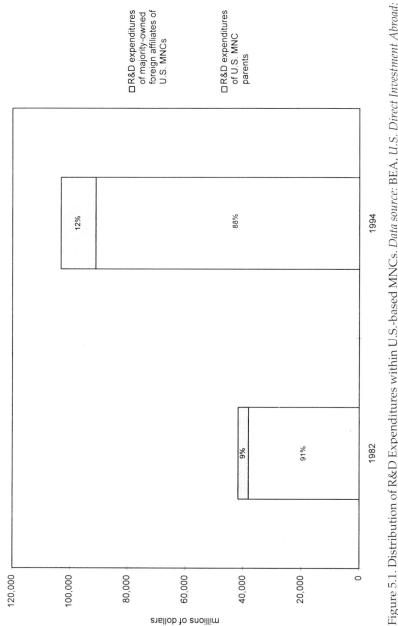

Figure 5.1. Distribution of R&D Expenditures within U.S.-based MNCs. *Data source:* BEA, *U.S. Direct Investment Abroad: 1994 Benchmark Survey* (January 1997): tables II.R 1, III.I 2; BEA, *Survey of Current Business* (June 1995): table 5, p. 36.

groups. For example, between 1982 and 1994 the annual growth rate in the R&D intensity of majority-owned foreign affiliates of U.S. MNCs averaged 10 percent, compared with 3 percent for their parent groups.[17]

Although low in absolute terms, the relatively rapid growth in overseas R&D by foreign affiliates does represent a gradual globalization of R&D. However, it is difficult to assess the significance of this trend, due to the lack of data regarding the technological and strategic contribution of the R&D conducted by foreign affiliates to the global competitiveness of MNCs.[18] Apparently, much of the growth in the R&D intensity of both foreign affiliates in the United States and U.S. affiliates abroad can be attributed to overseas acquisitions and/or joint ventures, and consequently may not represent a transfer of R&D operations from the home country to foreign markets.[19] The most challenging analytical task is to determine whether the R&D conducted by foreign affiliates contributes to the core technological competencies of the parent firms, or whether it contributes primarily to the affiliates' local process technology and product adaptation requirements.

Over time and across countries, the most significant reasons for conducting R&D in foreign markets are to customize products to accommodate local market conditions, improve foreign production processes, take advantage of local research competencies, assist parent companies in procurement, and keep abreast of competitors' technological and overall business strategies.[20] Firms usually take a long time to establish complex overseas R&D operations that fully support local production facilities. In the electronics industry—one of the most internationalized in terms of R&D as well as production—firms require at least a decade to establish an overseas research facility that can closely support affiliate manufacturing operations. For example, Philips Electronics NV has maintained a U.S. research facility at Briarcliff Manor, New York, for over two decades. The facility now accounts for approximately 15 percent of all corporate research activity, and is an integral part of Philips' laboratory network. The company maintains four laboratories in Europe—the central lab at corporate headquarters in Eindhoven, Netherlands, plus smaller facilities in France, Germany, and England. While each of the foreign facilities has its own technological capabilities and its own mix of research programs, most basic research continues to be conducted in Eindhoven. The U.S. facility focuses mostly on supporting Philips' substantial U.S. manufacturing facilities.[21]

Fully integrated affiliates that conduct independent product R&D are relatively rare, even for the largest and oldest MNCs. For instance, Siemens has a laboratory in Princeton, New Jersey, that conducts independent R&D in imaging, software engineering, multimedia, and learning systems. Much of this work involves missions tied to the central corporation, not just its U.S. divisions. At the same time, however, the Princeton facility's budget is only $21.8 million, less than 5 percent of Siemens' total R&D budget.[22] Similarly, Ford Motor Company, after many years of foreign production in Europe and elsewhere, only recently began to establish a single operating unit, Ford Automotive Operations, that would oversee five vehicle program centers, each with worldwide responsibilities for the development and production of independent product lines.[23]

In short, R&D moves overseas much more slowly than production, sourcing, and other business activities. Production facilities often can be established quickly and moved quickly, as market conditions change. By comparison, R&D facilities typically take a long time to set up and, once established, are relatively difficult to move.[24] Yet even in industries with extensive global production and sourcing networks as well as high R&D intensity levels—such as electronics, computers, and pharmaceuticals—R&D across the advanced industrial states remains fairly centralized. For instance, pharmaceutical firms conduct very little basic research and clinical evaluation outside of the home country,[25] and R&D in the computer industry is among the most highly centralized (a fact some analysts ascribe to domestic support programs that favor local firms).[26] The pattern is much the same in less R&D-intensive industries, especially those where core product technology varies little across national markets. For example, R&D in the auto industry remains relatively centralized, although design customization often is conducted locally.[27]

In general, most MNCs centralize core research and product development in the home market, while research oriented toward customization and foreign production support is gradually conducted locally as affiliates become more deeply integrated into foreign markets.[28] Indeed, many multinational firms have become more deeply integrated into local markets over time, which accounts in part for the rapid rate of increase in R&D conducted by foreign affiliates. Nevertheless, foreign affiliates that do conduct R&D abroad tend to do so at different levels and for different purposes.

R&D BY FOREIGN AFFILIATES IN THE UNITED STATES

Over the last decade, R&D spending by foreign affiliates in the United States has increased substantially. In 1980, foreign MNCs operating in the country spent $3.2 billion in real terms on R&D, equivalent to 6.4 percent of all R&D funded by U.S. businesses. By 1994 that level had risen to $14.9 billion, equivalent to 16 percent of all corporate

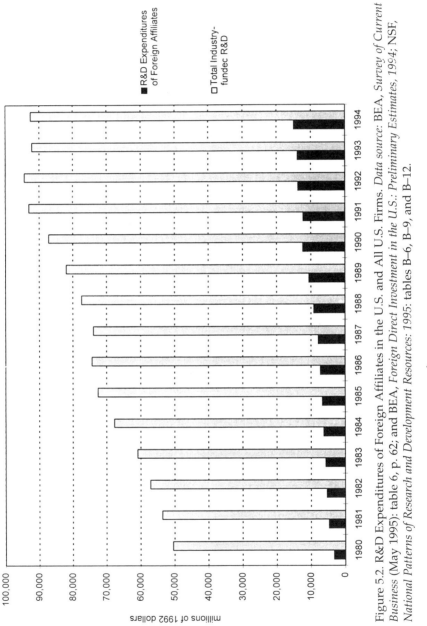

Figure 5.2. R&D Expenditures of Foreign Affiliates in the U.S. and All U.S. Firms. *Data source:* BEA, *Survey of Current Business* (May 1995): table 6, p. 62; and BEA, *Foreign Direct Investment in the U.S.: Preliminary Estimates, 1994;* NSF, *National Patterns of Research and Development Resources: 1995:* tables B–6, B–9, and B–12.

TABLE 5.1
R&D Expenditures of Foreign Affiliates in the U.S. by Country of Origin

	Japan	Germany	France	U.K.
R&D expenditures in 1994 (in billions of constant 1992 dollars)	$1.9	$2.3	$1.3	$2.4
Average percent of total R&D expenditures by all foreign affiliates in the U.S., 1983–1994	9.4%	15.1%	7.1%	15.5%
Average annual growth rate, 1983–1994	65.6%	17.2%	31.8%	19.0%

Source: Bureau of Economic Analysis, Foreign Direct Investment in the U.S.: 1994 (Washington, D.C.: U.S. Government Printing Office, 1996): table I-6.

R&D funding that year (Figure 5.2. R&D Expenditures of Foreign Affiliates in the U.S. and All U.S. Firms).[29] Although small relative to total R&D funding by U.S. firms—$92.6 billion in 1994—the rate of increase in R&D spending by foreign affiliates has been much more rapid than that of total U.S. business R&D. Between 1980 and 1994, R&D expenditures by foreign affiliates in the United States grew at an average annual rate of 26 percent, compared to 6 percent for R&D funding by all U.S. firms.[30]

Firms based in each of the major advanced industrial nations contributed to the rapid increase in total affiliate R&D during the 1980s and early 1990s (Table 5.1. R&D Expenditures of Foreign Affiliates in the U.S., by Country of Origin). During that period, U.K. and German affiliates consistently outspent French and Japanese affiliates in absolute terms, each accounting for approximately 15 percent of all R&D conducted by foreign affiliates in the United States.[31] Although average annual increases in affiliate R&D spending were strong across all countries, French and Japanese affiliates expanded their R&D spending particularly quickly, especially after 1987.

Over 80 percent of the R&D conducted by foreign affiliates in the United States has been in manufacturing industries, most of which is concentrated in three sectors—in 1994, 29 percent of all R&D by affiliates was in pharmaceuticals, while 17 percent was in electronic equipment and 13 percent in industrial chemicals.[32] The most rapid rate of growth has been in the pharmaceutical sector, where foreign affiliates increased their R&D spending from $716 million in 1985 to $4.3 billion in 1994 (in constant 1992 dollars)—a stunning average annual increase of 56 percent (Figure 5.3. R&D Expenditures of Foreign Affiliates in the U.S., by Industry). Indeed, the growth of foreign R&D in the pharmaceutical sector accounts for over one third of the total increase in R&D

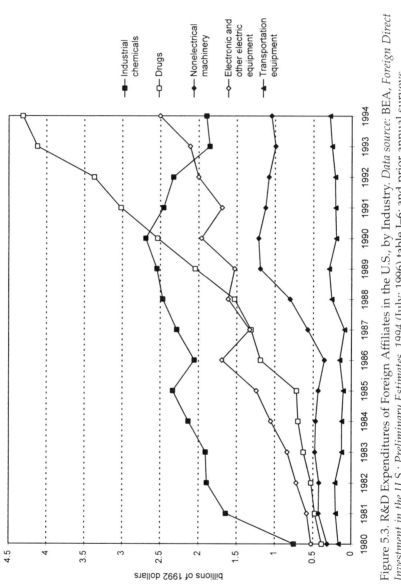

Figure 5.3. R&D Expenditures of Foreign Affiliates in the U.S., by Industry. *Data source:* BEA, *Foreign Direct Investment in the U.S.: Preliminary Estimates, 1994* (July: 1996) table J–6; and prior annual surveys.

conducted in the United States by foreign firms from 1980 to 1994. R&D spending by foreign affiliates has also grown significantly in industrial chemicals and machinery, again with fastest growth rates taking place in the late 1980s.

With only a few notable exceptions, such as NEC's laboratory in Princeton, most industrial laboratories run by foreign affiliates in the United States have been established not through new investment dedicated to R&D activities per se but rather through the merger and acquisition (M&A) strategies of foreign firms.[33] The rapid increase in R&D by foreign affiliates began in the late 1980s, corresponding to a very active period of M&A activity by foreign investors. Between 1986 and 1988, the value of foreign acquisitions in the United States jumped from $31.5 billion to $64.9 billion, and remained quite high during 1988–90.[34] The correspondence between this period of high acquisition activity and the rise in R&D spending by foreign affiliates after 1986 implies that part of the increase in affiliate R&D was due to acquisitions of U.S. research facilities, as opposed to the transfer of R&D activities from the home market to existing affiliates in the United States.[35] No sector illustrates this relationship better than pharmaceuticals, where the unusually high average annual growth rate in R&D by foreign affiliates—56 percent—corresponds to an even more remarkable average annual growth in direct investment of 106 percent (much of it related to the enormous amount of M&A as well as alliance activity in the industry during this period).[36]

Whether established through acquisition or direct establishment, foreign affiliates in the U.S. vary systematically in their levels of R&D per unit of sales, as seen in Figure 5.4 (R&D Intensity of Foreign Affiliates in the U.S.). Much of the difference in aggregate R&D intensity levels appears to be consistent with the sectoral distribution of foreign direct investment in the United States (FDIUS) by individual countries. For instance, the R&D intensity of European affiliates is above the average for all affiliates, which reflects in part the relatively high percentage of European FDIUS that is directed to R&D-intensive manufacturing sectors. In particular, German affiliates in the United States regularly have the highest R&D intensity level, as is consistent with the concentration of German affiliates in R&D-intensive manufacturing industries—in 1994, for instance, 38 percent of German FDIUS was in chemicals and allied products and industrial machinery (combined).[37] By comparison, the low R&D intensity of Japanese affiliates in the United States reflects in part the relatively low percentage of Japanese FDIUS directed to R&D-intensive manufacturing industries. In 1994, only 19 percent of Japan's FDIUS was in manufacturing industries altogether (and only 9

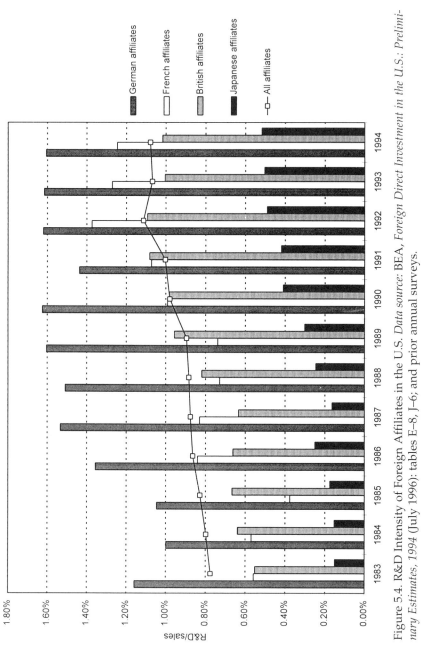

Figure 5.4. R&D Intensity of Foreign Affiliates in the U.S. *Data source: BEA, Foreign Direct Investment in the U.S.: Preliminary Estimates, 1994* (July 1996): tables E–8, J–6; and prior annual surveys.

percent in chemicals and industrial machinery), while 34 percent was in wholesale trade.[38]

Although the national variation in aggregate R&D intensity levels is consistent with the sectoral composition of FDIUS, a comparison of R&D intensities within sectors points toward another factor—consistent variation in the R&D strategies of MNCs along national lines. As Figure 5.5 (R&D Intensity of Foreign Affiliates in the United States, by Sector and by Country) shows, the R&D intensity levels of foreign affiliates in the United States vary significantly within as well as across sectors. In 1994, the average R&D intensity for all foreign affiliates in U.S. manufacturing industries was 2.6 percent. German affiliates in manufacturing industries were well above that average (at 3.5 percent), while French and U.K. affiliates were slightly above the average (at 2.8 and 2.7 percent, respectively). Japanese affiliates were well below average (at 1.1 percent). This pattern generally holds across the major industrial sectors: German, French, and U.K. affiliates share the highest R&D intensity levels across chemicals and allied products, metals, transportation, and instruments, while Japanese affiliates consistently have the lowest R&D intensity level (with the partial exception of machinery, where the R&D intensity of U.K. affiliates is lower).

In short, foreign affiliates operating in the United States have increased their R&D spending relatively quickly over the last 15 years, particularly in the pharmaceutical sector. In absolute terms, most of the R&D conducted by foreign affiliates is concentrated in pharmaceuticals, electrical and electronic machinery, and industrial chemicals. In general, affiliates of German MNCs have the highest R&D intensity levels in the United States, while affiliates of Japanese MNCs have the lowest. This difference appears to be consistent with the relative concentration of direct investment in R&D-intensive industries. However, consistent variation in the R&D intensity of German, Japanese, and other foreign affiliates operating in the same industry indicates that multinational firms based in different states tend to pursue distinct R&D strategies.

R&D BY U.S. AFFILIATES IN FOREIGN MARKETS

Like the R&D activity of foreign affiliates in the United States, the overseas R&D by affiliates of U.S. MNCs has increased steadily over time. Between 1989 and 1994, R&D expenditures by majority-owned foreign affiliates of U.S. MNCs increased by an average annual rate of 9 percent (from $7.9 billion to $11.5 billion, in real terms)—far slower than the growth rate of R&D spending by foreign affiliates in the United States

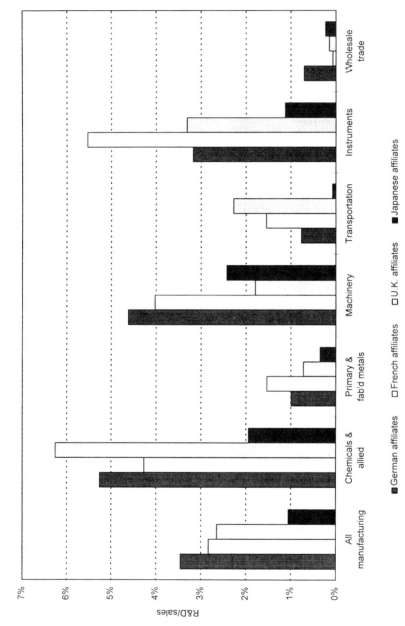

Figure 5.5. R&D Intensity of Foreign Affiliates in the U.S., by Sector and by Country. *Data source:* BEA, *Foreign Direct Investment in the U.S.: Preliminary Estimates, 1994* (July 1996): tables I-6, E-8.

TABLE 5.2
R&D Expenditures of U.S. Affiliates in Foreign Markets: Growth Rates and
Distribution across Countries

	Japan	Germany	France	U.K.
R&D expenditures in 1994 (in billions of constant 1992 dollars)	$1.1	$2.7	$1.3	$2.1
Average percent of total R&D expenditures by U.S. affiliates in all foreign markets, 1989–1994	7.0%	24.1%	9.3%	18.3%
Average annual growth rate, 1989–1994	19.4%	12.1%	22.6%	2.3%

Source: Bureau of Economic Analysis, *U.S. Direct Investment Abroad* (Washington, D.C.: U.S. Government Printing Office, 1997): table III.I 3.

Note: Data expressed in constant 1992 dollars. R&D data for U.S. affiliates in foreign markets are not available prior to 1989.

(26 percent), but faster than the real growth of R&D spending by all U.S. firms over the same period (6 percent).[39]

The distribution of R&D expenditures by U.S. affiliates across countries mirrors the relative level of R&D spending by foreign affiliates in the United States. R&D by U.S. affiliates is concentrated in Germany and to a lesser extent the United Kingdom, with comparatively little R&D in France and Japan (Table 5.2. R&D Expenditures of U.S. Affiliates in Foreign Markets: Growth Rates and Distribution across Countries). Between 1989 and 1994, U.S. affiliates on average spent $2.3 billion per year in Germany (24 percent of the total real R&D spending by U.S. affiliates in all foreign markets) and $1.9 billion per year in the United Kingdom (18 percent of the total), compared with $952 million (9 percent) in France and $716 million (7 percent) in Japan.

Most of the overseas R&D conducted by U.S. affiliates is in manufacturing industries. In 1994, manufacturing firms accounted for 84 percent of all R&D spending by U.S. affiliates in foreign markets, a level equivalent to that of foreign affiliates in the United States.[40] Also like their counterparts in the United States, a large percentage of the overseas R&D conducted by U.S. affiliates is concentrated in the pharmaceutical industry, which accounted for 17 percent of all foreign R&D by U.S. affiliates between 1989 and 1994. The industrial machinery sector accounts for an equivalent share of overseas R&D by U.S. firms. These two industries also display the strongest average annual real growth rates in affiliate R&D spending—16 and 25 percent, respectively. Quite unlike R&D by foreign affiliates in the U.S., however, the transportation equipment sector accounts for nearly a quarter of

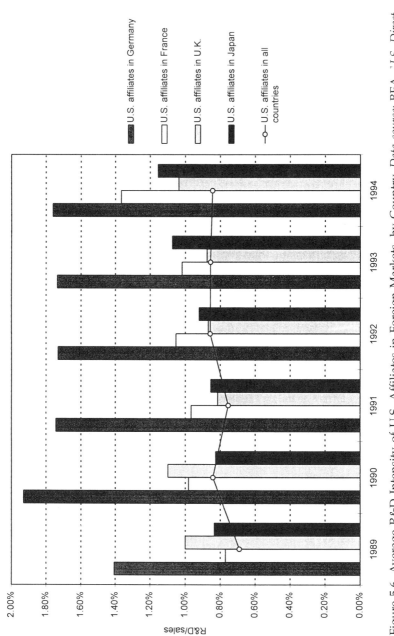

Figure 5.6. Average R&D Intensity of U.S. Affiliates in Foreign Markets, by Country. *Data source:* BEA, *U.S. Direct Investment Abroad: 1994 Benchmark Survey* (January 1997): tables III.I 3.; III.E 3.

TABLE 5.3

R&D Expenditures of U.S. Affiliates in Foreign Markets, by Sector and by Country, 1994

	Japan	Germany	France	U.K.
All industries ($ million)	$1,123	$2,808	$1,357	$2,179
Chemicals & allied products (% of all R&D by U.S. affiliates within country)	$397 (35%)	$296 (11%)	$543 (40%)	$616 (28%)
Primary & fabricated metals	$10 (1%)	$23 (1%)	$6 (0.5%)	$25 (1%)
Industrial machinery & equipment	$77 (7%)	$530 (19%)	$202 (15%)	$433 (20%)
Electronic & electric equipment	$136 (12%)	$128 (5%)	$41* (3%)	$46* (2%)
Transportation equipment	$6 (1%)	$1,435 (51%)	$27* (2%)	$383* (18%)
Wholesale trade	$307 (27%)	$87 (3%)	$120 (9%)	$120 (6%)

Source: Bureau of Economic Analysis, *U.S. Direct Investment Abroad: 1994* (Washington, D.C.: U.S. Government Printing Office, 1997): table III.I 3.

Note: Expenditure data expressed in millions of current dollars. (An asterisk represents 1993 data. 1994 data not available for these sectors.)

overseas R&D conducted by U.S. affiliates, although the average annual growth rate of R&D spending has been comparatively slow since 1989 (about 8 percent).[41]

Viewed across countries, the aggregate R&D intensity of U.S. affiliates is relatively similar but for one exception: Germany. As Figure 5.6 shows (Average R&D Intensity of U.S. Affiliates in Foreign Markets, by Country), the R&D intensity of U.S. affiliates in France, the United Kingdom, and Japan is within a narrow range, close to the average R&D intensity for U.S. affiliates in all markets. U.S. affiliates in Germany, however, consistently display substantially higher aggregate R&D intensity levels.

This pattern conforms in part to differences in the concentration of R&D by U.S. affiliates in R&D-intensive manufacturing industries. In 1994, fully 86 percent of all R&D expenditures by U.S. affiliates in Germany was concentrated in four R&D-intensive sectors—transportation equipment, chemicals and allied products, electronic and other electric equipment, and industrial machinery (Table 5.3. R&D Expenditures of U.S. Affiliates in Foreign Markets, by Sector and by Country). The equivalent concentration levels for U.S. affiliates in France and the United Kingdom was approximately 72 and 70 percent, respectively.[42]

Surprisingly (since the average R&D intensity of U.S. affiliates in Japan is close to or higher than those in France or the United Kingdom), only 55 percent of the R&D expenditures by U.S. affiliates in Japan is concentrated in these four sectors. In Japan, unlike all European countries, the largest share of R&D by U.S. affiliates takes place in the wholesale trade sector, where U.S. affiliates spend over four times the level that they do in the German and U.K. wholesale trade sectors.

Variation in the sectoral distribution of R&D only partially explains cross-national differences in the R&D intensity of U.S. affiliates. When viewed across industries in the same country, additional variation in the R&D intensity of U.S. affiliates suggests that local investment and technological circumstances may be a factor as well. As Figure 5.7 (R&D Intensity of U.S. Affiliates in Foreign Markets, by Industry and by Country) illustrates, the R&D intensity of U.S. affiliates operating in the same sector often varies substantially across countries. In most major manufacturing sectors, the R&D intensity of U.S. affiliates operating in Japan is noticeably higher than affiliates operating in Germany, France, or the United Kingdom. In the transportation equipment and industrial machinery industries, the R&D intensity of U.S. affiliates in Germany is particularly high. And in the category of wholesale trade, which typically is among the least R&D intensive sectors, the R&D intensity of U.S. affiliates in Japan is approximately four times that of U.S. affiliates in Germany, France, or the United Kingdom.

In sum, the R&D activities of both foreign affiliates in the United States and U.S. affiliates abroad have increased significantly in recent years, but the scope and intensity of that activity varies by sector as well as by country.

By sector, the highest levels of foreign R&D conducted by MNCs are in pharmaceuticals, chemicals, electronic equipment, and, for U.S. MNCs, transportation equipment. More than any other sector, rapid growth in overseas R&D in pharmaceuticals accounts for a large share of the increase in foreign R&D by MNCs—particularly by foreign affiliates operating in the United States.

By country, the magnitude and intensity of R&D activity is the highest between the United States and Germany, in both directions and across most sectors. The magnitude and intensity of R&D activity between the United States and Japan is the lowest in terms of Japanese affiliates in the United States. By contrast, U.S. affiliates in Japan have R&D intensity levels similar to or greater than those of U.S. affiliates in France, the United Kingdom, and, in some sectors, Germany. Generally, the magnitude and intensity of R&D activity is relatively similar between the United States and both France and the United Kingdom, in each direction. However, there are noticeably different

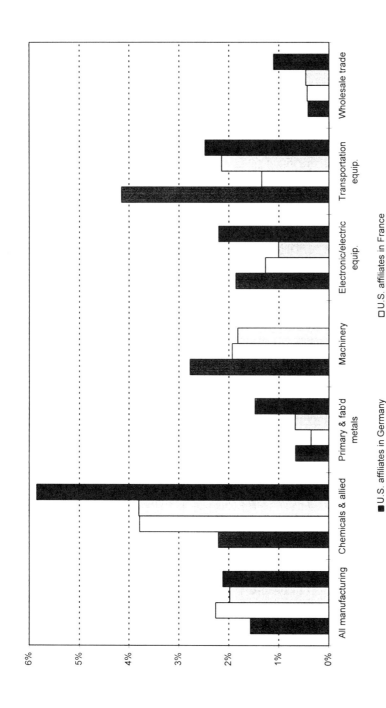

Figure 5.7. R&D Intensity of U.S. Affiliates in Foreign Markets, by Industry and by Country. *Data source:* BEA, *U.S. Direct Investment Abroad: 1994 Benchmark Survey* (January 1997): tables III.I 3.; III.E 3. *Note:* 1993 data for U.K. and France in electronic, electric equipment; transportation equipment (1994 data not available).

R&D intensity levels between French and U.K. affiliates operating in different U.S. industries.

These patterns can be viewed against other measures of the technology development strategies of MNCs, such as the direct sale or purchase of technology in the form of intellectual property. As described in the next section, trends in technology trade are consistent with the centralization of R&D by MNCs, and also point to additional variations in the tendency of foreign affiliates to develop and/or acquire technology in foreign markets.

Technology Trade

Beyond overt corporate R&D programs, technology can be transferred across national borders in different forms and through various mechanisms, many of which are difficult to measure. The best available quantitative indicator of technology exchange is the volume and direction of international royalty and license fee transactions.[43] Sales of intellectual property represent exports on the services account, and purchases represent imports; the net of sales less purchases constitutes the technology trade balance.

Outside of the United States, few countries have had a positive technology trade balance. In fact, with the exception of the United Kingdom until 1986, no other large OECD country has had a positive balance.[44] Figure 5.8 (Ratio of Technology Exports to Imports, by Country) shows the ratio of sales to purchases for the United States, Japan, France, Germany, and the United Kingdom. Throughout the 1980s and early 1990s, the ratio for most countries remained just under one, with the exception of the United Kingdom during the early 1980s. In other words, except for the United States, the major OECD countries export roughly the same amount of technology that they import. By contrast, U.S. technology exports have consistently outweighed imports by a substantial margin.[45]

Until the mid-1980s, many U.S. corporations did not treat their intellectual property as a productive asset—in fact, few corporations even included it on their balance sheets. Throughout the 1980s, however, U.S. companies gradually recognized and harnessed the financial power of their intellectual property. Sales of U.S. intellectual property increased steadily from $8.1 billion in 1986 to $27 billion by 1995.[46] Imports of intellectual property also increased, but remained at a substantially lower volume—over the same period, intellectual property imports increased from $1.4 to $6.3 billion. As a result, the technology trade balance remained decidedly positive, rising from a surplus of $6.7 billion in 1986 to $20.6 billion in 1995.

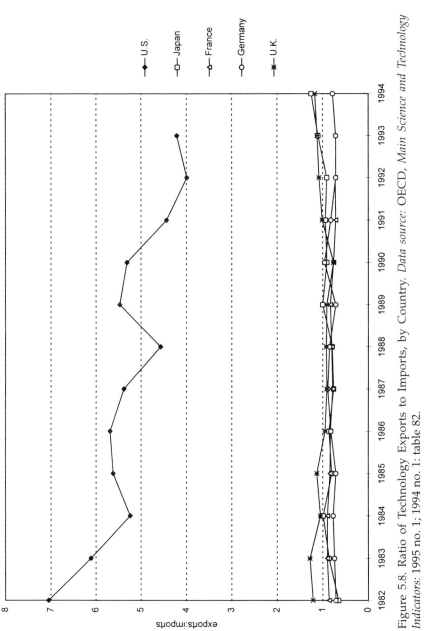

Figure 5.8. Ratio of Technology Exports to Imports, by Country. *Data source: OECD, Main Science and Technology Indicators: 1995 no. 1; 1994 no. 1: table 82.*

The unusually large U.S. surplus in technology trade could indicate that the U.S. technology base is very robust, producing valuable and highly marketable knowledge that contributes positively to the U.S. trade balance. On the other hand, the technology trade surplus also could indicate a relatively low willingness or ability of U.S. firms to import foreign technology.[47] Both interpretations may be correct, at least in part. Further analysis of the direction and composition of technology trade indicates that much of the volume of technology trade remains within multinational corporate networks, although firms vary along national lines in their tendency to trade technology within or outside of multinational corporate networks.

In terms of direction, Figures 5.9 (MNCs and U.S. Technology Exports) and 5.10 (MNCs and U.S. Technology Imports) indicate that a large percentage of both U.S. technology exports and imports is associated with MNCs. Between 1986 and 1994, U.S. MNCs and U.S. affiliates of foreign MNCs together sold 79 percent of all technology exports and bought 68 percent of all technology imports. However, U.S. MNCs sell virtually all of the MNC technology exports (Figure 5.9), while U.S. affiliates of foreign MNCs purchase most of the MNC technology imports (Figure 5.10). Between 1986 and 1994, 96 percent of all MNC technology exports was sold by U.S. MNCs to their foreign affiliates, while 4 percent was sold by affiliates in the United States to their foreign parents. The obverse pattern holds for imports: 8 percent of all MNC technology imports was purchased by U.S. MNCs from their foreign affiliates, while U.S. affiliates purchased 92 percent of all technology imports from their foreign parents.[48] In short, technology trade not only is dominated by MNCs, but also flows from parent firms to their foreign affiliates.[49]

These figures also illustrate the strong growth in both technology exports and imports since the mid-1980s, trends that can be linked to FDI flows during the same period. Between 1986 and 1994, technology exports from U.S. MNCs to their foreign affiliates increased at an average annual rate of 22 percent, which corresponds to the growth in U.S. direct investment abroad during this period. Similarly, during the same period, imports by U.S. affiliates from their foreign parents increased at an annual rate of 44 percent, corresponding to the rapid increase in FDI in the United States during the late 1980s.[50] Moreover, the geographical distribution of technology trade tends to conform to the geographical distribution of investment: in 1994, for instance, 44 percent of all U.S. technology exports were received by U.S. affiliates in Europe, while 11 percent were received by U.S. affiliates in Japan; likewise, 46 percent of all U.S. technology imports were by

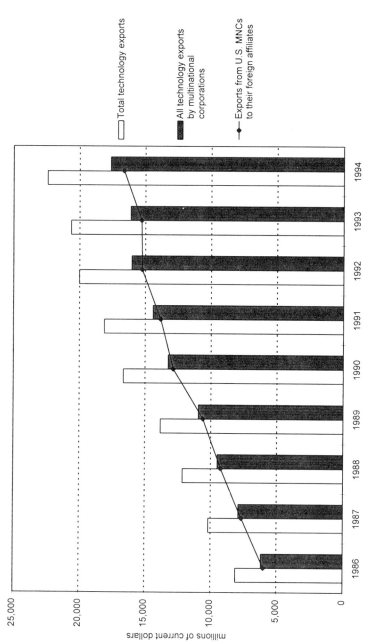

□ Total technology exports

■ All technology exports by multinational corporations

♦ Exports from U.S. MNCs to their foreign affiliates

Figure 5.9. MNCs and U.S. Technology Exports. *Data source:* BEA, *Survey of Current Business* (Sept. 1995), table 2.1, p. 76.

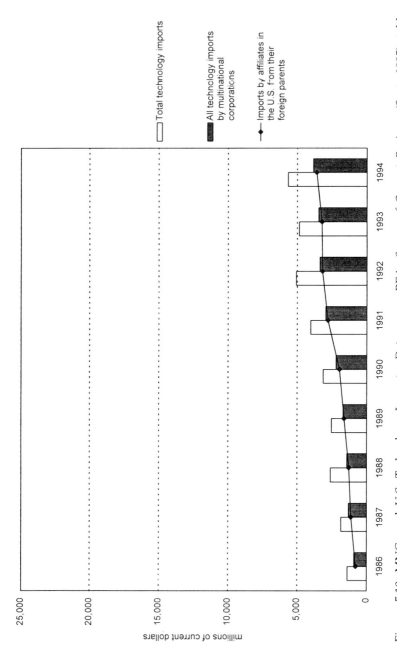

Figure 5.10. MNCs and U.S. Technology Imports. *Data source:* BEA, *Survey of Current Business* (Sept. 1995), table 2.1, p. 76.

U.S. affiliates of European firms, while 13 percent were by U.S. affiliates of Japanese firms.[51]

In essence, technology export and import patterns indicate that cross-border technology flows certainly have increased over time, yet those flows consistently have stayed within multinational corporate networks. In addition, the data imply that technology typically is developed in the home market operations of MNCs and gradually extends abroad in the wake of foreign direct investment.[52] In this respect, the technology trade data are consistent with the R&D data, which indicate that technology development remains relatively centralized in the home market operations of MNCs.

In terms of composition, unaffiliated technology trade patterns indicate that there are significant variances in the propensity of firms based in different nations to trade technology within or outside of multinational corporate networks. Unaffiliated or arms-length technology trade takes place among firms that have no economic relationship other than through the market. Since unaffiliated technology transactions take place through market-based bargaining, they reflect the market value of technology more accurately than trade among firms within multinational corporate networks. Moreover, unaffiliated transactions imply less control by the originator and more control by the purchaser. Consequently, cross-national differences in technology acquisition strategies should apply in the propensity of firms based in different states to purchase technology from unaffiliated sources.

The data on unaffiliated technology trade reveal that Japanese firms buy an unusually large percentage of U.S. technology through arms-length transactions. In 1994, 39 percent of all U.S. technology sales to Japan were purchased through arms-length transactions, compared to 12 percent of all U.S. technology sales to Europe and even lower percentages for firms in the larger European countries—13 percent for Germany, 12 percent for the United Kingdom, and 11 percent for France.[53] Consequently, since unaffiliated transactions impart a higher degree of control to the purchaser, Japanese firms retain greater control over the technology they purchase from the United States than do European firms.

Most of the unaffiliated U.S. technology exports are of industrial process technology. Between 1987 and 1994, industrial process technology accounted for 65 percent of unaffiliated U.S. technology exports. This subset of technology trade is particularly critical to commercial competitiveness, given the direct bearing of industrial process technology on production costs and productivity. Consequently, trends in the unaffiliated sale of industrial process technology provide an important

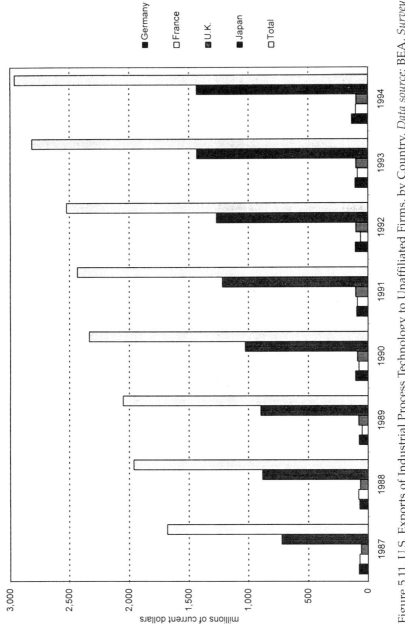

Figure 5.11. U.S. Exports of Industrial Process Technology to Unaffiliated Firms, by Country. *Data source:* BEA, *Survey of Current Business* (Sept. 1995), table 2.1, p. 76; (Sept. 1994); (Sept. 1993).

indicator of the near-term competitive strategies of MNCs across the advanced industrial states.

As with total technology trade, unaffiliated U.S. exports of industrial process technology have consistently outweighed U.S. imports, resulting in an average annual surplus of $1.6 billion between 1987 and 1994. Japan is the largest consumer of unaffiliated U.S. industrial process technology—in 1994, U.S. exports to Japan accounted for 48 percent ($1.4 billion) of all industrial process technology exports, compared with 5 percent for Germany, 3 percent for the United Kingdom, and 24 percent for Europe as a whole (Figure 5.11. U.S. Exports of Industrial Process Technology to Unaffiliated Firms, by Country). This same pattern has been consistent throughout the 1980s and 1990s.

The large percentage of unaffiliated industrial process technology purchased by Japanese firms is further reflected in the sources of the U.S. trade surplus in unaffiliated industrial process technology trade. As shown in Figure 5.12 (U.S. Trade Balance among Unaffiliated Firms in Industrial Process Technology, by Country), Japan consistently accounts for the bulk of this surplus: between 1987 and 1994, Japan's average annual surplus accounted for 60 percent of the total U.S. surplus in arms-length trading of industrial process technology. During this period, Japan ran average annual surpluses with the United States of $764 million, compared with $27 million for all of Europe combined. The only countries with which the United States has had a trade deficit in unaffiliated industrial process knowledge have been the United Kingdom and Germany, averaging -$18 million and -$45 million per year respectively from 1987 through 1994.

In sum, U.S. technology trade data reveal two important patterns in the international exchange of technology. First, most of the formal cross-border exchange of technology takes place within multinational corporate networks—in particular, most of the technology flows from parents to their affiliates. Like the distribution of R&D within multinational corporate networks, this pattern implies that the development of new technology remains centralized in the home market operations of MNCs. Second, there are notable differences in the tendency of firms based in different nations to acquire technology through unaffiliated channels. In particular, Japanese firms purchase far more U.S. technology through arms-length transactions than do European firms—in fact, the total U.S. surplus in the unaffiliated trade of industrial process knowledge is due largely to surpluses with Japan, while the United States has been a net importer of U.K. and German industrial process knowledge. This pattern is consistent with other comparative analyses showing that Japanese firms have a greater tendency to

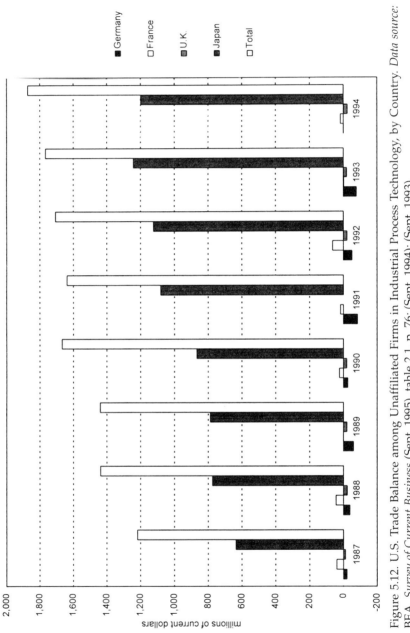

Figure 5.12. U.S. Trade Balance among Unaffiliated Firms in Industrial Process Technology, by Country. *Data source:* BEA, *Survey of Current Business* (Sept. 1995), table 2.1, p. 76; (Sept. 1994); (Sept. 1993).

acquire foreign technology through direct purchases than do U.S. and European firms.[54]

Although both the R&D and technology trade data indicate that technology development remains relatively centralized, technology can be globalized through other mechanisms such as international strategic alliances and related forms of intercorporate cooperation designed to spread investment costs and gain access to a wider range of technologies. Interfirm alliances and joint ventures in R&D and product development have become increasingly common, particularly in information technologies and biotechnology. At the same time, however, the density of alliances among U.S., European, and Japanese firms varies considerably.

International Technology Alliances[55]

Corporations can cooperate on technology development through a variety of mechanisms, some of which imply clear directions of technology flow either out of or into a national base. In the 1970s, the most common form of international technology collaboration was through joint ventures and research corporations, where firms shared equity ownership (and corresponding profits and losses) in a separate and distinct corporate entity. By the late 1980s, joint equity collaboration was eclipsed by non-equity alliances, in which firms forgo formal equity linkages and directly organize joint R&D activities to reduce the cost and risk of pursuing related innovations.[56] Whether through direct or indirect linkages, alliances tend not to displace but to complement firms' internal research activities, and generally work best between firms that have different but complementary technological assets.[57]

Technology alliances began to grow substantially during the late 1980s and continue to do so today.[58] Contemporary economic and technological conditions provide a variety of incentives for firms to engage in international technology alliances.[59] Many firms use alliance strategies to reduce rapidly rising R&D costs and associated risks, particularly in sectors with increasingly capital-intensive scientific and technological disciplines, shorter innovation to commercialization periods, accelerated product life cycles, and a rapid diffusion of technology across competing firms. In addition, many firms use alliances to better monitor and retain access to a wider array of technological and scientific developments, which is increasingly important as product and process technologies become more complex and geographically dispersed. Moreover, alliances can generate new business opportunities, improve access to foreign markets, and reduce time to market.

Alliances are most common in high-technology industries. Most alliances in fact are concentrated in a few industries, particularly information technologies, biotechnology, and new materials.[60] Alliances in information technologies have grown far faster than in any other area, owing in part to the rapid growth of information technology (IT) industries generally as well as the overlapping nature of technological developments in computer software and hardware, telecommunications, industrial automation, and microelectronics. Alliances also are quite common in biotechnology, largely because of the unique division of labor between small, specialized biotechnology firms and large pharmaceutical and agro-chemical firms: the latter are attracted to the specialized research capabilities of dedicated biotechnology companies, which in turn are attracted to the financial depth, production capacity, and marketing capabilities of diversified pharmaceutical and agro-chemical firms. Alliances are also fairly common in new materials, in part because of the concentrated costs of R&D in new materials and the relative dispersion within and across industries of technological advances in this area.

Between 1980 and 1994, there were over 2,800 technology alliances among U.S., European, and Japanese firms in information technology industries. Over the same period, there were less than half as many alliances in biotechnology (approximately 1,300), and considerably fewer in new materials (approximately 560).[61] Figure 5.13 (Distribution of Technology Alliances between Economic Regions, by Technology) conveys the relative magnitude of alliances in these three sectors from 1980 to 1994.

Figure 5.13 also indicates that technology alliance formation varies considerably across countries. In new materials, biotechnology, and especially information technologies, the largest number of alliances occurred between U.S. firms and other U.S. firms—not foreign firms. Information technology alliances among U.S. firms have grown steadily since the early 1980s, and account for 37 percent of all alliances in this area from 1980 to 1994. In 1994 alone, IT alliances among U.S. firms accounted for 56 percent of the total. Similarly, alliances among U.S. firms account for nearly 40 percent of all biotechnology alliances over the period. Intra-U.S. alliances in these two technologies account for most of the recent growth in strategic technology alliances among U.S., European, and Japanese firms.

Across each of the three technologies, the second most frequent alliance combination has been between U.S. and European firms. In information technologies, alliances between U.S. and European firms have accounted for 22 percent of all alliances in this category between 1980 and 1994, although the growth of IT alliances among U.S. firms has far

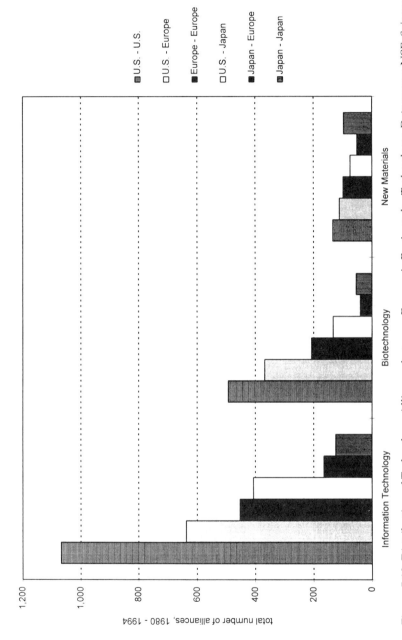

Figure 5.13. Distribution of Technology Alliances between Economic Regions, by Technology. *Data source: NSF, Science and Engineering Indicators* (1996): 158.

outstripped U.S.-European IT alliances since the mid-1980s. Biotechnology alliances have been more evenly distributed. Since 1989, biotechnology alliances between U.S. and European firms have been close to and occasionally greater than the number of alliances among U.S. firms. Over the entire time period, biotechnology alliances between U.S. and European firms accounted for 28 percent of the total.

In each technology, intraregional alliances among European firms represent the third most frequent alliance combination. Intraregional European alliances in each of the three technologies peaked in the late 1980s, most likely a product of strategic maneuvering prior to the European Union's 1992 market liberalization. Of all alliance combinations involving Japanese firms, the most frequent have been with U.S. firms in information technologies. In other technologies and other alliance combinations, however, Japanese firms are the least likely to engage in technology alliances, whether with U.S., European, or other Japanese firms.

In short, given a variety of technological and market pressures, firms have been turning to alliance strategies to reduce R&D costs, spread product development risks, and maintain access to a relatively broad portfolio of technologies and market opportunities while focusing their internal R&D efforts on core competencies. However, firms based in different states have different tendencies to form alliances, and tend to favor some technologies more than others. Most of the technology alliances over time and across technologies have involved U.S. firms and other U.S. firms. Of all combinations, the fastest growth in alliance formation has been among U.S. firms in information technology industries. Alliances between U.S. and European firms also have been quite frequent, particularly in biotechnology. By contrast, alliances involving Japanese firms have been relatively infrequent, with the exception of IT alliances with U.S. firms.

These variations in the tendency to use technology alliances complement the cross-national portrait of multinational corporate behavior that emerges from R&D and technology trade patterns. In the broadest view, the picture of technology development by multinational firms appears concentrated, not diffuse: most of the R&D conducted by MNCs takes place in the home market, and most international technology trade flows from parents to their affiliates. The fact that technology alliances are most frequent among U.S. firms is consistent with this central pattern.

On the periphery, much more variation appears. Sectoral detail indicates that the global spread of technology is far more extensive in some industries than others. The highest levels of foreign R&D conducted by MNCs are in pharmaceuticals, chemicals, electronic equipment, and, for U.S. MNCs, transportation equipment. More than any other sector, pharmaceuticals presents the clearest view of the diffusion of corporate R&D operations, showing both rapid growth and a large share of total R&D by foreign affiliates—particularly those operating in the United States. The concentration of international technology alliances in biotechnology and information technologies adds further resolution to this picture.

Country detail reveals even more variation. Generally, the R&D intensity of U.S. affiliates in different foreign markets varies less than the R&D intensity of different foreign affiliates in the United States. German affiliates have both the highest R&D expenditures and the highest R&D intensity of all foreign affiliates in the United States, while Japanese affiliates in the United States have the lowest levels in both respects. The magnitude of R&D is relatively similar for French and U.K. affiliates, although there are noticeably different R&D intensity levels between French and U.K. affiliates operating in different U.S. industries. By contrast, U.S. affiliates in Japan have R&D intensity levels similar to or greater than those of U.S. affiliates in France, the United Kingdom, and, in some sectors, Germany. Technology trade flows add further depth to this pattern. Japanese firms purchase far more U.S. technology through arms-length transactions than do European firms—in fact, the U.S. maintains a large export surplus in unaffiliated industrial process knowledge with Japan, while the United States has been a net importer of U.K. and German industrial process knowledge. Again, the distribution of technology alliances provides complementary color: alliances involving Japanese firms are infrequent, while alliances involving European and especially U.S. firms are common.

In sum, MNCs based in different states and operating in different sectors internationalize their technology development functions in different ways and to different degrees. The nature and identity of the base itself are mirrored in ultimate corporate behavior. As the following section demonstrates, such cross-national variations in foreign technology development strategies are similar in nature to cross-national variations in corporate investment, trade, and local production.

DIRECT INVESTMENT AND INTRAFIRM TRADE

Are the national patterns observed in the research and development activities of today's leading MNCs matched in other key areas of corporate strategy? This section compares the operations of MNCs along three closely related dimensions: the composition of direct investment, the volume and direction of intrafirm trade, and the domestic content of production by foreign affiliates. These indicators measure the types of industries in which MNCs operate outside their home markets, the degree to which they trade within or outside of their own internal networks, and the extent to which their foreign operations are integrated with host markets.

The evidence along each of these dimensions suggests that leading MNCs tend to pursue distinct operational styles in foreign markets and that these styles vary along national lines. U.S. MNCs represent one style, operating largely in foreign manufacturing and financial sectors, using intrafirm trade (IFT) channels relatively moderately, and displaying a comparatively high degree of integration in local markets. Japanese MNCs represent quite a different style, operating largely in foreign wholesale trade sectors, using IFT extensively, and displaying a comparatively low level of integration in local markets. If U.S. and Japanese MNCs can thereby be depicted at opposite ends on a spectrum of corporate behavior, German MNCs may be placed between the midpoint of that spectrum and the Japanese end. In addition, the evidence also suggests that French and British MNCs could be placed between the midpoint and the U.S. end of the spectrum (with British MNCs quite close to U.S. MNCs).

The Composition of Direct Investment[62]

The volume of FDI flows among advanced industrial states often varies substantially, in ways that tend to reflect different national approaches to inward direct investment. The largest variation is the relatively low level of direct investment in Japan, particularly in comparison to very high levels of outward investment by Japanese MNCs. For instance, although the ratio has declined slightly over time, in 1995 the volume of Japanese direct investment in the United States was almost three times the size of U.S. direct investment in Japan—$108.5 billion to $39.2 billion, respectively. This pattern reflects historically rooted structures in Japan's political economy, which tend to inhibit inward investment.[63]

As the evidence in this section illustrates, national patterns of direct investment differ not only in volume but also in composition, suggesting that both the home and host economies play a significant role in shaping FDI.

Figures 5.14 (Germany's Direct Investment Position in the U.S., by Sector) and 5.15 (Japan's Direct Investment Position in the U.S., by Sector) illustrate the composition of direct investment by German and Japanese MNCs in the United States.[64] In both cases, direct investment in the United States has increased over time, although at different rates:

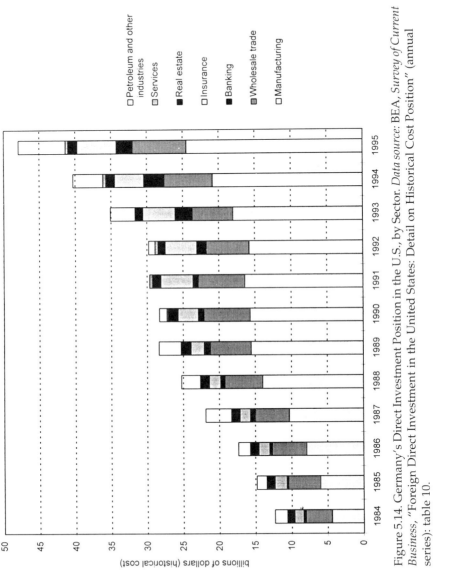

Figure 5.14. Germany's Direct Investment Position in the U.S., by Sector. *Data source:* BEA, *Survey of Current Business*, "Foreign Direct Investment in the United States: Detail on Historical Cost Position" (annual series): table 10.

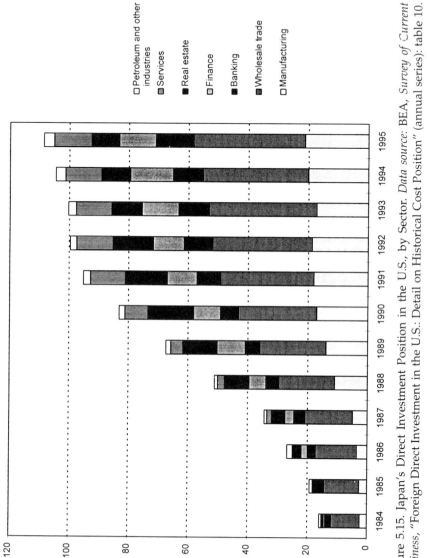

Figure 5.15. Japan's Direct Investment Position in the U.S., by Sector. *Data source:* BEA, *Survey of Current Business,* "Foreign Direct Investment in the U.S.: Detail on Historical Cost Position" (annual series): table 10.

German direct investment in the United States rose from $12.3 billion in 1984 to $47.9 billion in 1995, while Japanese direct investment increased very rapidly, from $16.0 billion to $108.6 billion (nearly twice the magnitude of German direct investment).[65] At the same time, direct investment from each nation has been placed in different segments of the U.S. economy.

Over the 1984–1995 period, half of all German direct investment in the United States was in manufacturing industries, slightly higher than the average for all European countries (43 percent). A sizable portion—22 percent—of German direct investment has gone into the U.S. wholesale trade sector, compared to just 9 percent for all European countries. As with other European countries, most other sectors account for fairly small shares of German direct investment in the United States.

By comparison, over the same period only 18 percent of Japanese direct investment in the United States was located in manufacturing industries. The wholesale trade sector consistently accounts for the largest share of Japan's direct investment—on average, 41 percent from 1984 to 1995. Compared to German and other European investors, fairly large shares of Japanese direct investment also have gone into banking (10 percent) and services (9 percent).

The composition of foreign direct investment flowing from the United States to both Germany and Japan also differs, but far less substantially than for foreign investment in the United States (Figure 5.16. U.S. Direct Investment Position in Germany, by Sector; and Figure 5.17. U.S. Direct Investment Position in Japan, by Sector). Over the 1984–1995 period, 60 percent of U.S. direct investment in Germany was in manufacturing industries, higher than the average for all European countries (40 percent).[66] Only 6 percent of U.S. direct investment went to Germany's wholesale trade sector, lower than the average for all European countries (12 percent). The composition of U.S. direct investment in Japan is close to the average for U.S. investment in Europe: 47 percent in manufacturing, and 18 percent in wholesale trade. Also, unlike German or Japanese investment in the United States, a substantial portion of U.S. direct investment abroad goes into the financial sector: finance accounts for 25 percent of U.S. direct investment in Europe, 12 percent in Germany, and 11 percent in Japan.

In short, the composition of direct investment flows across the Triad varies markedly. In general, there is far more variation in FDI in the United States than United States investment abroad. Japanese direct investment in the United States is unusually concentrated in the wholesale trade sector. Far more of German investment flows to U.S. manufacturing industries, although wholesale trade also accounts for a large

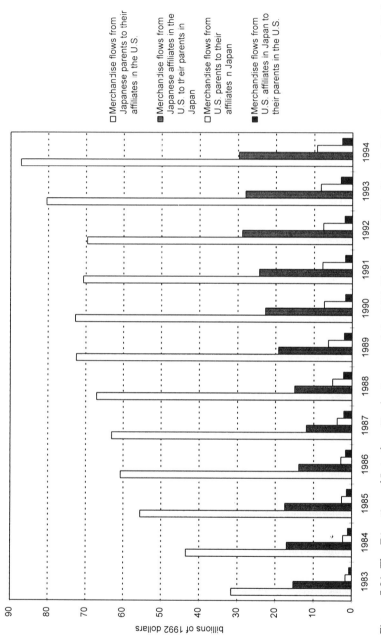

Figure 5.21. The Direction of Intrafirm Trade: Japan and the U.S. *Data source:* BEA, *Foreign Direct Investment in the U.S.* (annual series); BEA, *U.S. Direct Investment Abroad* (annual series); BEA, *Survey of Current Business* (June 1995).

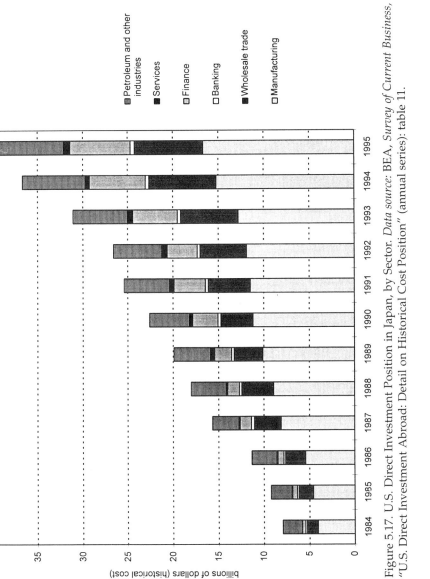

Figure 5.17. U.S. Direct Investment Position in Japan, by Sector. *Data source:* BEA, *Survey of Current Business,* "U.S. Direct Investment Abroad: Detail on Historical Cost Position" (annual series): table 11.

share. By comparison, European MNCs as a whole invest in U.S. manufacturing industries at levels comparable to German MNCs, but direct substantially less investment to the U.S. wholesale trade sector.

U.S. direct investment abroad is distinctive primarily by virtue of the large fraction that goes into the finance sector. In addition, U.S. direct investment in Germany is concentrated in manufacturing industries, while the share directed to wholesale trade is relatively small. Otherwise, the composition of U.S. direct investment in Europe as a whole, in Germany, and in Japan is relatively similar.

The fact that U.S. outward investment varies little across countries, while direct investment in the United States varies significantly across countries, suggests that multinational firms based in different states tend to engage foreign markets in distinct ways. At one end of the spectrum, U.S. MNCs place the majority of their direct investment abroad in manufacturing industries, comparatively little in wholesale trade, and a relatively large share in finance. At the other end of the spectrum, Japanese MNCs place the majority of their direct investment in wholesale trade, and comparatively little in manufacturing industries. German firms combine elements of both U.S. and Japanese styles of direct investment, with the majority in manufacturing industries but a large share in wholesale trade as well. Other European investors are closer to the U.S. model, with a considerably lower share in wholesale trade.

The sectoral distribution of direct investment is particularly significant because of its implications for the operational style of affiliates in foreign markets. By design, foreign affiliates in the wholesale trade sector import very large shares of their total output, as they primarily import finished goods for resale. Affiliates in manufacturing industries may or may not import large shares of their total output, as they can procure intermediate inputs (ranging from manufactured components to commodity-type bulk materials) through local suppliers.

Given the sectoral distribution of direct investment, this basic difference between wholesale trade and manufacturing industries implies that affiliates of Japanese MNCs, in the aggregate, are less likely than Europe and U.S.-based MNCs to be deeply integrated in local markets. Foreign affiliates of U.S. firms are more likely to be integrated in local markets. Affiliates of German MNCs are likely to represent a midpoint on this spectrum.

These expectations are borne out by national variations in the trade flows associated with MNCs. Data on trade among affiliated firms—that is, intrafirm trade—are largely consistent with cross-national differences in the composition of investment.

Intrafirm Trade

Intrafirm trade (IFT) represents cross-border transactions between affiliated units of MNCs. In the United States, the volume of intrafirm trade represents a substantial share of total merchandise trade: in 1994, IFT accounted for more than one third of all merchandise exports and over two fifths of all merchandise imports.[67]

Like many domestic firms, foreign affiliates in different markets import and export a mix of finished and intermediate goods, depending upon their production and marketing strategies, price differentials, and a variety of additional factors internal and external to the firm. However, IFT data indicate that affiliates based in different states use IFT to different degrees, in part reflecting differences in the composition of direct investment.

Figures 5.18 (The Volume of Intrafirm Trade: Germany and the U.S.) and 5.19 (The Volume of Intrafirm Trade: Japan and the U.S.) represent the volume of IFT between the United States and both Germany and Japan (respectively), relative to the total volume of merchandise trade in each bilateral relationship.[68] Together, the two figures illustrate that IFT accounts for a larger percentage of total merchandise trade between the United States and Japan. Between 1983 and 1994, IFT has averaged 72 percent of total merchandise trade between the United States and Japan, compared to 55 percent for U.S.-German trade. In both instances, the IFT share of total trade has increased over time: IFT between the United States and Germany increased from 52 percent of all merchandise trade in 1983 to 63 percent in 1994, while IFT between Japan and the United States increased from 68 percent to 77 percent. While U.S.-German IFT is lower than U.S.-Japan IFT, it is higher than the average for U.S. trade with all Europe generally: from 1983 to 1994, IFT accounted for 51 percent of all merchandise trade between the United States and Europe.[69]

Figures 5.18 and 5.19 also indicate that IFT within U.S. firms represents a relatively small share of total IFT within each bilateral trade relationship. In U.S.-Japan trade, IFT among Japanese MNCs accounts for 92 percent of all bilateral IFT. In U.S.-German trade, IFT among German MNCs accounts for 71 percent of all IFT. By comparison, IFT among European MNCs accounts for 57 percent of all IFT between the United States and Europe.

Further detail on the direction of trade within MNCs indicates that IFT, in all cases, flows primarily from parents to their foreign affiliates. Figures 5.20 (The Direction of Intrafirm Trade: Germany and the U.S.) and 5.21 (The Direction of Intrafirm Trade: Japan and the U.S.) portray

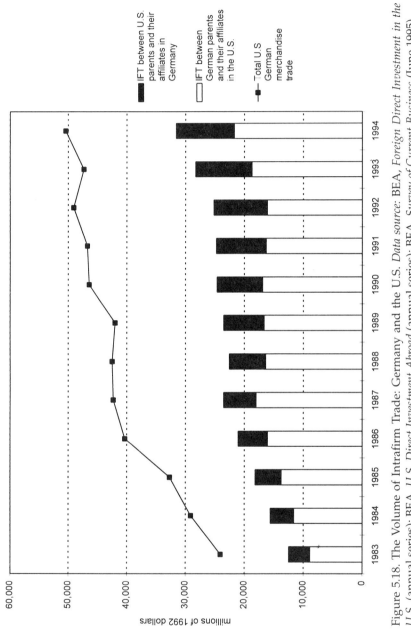

Figure 5.18. The Volume of Intrafirm Trade: Germany and the U.S. *Data source:* BEA, *Foreign Direct Investment in the U.S.* (annual series); BEA, *U.S. Direct Investment Abroad* (annual series); BEA, *Survey of Current Business* (June 1995).

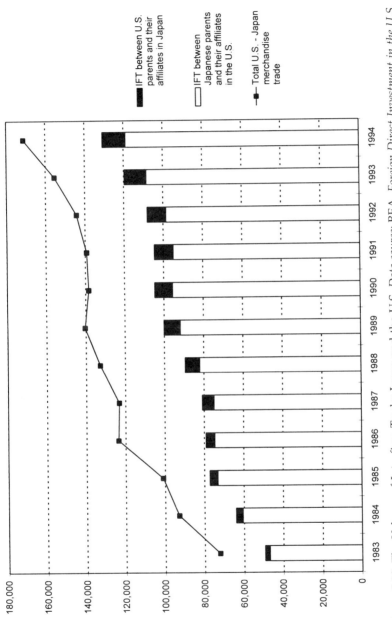

Figure 5.19. The Volume of Intrafirm Trade: Japan and the U.S. *Data source:* BEA, *Foreign Direct Investment in the U.S.* (annual series); BEA, *U.S. Direct Investment Abroad* (annual series); BEA, *Survey of Current Business* (June 1995).

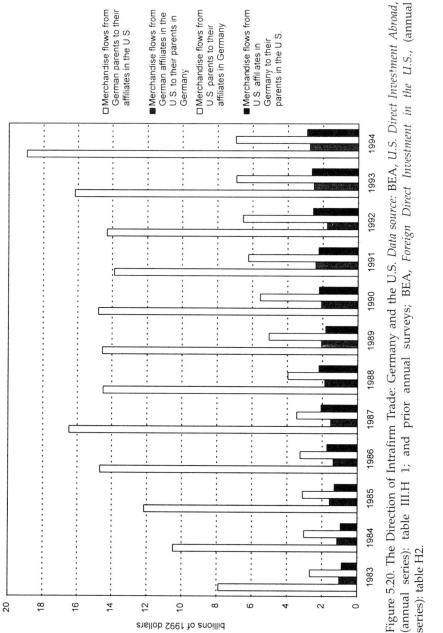

Figure 5.20. The Direction of Intrafirm Trade: Germany and the U.S. *Data source*: BEA, *U.S. Direct Investment Abroad*, (annual series): table III.H 1; and prior annual surveys; BEA, *Foreign Direct Investment in the U.S.*, (annual series): table H2.

IFT flows in each of four possible directions for U.S. trade with Japan and Germany: from parent to affiliate, and vice versa, for each country. In all cases, trade flows from multinational corporate parent groups to their foreign affiliates outweigh flows from foreign affiliates to their parent groups, suggesting that outward direct investment consistently creates trade. However, the relative magnitude character of IFT varies considerably across MNCs based in different states.

Most of the total IFT between the United States and both Japan and Germany flows from the foreign parent group to affiliates in the United States. Merchandise flows from German multinational corporate parents to their affiliates in the United States are approximately twice the size of flows from U.S. parents to their affiliates in Germany, while merchandise flows from affiliates to parents are similarly low in both directions (Figure 5.20). In the case of U.S.-Japan trade, merchandise trade flows from Japanese parents to their affiliates in the United States far outweigh any other IFT flow (Figure 5.21). In addition, unlike the U.S.-German trade relationship, IFT from Japanese affiliates in the United States to their foreign parents is over three times the volume of trade flows from U.S. parents to their affiliates in Japan.

These cross-national variations in the volume and direction of IFT are consistent with variations in the volume and composition of direct investment. Japanese direct investment in the United States is three times the size of U.S. direct investment in Japan. It is also far more concentrated in the wholesale trade sector, which characteristically involves a large share of finished goods imports. These direct investment patterns are consistent with the very large share of total U.S.-Japan trade that flows from Japanese parents to their affiliates in the United States. A similar but less stark pattern exists in the investment and trading relationship between the United States and Germany. German direct investment in the United States is about the same size as U.S. investment in Germany, although a larger share of it is in wholesale trade. In line with this investment pattern, more IFT flows from German parents to their affiliates in the United States than vice versa, while IFT flowing from affiliates to parents is similar in both directions.

In short, cross-national variation in the basic sectoral composition of direct investment provide some basis for understanding the net tendency of affiliates from individual countries to trade within or outside of multinational corporate networks. In general, overseas investment by U.S., German, and Japanese MNCs creates trade, through IFT flows from parents to affiliates. But U.S. MNCs invest abroad in ways that tend to create less IFT than either German or especially Japanese

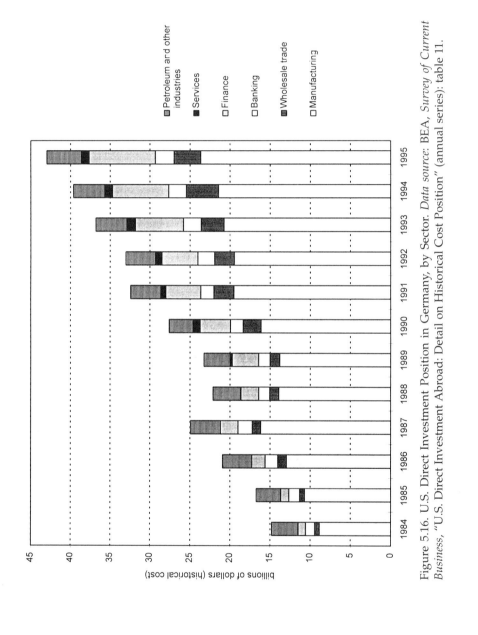

Figure 5.16. U.S. Direct Investment Position in Germany, by Sector. *Data source:* BEA, *Survey of Current Business*, "U.S. Direct Investment Abroad: Detail on Historical Cost Position" (annual series): table 11.

MNCs, both of which invest abroad in ways that tend to foster particularly high levels of IFT.

Further data on the intended use of intrafirm trade provide additional evidence that MNCs based in different states engage foreign markets in distinctive ways. IFT flows from parents to their foreign affiliates generally fall into two categories, goods for resale without further manufacture (typically, finished goods) and goods for further manufacture (typically, intermediate goods). The mix of these two types of goods provides an approximate measure of the degree to which affiliates are integrated in local markets: the higher the share of imports for further manufacture, the more likely that the affiliate is adding value through local production.

Table 5.4 (Intrafirm Trade of Foreign Affiliates in the U.S. and U.S. Affiliates Abroad, by Intended Use) presents data describing how affiliates from different countries use goods received from their foreign parent group. Of foreign affiliates in the United States, the share of imports used for further manufacture is lowest among Japanese and German affiliates, and highest among French and U.K. affiliates. Of the different foreign markets in which U.S. affiliates operate, the share of imports used for further manufacture is lowest in Japan, highest in the United Kingdom, and relatively similar for Germany and France. Moreover, in all cases, a considerably higher share of the goods sent from U.S. parents to their foreign affiliates is used for further manufacture in each country than is the case for the corresponding foreign MNCs operating in the U.S. market. This suggests that U.S. affiliates are more likely to add value in foreign markets than MNCs based in the United Kingdom, France, Germany, or Japan, collectively as well as individually.

These patterns are consistent with the basic composition of direct investment by affiliates operating in each market. Other factors, however, may play a role as well. For instance, variation in the share of IFT goods used for further manufacture between U.S. affiliates in Japan and U.S. affiliates in the United Kingdom could reflect the relative ease of production for U.S. MNCs in the United Kingdom because of commonalities of language and culture, standards, legal and regulatory systems, and other business climate factors. The variation also seems associated with the fact that the United Kingdom has traditionally been far more accommodating of inward investment than Japan.

In addition, variation in the use of IFT among different foreign affiliates operating in the relatively open U.S. market is consistent with cross-national variation in the sectoral composition of investment. IFT patterns could, however, also reflect cross-national differences in how foreign affiliates pursue local production. Differentiating these two

TABLE 5.4
Intrafirm Trade of Foreign Affiliates in the U.S. and U.S. Affiliates Abroad, by Intended Use

	Japan	Germany	France	U.K.	All countries
Imports of foreign affiliates in the U.S., from their foreign parent group (1992):					
Goods for resale without further manufacture, as a percent of total imported from foreign parent group	79	81	60	55	74
Goods for further manufacture, as a percent of total imported from foreign parent group	21	19	40	45	25
Exports to U.S. affiliates in foreign markets, from their U.S. parent group (1994):					
Goods for resale without further manufacture, as a percent of total exported by U.S. parent group	72	53	48	32	46
Goods for further manufacture, as a percent of total exported by U.S. parent group	28	43	49	67	52

Source: Bureau of Economic Analysis, *Foreign Direct Investment in the U.S.: 1992* (Washington, D.C.: U.S. Government Printing Office, 1994) table G-36; Bureau of Economic Analysis, *U.S. Direct Investment Abroad: 1994* (Washington, D.C.: U.S. Government Printing Office, 1997) table III.H 14.
Note: The two categories, goods for resale and goods for further manufacture, may not equal 100 percent due to the small fraction of intrafirm trade that consists of capital equipment.

factors requires observations of different affiliates operating within the same industry in the same foreign country. Domestic content data provide this degree of discrimination, and ultimately suggests that MNCs in different countries do indeed pursue different production strategies in foreign markets.

Domestic Content

The 1994 Benchmark Survey on Foreign Direct Investment in the United States, conducted by the Bureau of Economic Analysis of the U.S. Department of Commerce, provides detail on the imports of foreign affiliates by intended use. Such data allow observations of national differences across affiliates that otherwise appear very similar: they all operate in manufacturing industries and report high shares of goods intended for further manufacture. From this particular class of affiliates, one can observe whether affiliates based in different nations differ in their tendency to use local versus imported inputs for their U.S. production operations.[70]

Recent analyses of this class of affiliates provide findings quite similar to those reached in earlier sections of this chapter: foreign affiliates based in the United Kingdom have higher levels of domestic content across U.S. manufacturing industries, while foreign affiliates based in Germany and, to a greater extent, Japan, have considerably lower levels of domestic content.[71] In other words, affiliates based in the United Kingdom are more likely to be deeply integrated in the U.S. economy than are affiliates based in Germany. Japanese affiliates are least likely to be integrated.

Across all affiliates in all U.S. industries, the domestic content of production is slightly less than the estimated level for all firms—89 and 93 percent, respectively.[72] Across industries, domestic content tends to be lowest in machinery-intensive industries that have large amounts of manufactured intermediate goods, including construction, mining, and materials handling machinery; computer and office equipment; household audio and video; communications equipment; electronic components and accessories; and motor vehicles and equipment.

At the same time, domestic content rates in each of these industries vary across foreign affiliates based in different states. For instance, German-owned affiliates in the United States in nonelectrical machinery have a domestic content level of 79 percent, their British counterparts register a 95 percent level, while Japanese affiliates have a domestic content rate of 87 percent. In instruments and related products, 88 percent of production by German-owned affiliates is domestic content, French-owned affiliates register 95 percent, British-owned affiliates 97 percent, and Japanese affiliates 82 percent. In the electrical and electronic equipment sector, the domestic content for German-owned firms is 69 percent, while it is 96 percent for their French counterparts and 89 percent for Japanese affiliates.

Otherwise, in the construction, mining, and related machinery sector, the domestic content for Japanese-owned affiliates as a percentage of total output was 55 percent, compared to an average for all foreign affiliates of 89 percent. In computer and office equipment, the domestic content level for Japanese affiliates is 56 percent, compared to an average of 90 percent. In motor vehicles and equipment, the domestic content figure for Japanese affiliates was 63 percent, compared to 86 percent for other foreign affiliates.

Comparable domestic content data are not available for U.S. affiliates operating in foreign markets. However, the data on IFT exports by intended use (Table 5.4), which show comparatively high levels of exports for further manufacture, suggests that U.S. firms are likely to use local inputs more extensively than most foreign affiliates in the United States. Moreover, general domestic content data for all U.S. firms operating abroad, in all industries, show an average local content rate of 91 percent. The domestic content of U.S. affiliates is slightly higher in Europe (95 percent) than in Asia and the Pacific (90 percent), largely because of different levels of imports in the wholesale trade sector.[73]

In sum, there are consistent cross-national variations in the level and composition of direct investment, the degree to which MNCs maintain trade within their own corporate networks, and the extent to which foreign affiliates are integrated with local markets. Generally, U.S. MNCs are most likely to be located in manufacturing and service industries, to have comparatively low levels of IFT, and to be relatively well integrated within local markets. Japanese MNCs are most likely to be located in wholesale trade, to have comparatively high levels of IFT, and to be more independent from local markets. European MNCs generally represent different combinations of these two models, with German MNCs being closer in form to the Japanese style, and both French and U.K. MNCs being closer in form to the U.S. style.

These variations correspond to different strategies through which MNCs invest and produce in foreign markets, as well as to the relative openness of host economies to inward investment. We do not doubt the relevance of other factors, such as fundamental macroeconomic variables (for instance, the impact of different national savings rates on international trade and investment flows).[74] But the evidence surveyed in this chapter strongly suggests that there are inherent and enduring structural factors that profoundly influence the location decisions and operating styles of MNCs.

Such a conclusion could be tested further through a similar analysis of investment and trading patterns between Japan and the European Union. Unfortunately, data comparable to that considered in this chapter do not exist for this leg of the Triad. Anecdotal evidence, however, indicates that the patterns would be similar. Our own interviews with European corporate executives and officials of the Commission of the European Communities conducted in 1992 and 1993 suggested that similar structural imbalances in investment and IFT exist between many European countries and Japan.[75] In addition, in some key areas, such as automobiles in Germany, Japanese imports peaked at a much lower level than they did in the United States and stayed at that level despite the rising relative competitiveness of Japanese industry over time. Not only do the strategies of MNCs appear to vary by nationality when it comes to the investment and IFT, but states also appear to manage their own associated bilateral relations differently and with different results.

Together, national variations in MNC investment, trade, and local production patterns are consistent with the evidence presented on MNC innovation, technology trade, and international strategic alliances. Although both innovation and trade remain centralized in most MNCs, the degree of that centralization generally varies by corporate nationality. U.S. and U.K. firms tend to be more integrated with the foreign economies in which they operate, while German and especially Japanese MNCs tend to retain large shares of their innovation and trading operations within their own networks. These variations partly reflect the orientation and competencies of the foreign systems in which they operate, but taken together they seem mainly related to the structure and character of the national systems in which they are based.

INTERACTION OF CORPORATE INVESTMENT, TRADE AND INNOVATION

In light of the above findings, it is important to note that national innovation systems are not entirely independent, nor are they static. Elements of some systems were explicitly modeled on others, and there are numerous interdependencies and linkages across systems.[76] In addition, national systems exhibit different capacities to learn and adapt to changing technological and economic conditions.[77] Indeed, linkages across innovation systems are likely to deepen over time, as technology and industry spread across national borders. Higher rates of external patenting, more rapid diffusion of technology across borders, increasing rates of overseas R&D activity, and other trends such as the increasing prevalence of international technology alliances all point toward the increasing openness of many national technology bases. MNCs are typically at the heart of that process of opening.

In fact, MNCs may be diffusing technology more extensively through their overseas production facilities than can be captured by such measures as foreign R&D, technology trade, and strategic technology alliances. Some analysts have argued, for instance, that tacit knowledge—that is, technical knowledge and know-how embodied in both people and organizations—can be central to successful technology development, commercialization, and production (although in ways that are intrinsically difficult to measure and evaluate).[78] In addition, technology also can be transferred abroad in the form of goods themselves.[79] Given their extensive international production and sourcing networks, MNCs are particularly likely to transfer technology abroad in the form of people, organizational assets, and intermediate goods.

If MNCs were thoroughly and relentlessly integrating national innovation systems through the systematic diffusion of technology abroad, however, it would register in the overseas R&D data as well as the technology trade data. By these and related measures, MNCs still retain the bulk of their innovative capabilities in their home markets, and technology that does flow overseas tends to stay within multinational networks as it moves from parent firms to their foreign affiliates. Again, inside the corporation—where the vast majority of commercially significant innovation takes place—R&D remains relatively centralized.[80] Overseas R&D by affiliates appears quite limited when compared to both the R&D activities of the parent group and the more extensive global spread of production and sourcing, while the R&D that does move overseas tends to be associated with product customization and local production processes. Only very rarely do companies transfer basic research functions to foreign markets.[81]

The tendency of MNCs to move R&D overseas in a measured fashion, mainly through their foreign direct investment and local production, suggests to some an R&D life cycle analogous to the life cycle of foreign direct investment.[82] According to such a model, firms in the early stages of overseas production will tend to use product and process technology developed in the home market; as overseas production units become more established, local R&D activities emerge to customize products in accordance with local market conditions and, eventually, to support affiliate production operations. In advanced stages, as affiliates become deeply integrated into local economies, they may undertake more substantial forms of R&D to develop products exclusively for the local market. In fact, however, few firms reach such stages.

If an R&D life cycle were the rule rather than the exception, one would expect overseas R&D to be more pronounced for European affiliates in the United States than for their Japanese counterparts, and relatively similar for U.S. affiliates in Europe and Japan. The evidence is consistent with this expectation. Both the magnitude and intensity of R&D conducted by German, French, and U.K. affiliates in the United States is substantially higher than R&D by Japanese affiliates. Studies of Japanese investment in Europe indicate that Japanese affiliates conduct substantially less R&D there than do U.S. affiliates.[83] In addition, the average intensity (but not the magnitude) of R&D is relatively similar for U.S. affiliates operating in different sectors in France, the United Kingdom, and Japan. But these observations more plausibly reflect differences in the composition of foreign direct investment, not life cycles. By this account, the difference in average R&D intensities between European and Japanese affiliates in the United States is related to the comparatively large percentage of European investment in technology-intensive manufacturing sectors, that is, sectors with far more R&D per unit of sales than other areas of FDI. Furthermore, such observations are consistent with the idea that MNCs conduct R&D overseas as one among a number of possible means of acquiring technology in foreign markets.

Altogether, the evidence considered in this chapter suggests that variations in the foreign technology development practices of MNCs are not a straightforward function of investment composition or life-cycle effects. Sectoral variations in the R&D intensity of foreign affiliates in the United States suggest that investment composition does not explain MNC behavior. In each of the major manufacturing sectors, either German, British, or French affiliates have the highest R&D intensities, while Japanese affiliates consistently have the lowest. In addition, variations in technology trade as well as strategic technology alliances indicate that firms based in different nations use very different methods for gaining access to foreign technology. Compared to European firms, Japanese firms tend to acquire U.S. technology through unaffiliated channels; they also tend to avoid international technology alliances. These measures, along with the relatively low level of R&D by Japanese affiliates in the United States, support the contention that Japanese MNCs pursue far more centralized technology development strategies than their European counterparts.

It is true that the degree to which R&D is centralized or decentralized often conforms to the particular characteristics of individual technologies and markets. For instance, one of the reasons pharmaceutical companies conduct R&D overseas is to accommodate different national regulatory standards and practices.[84] In the consumer electronics industry, firms often conduct R&D abroad to keep in touch with leading-edge technological developments as well as to adapt technologies to local standards, such as different voltages or broadcasting systems.[85] In the automotive industry, the uniform nature of core technologies tends to encourage centralized R&D, even though production has become highly decentralized.[86] In the semiconductor industry, moreover, the high R&D component of new product costs leads firms from different countries to collaborate on next-generation product development.[87]

At the same time, however, MNCs from different locations do respond to such industry characteristics in unique ways. For instance, in the pharmaceutical industry, U.S. firms have set up more secondary R&D facilities than MNCs based elsewhere. European pharmaceutical firms tend to locate their secondary R&D facilities in the United States, while Japanese pharmaceutical firms have very little exposure in foreign markets.[88] In the consumer electronics industry, Japanese firms conduct the bulk of their R&D at home, unlike European firms.[89] And in the automotive industry, U.S. firms have long had independent operations in Europe that conduct advanced R&D work. By contrast, Japanese auto producers have only recently begun to establish local technological support operations for their foreign assembly plants.[90]

Only the passage of time will fully reveal the impact of life-cycle effects on the distinctive technology acquisition style of Japanese MNCs. But if the length of investment is a powerful explanatory factor in itself, then one would expect the R&D intensity of U.S. affiliates to be relatively similar in most European economies, and perhaps slightly lower in Japan. To the contrary, the R&D intensity of U.S. affiliates in Germany actually is far higher than in other countries, and in many individual sectors the R&D intensity of U.S. affiliates operating in Japan is noticeably higher than affiliates operating in France, the United Kingdom, and in some cases Germany as well.

The fact that U.S. affiliates operating in the same sector have different R&D intensities in different foreign markets suggests that the technological orientation of national innovation systems very likely has a significant bearing on the location and level of technology development by foreign affiliates. Indeed, the R&D intensity of U.S. affiliates in Germany and Japan is unusually high in precisely those scale-intensive, medium-technology sectors that those nations specialize in—transportation equipment, and electronic and other electric equipment. Similarly, the level and intensity of R&D by foreign affiliates in the United States is most pronounced in the pharmaceutical sector, which accounts for a large and rapidly growing share of the nation's scientific and technological resources.

Cross-national variations in the foreign technology development strategies of MNCs are consistent with broader patterns in overseas investment, trading, and production styles. Generally, U.S. MNCs invest abroad primarily in manufacturing industries, and do so in a way that involves deeper levels of integration with the local economy. Japanese MNCs invest far more in wholesale trade, and tend to pursue strategies that involve high degrees of IFT and comparatively low levels of local market integration. German firms represent a hybrid case, investing heavily in manufacturing as well as wholesale trade operations, trading relatively heavily through IFT, and integrating with local markets at comparatively modest levels.

National innovation systems and national investment styles convey different degrees of attractiveness and different degrees of access to foreign MNCs. The degree of attractiveness is partly a function of nationally distinctive resources, as well as of the fundamental governing and financial structures embedded within firms. The degree of access is itself partly a function of the structure of the national political and economic system. Among other things, that structure conditions the extent to which science and technology resources are centralized within firms or dispersed more broadly. The next and last chapter of this book summarizes such linkages between national structural context and MNC behavior and sketches analytical and policy implications.

Chapter 6

CORPORATE DIVERSITY AND PUBLIC POLICY

GLOBALIZATION AT BAY

THE OPENING chapters of this book brought together important strands of research from the fields of comparative political economy and comparative business studies. The empirical chapters then surveyed and analyzed evidence on the question of structural and strategic convergence of multinational business across the three major economies of the advanced industrial world. Our findings are at odds with conventional liberal and radical views on the trajectory and impact of cross-national economic integration. They are problematic for those observers who, for better or for worse, envisage a world where gigantic corporations are truly global, and where the state is in retreat. For them the relocation of authority to either the supranational or subnational levels offers the only realistic hope for regaining political control over a dynamically changing economy.

In contrast to such views, we sketched in chapter 3 remarkably enduring diversity across the United States, Germany, and Japan in corporate governance arrangements and in long-term corporate financing. In short, MNCs based in these three leading home markets continue to govern and finance themselves quite differently. Although there are some changes at the margins, there is scant evidence that basic patterns of corporate control, which is what governance and financing arrangements are ultimately about, are shifting fundamentally. Similarly, we observed in chapter 4 enduring diversity in the national innovation and investment systems within which the world's most prominent MNCs are based.

In chapter 5, and in light of widely held expectations that multinational firms and the markets within which they operate must become more alike as they expand their global activities, we examined extensive evidence touching on core aspects of corporate behavior. In our examination of the diffusion of R&D spending abroad by MNCs, we identified a convergent tendency of sorts, but not the kind expected by many observers. Leading MNCs across the Triad continue to maintain the vast majority of their R&D activity at home. We also found striking national differences in the sectoral composition of corporate R&D and in the technological activities of foreign affiliates.

Finally, we examined the linked areas of strategic corporate investment and intrafirm trade, with Japanese MNCs positioned as clear outliers in comparison to American (and British) firms, but with German MNCs often tending toward the approach of their Japanese counterparts. In this regard, the evidence indicated not convergence, but rather consistent divergence among quite distinctive approaches.

Table 6.1 (National Context and Multinational Corporate Behavior) summarizes the most important patterns in corporate structures and strategies elucidated in the book for leading MNCs based in the United States, Germany, and Japan.

Even when government policy in a host economy is based on the principle that all incoming firms should be treated as nationals, striking differences in firm behavior persist. These differences correlate most obviously with corporate nationality, not with sectoral characteristics or investment maturity. For example, despite the comparative constancy of governmental policy on incoming FDI in the United States, marked differences recur in the strategies and activities of MNCs. Even when they compete in the same domestic U.S. markets and in the same sectors, MNCs based in Japan, Germany, and other industrial countries behave quite differently. Those differences, we contend, are systematic. Across firms, sectors, and in the aggregate, only one set of behavioral variations shines through—national ones.

In chapter 2, we surveyed a broad range of scholarship relevant to a putative link between domestic structures in the home bases of MNCs and their ultimate activities in key markets throughout the world. The evidence set out and examined in subsequent chapters and summarized above suggests a logical chain that begins deep in the idiosyncratic national histories behind durable domestic institutions and ideologies and extends to firm-level structures of internal governance and long-term financing. Those structures, in turn, are then linked to continuing diversity in patterns of corporate R&D operations and in the complex connections between corporate FDI and IFT strategies. In short, the empirically delineated patterns summarized in Table 6.1 correspond closely to the national institutional and ideological distinctions arrayed in the companion table in chapter 2. That correspondence supports the basic linkage we have documented in this book. Distinctive national institutions and ideologies shape corporate structure and vitally important policy environments in home markets. The external behavior of firms continues to be marked by their idiosyncratic foundations.

We have looked mainly but not exclusively at the three leading home states of contemporary MNCs: the United States, Japan, and Germany. We have examined a range of key industrial sectors. And we have

TABLE 6.1
National Context and MNC Behavior

	United States	Germany	Japan
CONTEXT			
Corporate governance	Short-term shareholding; managers highly constrained by capital markets; risk-seeking, financial-centered strategies	Managerial autonomy except during crises; little takeover risk; conservative, long-term strategies	Stable shareholders; network-constrained managers; takeover risk only within network; aggressive market-share-centered strategies
Corporate financing	Diversified, global funding; highly price sensitive	Concentrated, regional funding; limited price sensitivity	Concentrated, national funding; low price sensitivity
Innovation system	Mission-oriented policy environment; mixed public and private funding and R&D performance; strong linkages across higher education and industry; high foreign R&D funding; national focus on science-intensive, high-tech industries	Diffusion-oriented policy environment; industry-centered funding and R&D performance with moderate public sector role; strong inter-industry linkages; low foreign funding of R&D; national focus on specialized supplier and scale-intensive medium-tech industries	Mixed policy environment (diffusion; mission); industry-centered funding and R&D performance, with low public sector role; strong inter-industry linkages; very low foreign funding of R&D; national focus on specialized supplier and scale-intensive medium-tech industries
Investment system	Liberal; no constraints on inward or outward direct investment	Modified liberal; indirect constraints on inward, no constraints on outward	Resistant; formal and informal constraints on inward; selective constraints on outward
BEHAVIOR			
Research & development	Centralized; larger overseas presence (especially in Germany and U.K.); growing slowly; high R&D intensity of foreign affiliates (especially in Germany)	Centralized; moderate overseas presence, growing steadily; high R&D intensity of foreign affiliates	Centralized; smaller, quickly growing overseas presence; low R&D intensity of foreign affiliates

TABLE 6.1 *(cont.)*

	United States	Germany	Japan
Technology trade	Centralized; export oriented (large trade surplus)	Centralized; exchange oriented (balanced trade)	Centralized; acquisition oriented (large unaffiliated imports, low exports)
Technology alliances	Large number; mostly intra-U.S.	Moderate number, mostly Europe–U.S. and regional	Small number, mostly Japan–U.S.
Outward investment	Manufacturing, finance, services	Manufacturing, wholesale trade	Wholesale trade
Intrafirm trade	Moderate	Moderate to high	High
Local production	High integration	Moderate integration	Low integration

analyzed core aspects of firm strategy in a comparative light. Neither liberal nor radical approaches to understanding multinational corporate behavior and its ultimate political and social outcomes led us to expect the degree of continuing diversity we found at the level of the firm. A straightforward realist alternative, moreover, might have led us to expect much stronger convergence in a nationalist direction when it comes to the question of final outcomes in public policy terms. The overarching story is one of increasing economic openness in national economies and deepening integration across dynamic markets—all conditioned and ultimately constrained by the extent to which still-divergent national governing structures can accommodate themselves to one another.

Consider several counterarguments. On the basis of the evidence, for example, it seems to us quite implausible to imagine that the remarkable persistence evident in Japanese corporate technology development programs, notwithstanding dramatic fluctuations in exchange rates, gross earnings, and net corporate profitability, are becoming disconnected from the stabilizing influence of cross-held corporate equity bases in Japan. Similarly, it is equally implausible to argue that the investment behavior of leading German MNCs and the particular modes of their restructuring in markets around the world is becoming unhinged from structures of corporate control back home. Finally, it is not credible to contend that the more cosmopolitan behavior exhibited by American firms in both their R&D and strategic investment is unrelated to their own efforts to compensate for the volatility of their financial foundations and for the relative openness of their home market. In light of the evidence presented, it is much more plausible to argue that the strategic behavior of MNCs based in the leading markets of the Triad divide into distinctive and national patterns.

Our answer to Alfred Chandler's question discussed in chapter 1—whether the kinds of vitally important differences in corporate structure and strategy sketched in *Scale and Scope* endure—is therefore in the affirmative. We took into account the diversification of large-scale British enterprises from their traditional industrial base, a movement that now bears some similarities to the adaptive external expansion of firms originally based in small European states. Among MNCs from the United States, Germany, and Japan, however, we uncovered little evidence to support the opposite answer to Chandler's question—that core national patterns of corporate structure and strategy are inevitably eroding as a single, global system of industrial enterprise and technological innovation inevitably emerges.

THE POLITICS OF DEEPENING ECONOMIC INTEGRATION

If the liberal or radical image of economic globalization provided the more accurate guideline for interpreting recent developments inside MNCs, national policymakers and ordinary citizens would have reason to be concerned. The legitimate authority to respond to the social, economic, or cultural demands of citizens would be slipping away to politically unaccountable actors as a process of transnational corporate integration advanced.[1] If, conversely, realists were right, policymakers and citizens would be shortsighted in the extreme if they failed to heed indications of shifts in international power, especially in key industrial sectors where MNCs are most active.

The world of international business is indeed changing, and it is easy to find selective evidence to support the most straightforward arguments of liberals, radicals, or realists. The evidence assessed in this book, however, supports an approach that dissents from all of them. It is indeed time for scholars of international relations to bring the corporation much more fully into their studies. At least with respect to MNCs from the three leading industrial states, however, we believe that the term *globalization* obscures much more than it enlightens.

The United States, Germany, and Japan—the dominant states within which leading MNCs across a full range of industrial sectors are based—all reduced their own room for policy maneuver in the years after World War II. In short, they sought the benefits promised by intensified international economic interaction. This created the political space within which corporations chartered by them, as well as by other states, flourished. The transformation of many into multinational corporations was, in this sense, clearly intended, even if no policy visionary foresaw the outcome precisely. But the multinationalization of firms within this political space did not occur unsystematically. It was less market driven than state driven. Variations by industrial sector and product line clearly exist across the world's leading MNCs. More importantly, however, variations by nationality—thought by many observers to be of receding importance—in fact endure.

Our research suggests that a commitment remains even at the level of the firm within Germany, and especially within Japan, to resist a diminishment of unique national values and institutions. That commitment is not necessarily stated in explicit corporate policy, but it is embedded in corporate structure. In other words, compared to many American corporations, German and Japanese firms retain a much clearer sense of their distinct national identities, a clearer commitment to national and regional prosperity in a changing international environment, and a much more realistic sense of the capacity of the rest of the world to adapt to the internal behavioral norms of their homelands. Furthermore, the difficulty the leaders of American MNCs often seem to have with the notion of national corporate identity seems peculiarly and typically American. As students of American history might suggest, this is consistent with, and reflective of, a long and much deeper struggle over collective identity and collective interest in a quite exceptional political environment.[2] We make a similar suggestion. The global corporation is mainly an American myth.

Consider the different meanings business leaders from different nations associate with the phrases "free trade," "deregulation," and even "globalization." In their public pronouncements, and certainly in their private interviews with us, American corporate leaders in many sectors use the phrases to imply a commitment to more openness and unhindered competition, both at home and abroad, as well as a sense of "letting the chips fall where they may." To German and especially Japanese executives, conversely, the phrases typically imply a commitment to keeping American and other external markets open to their exports and, increasingly, to their own direct investment in production or distribution facilities. The phrases are not without intellectual content, but in public arenas in Germany and Japan, they seem mainly to have become mantras to ward off any prospect of closure in American markets. Indeed, either publicly or privately, German and Japanese corporate leaders rarely imply support for truly laissez-faire policies, the restriction of cartel-like behavior across the board, or other actions that might expose their home markets fully to the bracing winds of global competition. Mantras aside, nontariff and structural barriers remain, and often in very subtle forms. Across American, Japanese, and German markets, the shape of basic economic institutions, the actual modus operandi of core industries, the endurance of historical business relationships, and the ideological foundations of those relationships—these and other national structures continue to reflect fundamental differences in social values and worldviews.

The phenomenon of corporate multinationalization examined in this book essentially describes a process through which still-national corporations, and the innovation and investment systems in which they remain embedded, are inserted into one another's home markets. Those corporations then adapt themselves at the edges, for example, to make their products and sales operations more consistent with local tastes or to garner some advantage that may prove useful in other markets or back home. But at their cores, our research underlines the durability of such factors as German systems of corporate control, the historical drive behind Japanese technology and investment strategies as well as corporate organizational forms, and the persistence of institutional disincentives to long-term planning inside American corporations.

At a very basic level, and however lustily they sing from the same hymnbook when they gather together in Davos or Aspen, the leaders of the world's great business enterprises continue to differ in their most fundamental strategic behavior and objectives. Moreover, they differ systematically in the ways they deal with common challenges. But what do those differences mean for the leaders of states?

PUBLIC POLICY AND INCREASING COMPLEXITY

A modicum of norms and rules needed to foster mutually beneficial international economic interaction emerges when the ideologies and institutional structures that differentiate states and their societies are rendered sufficiently compatible. In the past, this has occurred only with difficulty, especially in periods when no single state or national market has dominated world production and when specific modes of economic interaction have been delimited.

The negotiation of an effective international regime for trade in goods, for example, took many decades. It remains imperfect, but basically shared national understandings of fair play, appropriate means for redressing grievances, and principles by which specific transactions may be judged—all depended not on some automatic market mechanism promoting deep structural convergence, but on painstaking and often painful political negotiation. Barring systemic military instability, the question of whether similar negotiations can with equal success craft a solid basis for the deepening interaction of national innovation, investment, and corporate control systems remains very much an open one.[3] In this regard, the evidence presented in this book challenges the optimism of global market enthusiasts who prefer not to confront that interaction head-on. The operations of globe-spanning MNCs create no automatic or straightforward mechanisms for regime formation. Their intensifying competition, in fact, makes enduring national differences in the rules of the game more obvious, not less. Likewise, it renders the necessity for political negotiations to hammer out common understandings on at least some of those rules more, not less, pressing.

In the absence of such intervention in international markets, we will not inevitably enter a world of more perfect competition and more convergent policies. We will more likely end up with sanctuary markets in some countries and regions. In such markets, inward investment is effectively restricted and local markets are protected in opaque ways. Cartel-like behavior in corporate networks would favor competitive markets only in rhetorical terms, with market-sharing arrangements implicitly negotiated among MNCs themselves. In such a world, even the citizens of large, powerful states would rightly begin to ask, "Who makes the rules?"

Although smaller states have often found their room for rule-differentiation to be more limited than it is for more powerful nations, the three big industrial states at the center of this book are in fact now involved in ever more intricate bargaining over the rules that will govern the future world economy. Certainly questions of grand strategy enter into that negotiation at times. In the main, however, and on the complex agenda posed by the spread of differentially structured MNCs, the negotiation has mainly taken a tacit form. It is an agenda framed by the mutual compatibility or incompatibility of relatively rigid, or very slowly changing, national governing structures. Ultimately, domestic politics and international markets cannot easily be disengaged. Several implications follow.

Since MNCs are indeed key actors in the development and diffusion of new technologies, their national roots remain a vital determinant of where future innovation will take place. Innovation systems are dynamic and evolving, but their corporate cores remain national in a meaningful sense. The renewed interest of social scientists in the field of economic geography is justified.[4] In this regard, the main danger for policymakers is to infer that a global technology base is emerging on the basis of exceptional cases. The geographical diversification of firms like Nestle, ABB Asea Brown Boveri, and Philips outside their small home bases are exceptions that prove the rule. They are not harbingers of things to come. Their actions do not vitiate the mandate of national governments to nurture systems of innovation responsive to the interests and long-term goals of the citizens to whom they are accountable.

Our analysis also suggests the possibility that increasing openness in the corporate markets of leading states must be associated with explicit or implicit efforts to manage the consequences.[5] Where such efforts fail, measured closure may be a likely response. We see a continuous stream of evidence indicating that even as tariffs and other barriers to trade are formally discarded, leading states are still unwilling to stand idly by when basic corporate structures and technological capabilities are at risk.

At the beginning of 1997, for example, key European states collectively set a floor on the price that foreign producers can charge for DRAM memory chips sold in their markets. The objective of the new policy was to provide indigenous firms with breathing space in an environment widely viewed as hypercompetitive and prone to excess production. The policy, in short, was designed to preserve in Europe core national economic and technological capacities in a key sector.

The alternative idea, that mobile corporations freed from political interference are now somehow arbitraging diverse national structures and forcing an involuntary process of convergence or an inevitable trend toward openness, in our view, marks a road to discord. On the surface, there is indeed a certain process of homogenization at work in a world where Americans drive BMWs, Germans listen to Sony CD players, and Japanese eat McDonald's hamburgers. But below the surface, where the roots of leading MNCs remain lodged, our research indicates durable sources of resistance to fundamental economic convergence.

Efficient global markets with a modicum of stability will not likely evolve through the unhindered competition of globe-spanning firms if national institutions and ideologies remain decisive inside those firms. Those institutions and ideologies are not static, but they surely change slowly. Since they continue to be mirrored inside the worlds' leading corporations, therefore, they will continue to define the limits of a truly global economy more than that economy will redefine them.

If, therefore, roughly comparable governmental policies on increasingly complex aspects of corporate life are required to achieve the ultimate objective of a peaceful world where economic prosperity spreads widely—and the authors of this book believe that they are— more effective commercial diplomacy will be required. Markets are a tool of policy, not a substitute for it. Even among MNCs, where international competition is most obvious and most intense, there is no inevitable destination. Cross-national differences on such basic issues as the purpose of corporate growth and technological innovation will not evaporate.

More effective intergovernmental negotiations to manage intensifying corporate competition can be organized in many different ways. If there are good reasons to center them in multilateral forums, there needs to be a great deal more thought given to the appropriateness of existing institutional models. The model used in the field of trade policy in the post-World War II era, which led to the GATT and ultimately to the World Trade Organization, may not be sufficiently flexible. At base, that model depended upon a common goal (increased trade through lower national trade barriers) and upon a common set of principles (mutual nondiscrimination, diffuse reciprocity, transparency) that are immensely more difficult to agree upon when the discussion necessarily turns to issues of investment, innovation, and internal corporate structure.[6]

The evidence of this book suggests broad differences, even among leading industrial states, in policy fundamentals—the supervision of cartels and other forms of corporate networking in certain industrial sectors, the purpose and direction of national innovation systems, and the nature of the intimate interaction of intrafirm trading and long-term investment strategies. If MNCs reflect such differences in their core structures and strategies, the kinds of nationalist economic policy orientations witnessed so clearly early in the twentieth century are not precluded in the modern era of intensifying international competition, only transmuted. The issues thereby raised should not be obscured by the language of globalization.

The nascent understanding of the immense importance of such differences helps to explain the primarily low-level, analytical, and restricted negotiations that are beginning to occur on the issues raised in this book. On questions of the international impact of differences in national competition policies, of the effective creation of sanctuary markets because of divergences in inward investment regimes, or of the external consequences of domestic corporate-financial linkages, for example, early discussions are underway. In the main, these discussions are taking place on a bilateral or regional basis and in such forums as the Organization for Economic Cooperation and Development, which have limited memberships. It is worth pondering what this means for states and societies not represented therein.

In this regard, the analysis of this book is relevant to the growing debate over whether markets, or more precisely, huge sprawling commercial hierarchies, are replacing states as the world's effective government. Although our evidence does not speak directly to this debate, it does imply that for leading societies any such shift is primarily an internal matter. To put it bluntly, power, as distinct from legitimate authority, may indeed be shifting within those societies, but it is not obviously shifting outward into some supranational corporate ether. Some of those societies may be structurally better equipped than others to deal with the consequences of such power shifts, but there is little reason to make the challenge more difficult by accepting the now-conventional corporate line that nothing can really be done because they are global phenomena. If certain domestic structures in advanced industrial states are evolving in ways that make it more difficult to constrain corporate power, they should be adjusted internally.

As the basic argument at the center of this book suggests, such adjustments will likely entail modifying and adapting idiosyncratic state and social structures. Nowhere, for instance, is it written in stone that the short-term interests of corporate shareholders in the United States deserve a higher priority than all other corporate "stakeholders." But only open and informed national debate over fundamental rules of the American economic system in a new era can lead to a change in the status quo. Similarly, there is no reason why German corporate norms are fixed for all eternity; German citizens themselves are fully capable of reconsidering them directly, just as they can adapt basic structures of national governance to the needs of their partners in the European Union.[7]

The situation would seem quite different, however, for societies not in possession of a large, diversified, and rooted industrial base. From their point of view, power may indeed be shifting in the direction of a few leading states and increasingly concentrated commercial hierarchies durably nested within those states. Such perceptions may help explain the apparently increasing efforts of many smaller states to negotiate adjustments and seek redress through multilateral institutions. They may also help to explain why leading states might not want to erode the capacity of such institutions, at the very least, to provide legitimation for movement toward deeper international economic integration.

There is no doubt that efficiency gains are promised by the integration of national markets. But as those gains are pursued, cross-national and intranational distributive questions will become more pressing. The strain between the international economic logic of integration and the enduring national logic of political governance will become more evident. Given scope, nationalist tendencies inherent in the investment, technology, competition, and financial policies that governments of states actually pursue in our time could become more acute and more dangerous.

Notwithstanding the sanguine prognostications of global market enthusiasts, the possibility of global economic disintegration has not been banished. Such a vision is rightly to be feared. But the quickest way to get there is to accept the chimerical and too facile notion that intensifying competition among rootless global corporations will automatically and inevitably generate a more stable and more prosperous world.

NOTES

CHAPTER 1

1. Our focus is on home countries, but we will refer occasionally to similar structural political influences on corporate behavior that emanate from host countries. Notwithstanding the explosion in inward investment into many national economies in the late twentieth century, it remains the case that host governments continue to impede, steer, or redirect that investment in such a way that it bolsters indigenous national economic capabilities. The phenomenon is particularly obvious in East Asia in various high-technology sectors.

2. Most often, the term *globalization* refers to the worldwide spread of production facilities and processes, which brings in its wake a new international division of labor. A fuller and commonly accepted definition refers to the spread of corporate finance, investment, production, management, sales, labor, information, and technology across national borders and, by virtue of the efficiency-driven, competitive forces thereby put in place, the resulting tendency for economic and political variables to converge toward global norms. See Martin Carnoy et al., *The New Global Economy in the Information Age: Reflections on Our Changing World* (University Park, Penn.: Penn State Press, 1993) pp. 4–5.

3. Contrast Walter Wriston, *The Twilight of Sovereignty* (New York: Scribner, 1992) and William Greider, *One World, Ready or Not: The Manic Logic of Global Capitalism* (New York: Simon & Schuster, 1997).

4. Ian Angell, "Winners and Losers in the Information Age," *LSE Magazine*, vol. 7, no. 1 (Summer 1995): p. 10. For compatible views, see Richard O'Brien, *Global Financial Integration: The End of Geography* (London: Pinter, 1992); and Walter Wriston, *The Twilight of Sovereignty: How the Information Revolution Is Transforming Our World* (New York: Scribner, 1992). The concept of a global economy and technology base was popularized by Kenichi Ohmae in *The Borderless World* (New York: Harper, 1991) and *The End of the Nation State* (New York: Free Press, 1996).

5. Derrick de Kerckhove, *The Skin of Culture* (Toronto: Somerville House, 1995) p. 139.

6. Greider, *One World, Ready or Not*. Also see Richard J. Barnet and John Cavanagh, *Global Dreams: Imperial Corporations and the New World Order* (New York: Simon & Schuster, 1994); and David C. Korten, *When Corporations Rule the World* (West Hartford, Conn.: Kumarian Press, 1995).

7. Philip G. Cerny, "Globalization and the Changing Logic of Collective Action," *International Organization*, vol. 49. no. 4 (Autumn 1995) pp. 595–626. See also Edward M. Graham, *Global Corporations and National Governments* (Washington, D.C.: Institute for International Economics, 1996); Paul Hirst and Grahame Thompson, *Globalization in Question: The International Economy and the Possibilities of Governance*, Cambridge, U.K.: Polity, 1996); and Dani Rodrik, *Has Globalization Gone Too Far?* (Washington, D.C.: Institute for International Economics, 1997).

8. For a survey of the economic literature on the relationship between technological change and variations in international growth, see Jan Fagerberg, "Technology and International Differences in Growth Rates," *Journal of Economic Literature* (Sept. 1994), pp. 1147–75.

9. The concept of national innovation systems has become well established in the literature on the political economy of technological change. For some of the major contributions, see: P. Patel and K. Pavitt, "National Systems of Innovation," in P. Bianci and M. Quere, eds., *Interacting Systems of Innovation: The Sources of Growth?* (London: Kluwer, forthcoming); R. Nelson, ed., *National Innovation Systems: A Comparative Analysis* (New York: Oxford University Press, 1993); Bengt-Åke Lundvall, *National Systems of Innovation* (New York: St. Martins Press, 1992); and G. Dosi et al., *Technical Change and Economic Theory* (London: Pinter Publishers, 1988).

10. ABB Asea Brown Boveri, in particular, is widely cited as the prototype of the truly global, nationality-free corporation. In truth, the character of ABB reflects its peculiar history, which combined the fortunes and roots of its original Swedish and Swiss owners. It is, in any case, unusual.

11. Morgan Stanley database; rankings as of July 31, 1995, reported in *Wall Street Journal*, October 2, 1995, p. R32.

12. A similar point is made in Joseph S. Grieco, *Cooperation Among Nations* (Ithaca, N.Y.: Cornell University Press, 1990).

13. Data from Commission of the European Communities, *Panorama of EC Industry* (Brussels: Office for Official Publications of the European Communities, 1993).

14. These include motor vehicles (19% of OECD production), nonelectrical equipment (18%), electrical machinery (17.5%), fabricated metal products (14.4%), chemicals and pharmaceuticals (14%), and communications equipment (13%). In computing equipment, their share is comparable to the share of British and French firms, while in aircraft, joint production between German and French firms far exceed that of any other European firms. OECD/Directorate for Science, Technology and Industry (DSTI), *Structural Analysis Industrial Database* (Paris: OECD, 1994).

15. Alfred D. Chandler, Jr., *Scale and Scope: The Dynamics of Industrial Capitalism* (Cambridge, Mass.: Belknap Press, 1990).

CHAPTER 2

1. George Ball, "Cosmocorp: The Importance of Being Stateless," *The Columbia Journal of World Business* (November–December 1967).

2. Raymond Vernon, *Sovereignty at Bay* (New York: Basic Books, 1971); C. P. Kindleberger, ed., *The International Corporation* (Cambridge: The MIT Press, 1970); Raymond Vernon, *Storm Over the Multinationals* (Cambridge: Harvard University Press, 1977); Mira Wilkins, *The Maturing of Multinational Enterprise: American Business Abroad From 1914 to 1970* (Cambridge: Harvard University Press, 1974); C. Fred Bergsten, Thomas Horst, and Theodore Moran, *American Multinationals and American Interests* (Washington, D.C.: Brookings, 1978).

3. Seminal works included: Richard Cooper, *The Economics of Interdependence*

(New York: McGraw Hill, 1968); Edward Morse, "The Transformation of Foreign Policies", *World Politics*, 22,3 (April 1970); Robert O. Keohane and Joseph Nye, eds., *Transnational Relations and World Politics* (Cambridge: Harvard University Press, 1972); Robert Keohane and Joseph Nye, *Power and Interdependence* (Boston: Little, Brown, 1977). Later research focused more exclusively on the linkage between interdependence and MNCs, for example: Robert T. Kudrle, "The Several Faces of the Multinational Corporation," in W. Ladd Hollist and F. Lamond Tullis, eds., *An International Political Economy* (Boulder, Colo.: Westview, 1985); Theodore Moran, ed., *Governments and Transnational Corporations* (London: Routledge, 1993); John Robinson, *Multinationals and Political Control* (New York: St. Martin's Press, 1983).

4. J. J. Servan-Schreiber, *Le Défi Americain* (Paris: Denoël, 1967).

5. Lawrence G. Franko, *The European Multinational* (London: Harper & Row, 1976).

6. See, for example, Peter Hertner and Geoffrey Jones, eds., *Multinationals: Theory and History* (Aldershot, England: Edward Elgar, 1986).

7. John M. Stopford and Louis Turner, *Britain and the Multinationals* (New York: John Wiley & Sons, 1985); John H. Dunning, *American Investment in British Manufacturing* (London: Allen & Unwin, 1958); W. B. Reddaway et al., *UK Investment Overseas: Volumes I and II* (Cambridge: Cambridge University Press, 1968); Louis Turner, *Invisible Empires: Multinational Companies and the Modern World* (London: Hamish Hamilton, 1970). Dunning's later research and his "eclectic" theorizing on the causes and consequences of the multinational corporate phenomenon is summarized in *Multinational Enterprises and the Global Economy* (Reading, Mass.: Addison-Wesley, 1992); and *The Globalization of Business: The Challenge of the 1990s* (London: Routledge, 1993).

8. Stopford and Turner, *Britain and the Multinationals*, p. 248.

9. Yoshi Tsurumi, *Multinational Management: Business Strategy and Government Policy* (Cambridge, Mass.: Ballinger, 1983).

10. Sanjaya Lall et al., *The New Multinationals: The Spread of Third World Enterprises* (New York: John Wiley & Sons, 1983) p. 267–68.

11. Wells' work gradually covered a much wider terrain. See his *Third World Multinationals* (Cambridge: The MIT Press, 1983).

12. Geoffrey Jones and Harm G. Schröter, eds., *The Rise of Multinationals in Continental Europe* (Aldershot, England: Edward Elgar, 1993) p. 21; Lawrence Franko, "Global Corporate Competition," *Business Horizons* (November–December 1991); Jan Evert Nilsson, ed., *The Internationalization Process: European Firms in Global Competition* (London: Chapman, 1996).

13. Rob van Tulder and Gerd Junne, *European Multinationals in Core Technologies* (New York: Wiley, 1988); Gerd Junne, "Multinational Enterprises as Actors," in Walter Carlsnaes and Steve Smith, eds., *European Foreign Policy* (London: Sage Publications, 1994) pp. 84–102; W. Ruigrok and Rob Van Tulder, *The Logic of International Restructuring* (London: Routledge, 1995).

14. See, for example, Robert B. Reich, "Who Is Us?", *Harvard Business Review* (January–February 1990); Laura D. Tyson, "They Are Not Us: Why American Ownership Still Matters," *The American Prospect* (Winter 1991); United States Congress, Joint Economic Committee, " 'Who Is Us?'—National Interests in an

Age of Global Industry," *Hearings*, September 5 and 13, 1990; Daniel F. Burton, Jr. et al., "Multinationals: the 'Who Is Us' Debate," *Challenge* (Sept./Oct. 1994); Lorraine Eden and Maureen Molot, "Insiders and Outsiders: Defining "Who Is Us?" in the North American Auto Industry," *Transnational Corporations* (December 1993) pp. 31–64.

15. Lynn K. Mytelka, *Strategic Partnerships and the World Economy* (London: Pinter, 1991); Leonard Waverman, ed., *Corporate Globalization through Mergers and Acquisitions* (Calgary: University of Calgary Press, 1991); Michael Y. Yoshino and U. Srinivasa Rangan, *Strategic Alliances: An Entrepreneurial Approach to Globalization* (Boston: Harvard Business School Press, 1995); Harvey S. James and Murray Weidenbaum, *When Businesses Cross International Borders: Strategic Alliances and their Alternatives* (New York: Praeger, 1993); Peter F. Cowhey and Jonathan D. Aronson, *Managing the World Economy: The Consequences of Corporate Alliances* (New York: Council on Foreign Relations, 1993); Joel Bleeke and David Ernst, eds., *Collaborating to Compete: Using Strategic Alliances and Acquisition in the Global Marketplace* (New York: John Wiley, 1993).

16. David Yoffie, ed., *Beyond Free Trade: Firms, Governments, and Global Competition* (Boston: Harvard Business School Press, 1993).

17. Robert Gilpin, *U.S. Power and the Multinational Corporation: The Political Economy of Foreign Direct Investment* (New York: Basic Books, 1975) pp. 5–6. It is interesting to note that Gilpin's study began as a report commissioned by the Committee on Labor and Public Welfare of the U.S. Senate.

18. Gilpin himself began this task in *The Political Economy of International Relations* (Princeton, N.J.: Princeton University Press, 1987) chapter 6.

19. In this context, note that our argument and evidence are not incompatible with a constructivist theoretical agenda, but they do challenge scholars probing the connection between global economic transformation and political identity to make clearer distinctions among states. See John Gerard Ruggie, "Territoriality and Beyond: Problematizing Modernity in International Relations," *International Organization*, vol. 47, no. 1 (1993) pp. 139–74.

20. Stephen D. Krasner, "Power Politics, Institutions, and Transnational Relations," in Thomas Risse-Kappen, ed., *Bringing Transnational Relations Back In* (Cambridge: Cambridge University Press, 1996). Also see Razeen Sally, "Multinational Enterprises, Political Economy and Institutional Theory: Domestic Embeddedness in the Context of Internationalization," *Review of International Political Economy*, vol. 1, no. 1 (Spring 1994) pp. 161–92.

21. Although he did not work out a complete theoretical model, Philip Wellons' study of international banking comes close to our approach. In one of the most global of industries, Wellons showed how banks from different home states did not behave alike in the face of similar opportunities and challenges. See *Passing the Buck: Banks, Governments and Third World Debt* (Boston: Harvard Business School Press, 1987); and "International Debt: The Behavior of Banks in A Politicized Environment," in Miles Kahler, ed., *The Politics of International Debt* (Ithaca, N.Y.: Cornell University Press, 1986). Also see Thomas J. Biersteker, *Multinationals, the State, and Control of the Nigerian Economy* (Princeton, N.J.: Princeton University Press, 1987).

22. The point is well made in John Stopford and Susan Strange, *Rival States, Rival Firms* (Cambridge: Cambridge University Press, 1991), and in Lorraine Eden and Evan Potter, eds., *Multinationals in the Global Political Economy* (New York: St. Martin's Press, 1993).

23. Contemporary theorizing along this line begins with Stephen Hymer, *The International Operations of National Firms* (Cambridge: MIT Press, 1976) (based on a Ph.D. dissertation from 1960); and Hymer, *The Multinational Corporation* (New York: Cambridge University Press, 1979).

24. Paul Krugman, ed., *Strategic Trade Policy and the New International Economics* (Cambridge: MIT Press, 1986); G. M. Grossman and J. D. Richardson, "Strategic Trade Policy: A Survey of Issues and Early Analysis," *Essays in International Finance*, no. 15 (Princeton University, Department of Economics, International Finance Section, 1985).

25. See David Yoffie, ed., *Beyond Free Trade*, p. 17.

26. Peter J. Katzenstein, ed., *Between Power and Plenty* (Madison: University of Wisconsin Press, 1977).

27. Emanuel Adler, *The Power of Ideology* (Berkeley: University of California Press, 1987) p. 17. Also see George Lodge and Ezra Vogel, *Ideology and National Competitiveness* (Boston: Harvard Business School Press, 1987); Judith Goldstein and Robert O. Keohane, eds., *Ideas and Foreign Policy* (Ithaca, N.Y.: Cornell University Press, 1993); Judith Goldstein, *Ideas, Interests, and American Trade Policy* (Ithaca, N.Y.: Cornell University Press, 1993); Ellis S. Krauss and Simon Reich, "Ideologies, Interests, and the American Executive," *International Organization*, vol. 46, no. 4 (1992) pp. 857–97; Alexander Wendt, "Collective Identity Formation and the International State," *American Political Science Review*, vol. 88, no. 2 (1994) pp. 384–96.

28. For example, Alexander Gerschenkron, *Economic Backwardness in Historical Perspective* (Cambridge: Harvard University Press, 1962); Andrew Shonfield, *Modern Capitalism* (New York: Oxford University Press, 1965); Alfred D. Chandler, Jr., *Strategy and Structure* (Cambridge: MIT Press, 1962); *Giant Enterprise* (New York, Harcourt Brace & World, 1964); *The Visible Hand* (Cambridge: Harvard University Press, 1977).

29. See, for example, Stephen Krasner, *Defending the National Interest* (Princeton, N.J.: Princeton University Press, 1978); John Zysman, *Governments, Markets and Growth* (Ithaca, N.Y.: Cornell University Press, 1983); Peter Gourevitch, *Politics in Hard Times* (Ithaca, N.Y.: Cornell University Press, 1986); Peter Hall, *Governing the Economy* (Oxford: Oxford University Press, 1986); Richard Samuels, *The Business of the Japanese State* (Ithaca, N.Y.: Cornell University Press, 1987); Peter Katzenstein, *Small States in World Markets* (Ithaca, N.Y.: Cornell University Press, 1984); David Vogel, *National Styles of Regulation* (Ithaca, N.Y.: Cornell University Press, 1986); Sven Steinmo et al., *Structuring Politics* (Cambridge: Cambridge University Press, 1992); Geoffrey Garrett and Peter Lange, "Internationalization, Institutions, and Political Change," *International Organization*, vol. 49, no. 4 (Autumn, 1995) pp. 627–656; and Andrew Sobel, *Domestic Choices, International Markets* (Ann Arbor, Mich.: University of Michigan Press, 1994).

30. Richard Samuels, whose use of the term "technonationalism" we adapt above, provides an exemplary model of how ideology and institutions can be mutually constitutive and mutually reinforcing. See Samuels, *"Rich Nation, Strong Army": National Security and the Technological Transformation of Japan* (Ithaca, N.Y.: Cornell University Press, 1994) pp. 33–78.

31. See Robert Cox, *Production, Power and World Order* (New York: Columbia University Press, 1987), Richard J. Barnet and John Cavanagh, *Global Dreams: Imperial Corporations and the New World Order* (New York: Simon & Schuster, 1994). Especially as it relates to developing countries, the tradition is surveyed by Peter Evans in his book *Dependent Development: The Alliance of Multinational, State, and Local Capital in Brazil* (Princeton, N.J.: Princeton University Press, 1979) pp. 14–54; Dennis J. Encarnation, *Dislodging the Multinationals: India's Strategy in Comparative Perspective* (Ithaca, N.Y.: Cornell University Press, 1989); and Joseph La Palombara and Stephen Blank, *Multinational Corporations and Developing Countries* (New York: Conference Board, 1979). For a compelling and related analysis related to the United States, see William Greider, *Who Will Tell the People: The Betrayal of American Democracy* (New York: Simon & Schuster, 1992).

32. For straightforward expositions of the classic liberal view, see Lawrence Krauss, "Private International Finance," *International Organization*, vol. 25 (1971) pp. 523–40; Mark Casson, ed., *The Growth of International Business* (London: George Allen and Unwin, 1983); Richard E. Caves, *Multinational Enterprise and Economic Analysis* (New York: Cambridge University Press, 1982); Richard McKenzie and Dwight Lee, *Quicksilver Capital: How the Rapid Movement of Wealth Has Changed the World* (New York: Free Press, 1991); Richard O'Brien, *Global Financial Integration: The End of Geography* (London: Pinter, 1992); and Walter Wriston, "Technology and Sovereignty," *Foreign Affairs*, vol. 67 (1988) pp. 63–75.

33. Francis Fukuyama, *The End of History and the Last Man* (New York: Free Press, 1992) p. xii.

34. Helen Milner, *Resisting Protectionism* (Princeton, N.J.: Princeton University Press, 1988); Robert Z. Lawrence, *Regionalism, Multilateralism and Deeper Integration* (Washington, D.C.: The Brookings Institution, 1996).

35. Ronald Rogowski, *Commerce and Coalitions* (Princeton, N.J.: Princeton University Press, 1989); Jeffry Frieden, "Invested Interests: The Politics of National Economic Policies in a World of Global Finance," *International Organization*, vol. 45, no. 4 (Autumn 1991) pp. 425–52.

36. See, for example, Geoffrey Garrett and Peter Lange, "Political Responses to Interdependence: What's 'Left' for the Left?," *International Organization*, vol. 45, no. 4 (Autumn 1991) pp. 539–64; Mitchell Bernard, "Post-Fordism, Transnational Production, and the Changing Global Political Economy," in Richard Stubbs and Geoffrey Underhill, eds. *Political Economy and the Changing Global Order* (Toronto: McClelland and Stewart, 1994) pp. 216–29; Stephen Gill, "Economic Globalization and the Internationalization of Authority: Limits and Contradictions," *Geoforum*, vol. 23, no. 3 (1992) pp. 269–83; Ash Amin and Nigel Thrift, eds., *Globalization, Institutions, and Regional Development in Europe* (New York: Oxford University Press, 1994); Hans-Henrik Holm and Georg Sorensen,

Whose World Order? Uneven Globalization and the End of the Cold War (Boulder, Colo.: Westview Press, 1995); R. J. Barry Jones, *Globalization and Interdependence in the International Political Economy: Rhetoric and Reality* (London: Pinter, 1995); Paul Hirst, *Globalization in Question: The International Economy and the Possibilities of Governance* (Cambridge, Mass.: Blackwell, 1996); Razeen Sally, *States and Firms: Multinational Enterprises in Institutional Competition* (London: Routledge, 1995); and Susan Strange, *The Retreat of the State: The Diffusion of Power in the World Economy* (Cambridge: Cambridge University Press, 1996).

37. Helen Milner and Robert Keohane, for example, have recently likened its constraining effects to the notion of anarchy in the security arena. See Helen Milner and Robert Keohane, eds., *Internationalization and Domestic Politics* (Cambridge: Cambridge University Press, 1996) chapter 1; also see David Andrews, "Capital Mobility and State Autonomy: Toward a Structural Theory of International Monetary Relations," *International Studies Quarterly*, vol. 38, no. 1 (1994); and Michael Webb, *The Political Economy of Policy Coordination: International Adjustment Since 1945* (Ithaca, N.Y.: Cornell University Press, 1995). For a skeptical view, see Ralf Dahrendorf, "A Precarious Balance: Economic Opportunity, Civil Society, and Political Liberty," *The Responsive Community*, vol. 5, no. 1 (Summer 1995).

38. See, for example, Milner and Keohane, eds., *Internationalization and Domestic Politics*.

39. Robert Gilpin, "No One Loves a Political Realist" (manuscript, Princeton University, 1994). Also see Stephen D. Krasner, *Structural Conflict: The Third World Against Global Liberalism* (Berkeley: University of California Press, 1985).

40. For prominent versions of such a view, a view which we share, see Michael Porter, *The Competitive Advantage of Nations* (New York: Free Press, 1990); and Peter Gourevitch, "The Macropolitics of Microinstitutional Differences in the Analysis of Comparative Capitalism," in Suzanne Berger and Ronald Dore, eds., *National Diversity and Global Capitalism* (Ithaca, N.Y.: Cornell University Press, 1996) pp. 239–59.

CHAPTER 3

1. The theme is central to the seminal work of Alfred Chandler. Its conceptual evolution may be traced from *Strategy and Structure* (Cambridge: MIT Press, 1962) to *The Visible Hand: The Managerial Revolution in American Business* (Cambridge: Harvard University Press, 1977) to *Scale and Scope: The Dynamics of Industrial Capitalism* (Cambridge: Belknap Press, 1990).

2. Building on Ronald Coase's classic "The Nature of the Firm," *Economica*, vol. 4 (1937) pp. 386–405, and highlighting the importance of transactions costs and imperfect flows of information, Oliver Williamson provides systematic analysis of corporate governance along these lines. See, for example, his "The Modern Corporation: Origins, Evolution, Attributes," *Journal of Economic Literature*, vol. 19 (December 1981) pp. 1537–68; "Corporate Finance and Corporate Governance," *The Journal of Finance*, vol. 43, no. 3 (1988) pp. 567–91, and *The Economic Institutions of Capitalism* (New York: Free Press, 1985); also see

R. Glenn Hubbard, ed., *Asymmetric Information, Corporate Finance, and Investment* (Chicago: University of Chicago Press, 1990).

3. For relevant debate, see Robert B. Reich, "Who Is Us?" *Harvard Business Review* (January–February 1990); and Laura D. Tyson, "They Are Not Us: Why American Ownership Still Matters," *The American Prospect* (Winter 1991).

4. On the notion of "system friction," see Sylvia Ostry, *Governments and Corporations in a Shrinking World: Trade and Innovation Policies in the United States, Europe and Japan* (New York: Council on Foreign Relations Press, 1990). Also see John H. Dunning, "The Global Economy, Domestic Governance, Strategies and Transnational Corporations: Interactions and Policy Implications," *Transnational Corporations*, vol. 1, no. 3 (1992) pp. 7–45.

5. See John B. Goodman and Louis W. Pauly, "The Obsolescence of Capital Controls? Economic Management in an Age of Global Markets," *World Politics*, vol. 46. no. 1 (1993) pp. 50–82.

6. The comparative literature on this topic is developing rapidly. For recent analytical and practical surveys, see United States General Accounting Office, *Competitiveness Issues: The Business Environment in the United States, Japan, and Germany* (GAO/GGD-93-124, August 1993); Stephen Prowse, "Corporate Governance in an International Perspective," *BIS Economic Papers*, no. 41 (July 1994); William D. Coleman, "Banking, Interest Intermediation, and Political Power," *European Journal of Political Research*, vol. 26 (1994) pp. 31–58; Mitsuhiro Fukao, *Financial Integration, Corporate Governance, and the Performance of Multinational Companies* (Washington, D.C.: Brookings, 1995); International Capital Markets Group, *Who Holds the Reins?* (London: International Bar Association, 1995); Andrei Schleifer and Robert W. Vishny, "A Survey of Corporate Governance," *Working Paper Series*, no. 5554, National Bureau of Economic Research, (April 1996).

7. Adolph Berle and Gardiner Means, *The Modern Corporation and Private Property* (New York: Macmillan, 1932).

8. Mark J. Roe, *Strong Managers, Weak Owners: The Political Roots of American Corporate Finance* (Princeton, N.J.: Princeton University Press, 1994) p. 4.

9. Chandler, *Scale and Scope*, p. 12.

10. Organization for Economic Cooperation and Development, *National Systems for Financing Innovation* (Paris: OECD, 1995) p. 74.

11. Jay W. Lorsch and Elizabeth MacIver, "Corporate Governance and Investment Time Horizons," background paper prepared for M. Porter et al., *Capital Choices*, A Report to the Council on Competitiveness and co-sponsored by the Harvard Business School (June 1992). Senior executives of several leading U.S.-based MNCs told us that their investment planning was frequently constrained by the need to satisfy the expectations of temporary shareholders as expressed in current stock prices. They admitted that their R&D budgets, in particular, commonly suffered as a result. Several executives expressed concern that many of their foreign-based competitors faced a much-less-binding constraint and were therefore better able, for example, to maintain R&D expenditure levels over a full economic cycle. They suspected, for example, that differences in corporate governance helped significantly to explain the maintenance, or, at most, marginal trimming, of R&D spending by many Japanese

MNCs even as their earnings came under severe pressure in the early 1990s. For related analysis, see Michael T. Jacobs, *Short-Term America: The Causes and Cures of Our Business Myopia* (Boston: Harvard Business School Press, 1991) chapters 2 and 3.

12. Franklin R. Edwards and Robert A. Eisenbeis, "Financial Institutions and Corporate Investment Horizons: An International Perspective," background paper prepared for M. Porter et al., *Capital Choices.*

13. See Rondo Cameron et al., *Banking in the Early Stages of Industrialization* (New York: Oxford University Press, 1967); Walter Adams, ed., *The Structure of American Industry* (New York: Macmillan, 1982); Raymond Goldsmith, *Financial Structure and Development* (New Haven: Yale University Press, 1969).

14. As Edwards and Eisenbeis ("Financial Institutions and Corporate Investment Horizons") put it, "It was the legacy of the 1870–1911 period, however, that cemented concerns with the evils of 'bigness.' The creation of a decentralized Federal Reserve System in 1913 was in deference to fears about the concentration of banking power. In addition, the passage of the Bank Holding Company Act of 1956 was rooted in the failure of the Supreme Court to break up the Trans-America Corporation and prevent its attempt to monopolize banking in the western part of the country; and it was a fear of so-called 'congeneric' or 'near zaibatsu' banking companies that resulted in the restrictions contained in [the Douglas] amendments of 1970."

15. Roe, *Strong Managers, Weak Owners*, p. 49.

16. Louis W. Pauly, *Opening Financial Markets: Banking Politics on the Pacific Rim* (Ithaca, N.Y.: Cornell University Press, 1988) chapter 3.

17. Jacobs, *Short-Term America*, p. 153.

18. Alexander Gerschenkron, *Economic Backwardness in Historical Perspective* (Cambridge, Mass.: Belknap, 1962); Richard H. Tilly, *Financial Institutions and Industrialization in the Rhineland, 1815–1870* (Madison: University of Wisconsin Press, 1966); Kenneth Dyson, *Industrial Crisis: A Comparative Study of the State and Industry* (Oxford: Robertson, 1983); Christopher Schmitz, "Cooperative Managerial Capitalism: Recent Research in German Business History," *German History*, vol. 10 (1992) pp. 91–103.

19. For background, see Peter J. Katzenstein, *Politics and Policy in the Federal Republic of Germany: The Semi-Sovereign State* (Philadelphia, Penn.: Temple University Press, 1987); Andrei S. Markovits, *The Politics of the West German Trade Unions* (Cambridge: Cambridge University Press, 1986); and Kathleen Thelen, *Union of Parts: Labor Politics in Postwar Germany* (Ithaca, N.Y.: Cornell University Press, 1991).

20. See Kirsten Wever and Christopher S. Allen, "The Financial System and Corporate Governance in Germany: Institutions and the Diffusion of Innovations," *Journal of Public Policy*, vol. 12, no. 3 (1993); and J. Nicholas Ziegler, "Institutions, Elites, and Technological Change in France and Germany," *World Politics*, vol. 47 (April 1995) pp. 341–72.

21. See Herbert Giersch, Karl-Heinz Paque, and Holger Schieding, *The Fading Miracle: Four Decades of Market Economy in Germany* (Cambridge: Cambridge University Press, 1992).

22. The point is made explicitly by a Deutsche Bank executive in Ellen R. Schneider-Lenné, "The Role of German Capital Markets, the Universal Banks' Supervisory Boards, and Interlocking Directorships" (paper prepared for National Economic Development Office Policy Seminar, London, November 21–22, 1991).

23. For a detailed analysis, see Rolf Ziegler, Donald Bender, and Herman Biehler, "Industry and Banking in the German Corporate Network," in Fruns N. Stokeman et al., eds., *Networks of Corporate Power* (Cambridge: Polity, 1985).

24. Under the terms of new legislation, public companies will be required to disclose the identities of shareholders owning stakes of more than 5%. *The Economist* (December 18, 1993) p. 73.

25. The auto-parts and equipment maker, Robert Bosch, provides an illustrative example. When the company's founder died thirty years ago, most of his shares were transferred to a foundation that bears his name. Among other things, the foundation now provides the bulk of the financial requirements for a hospital located in the town where the company is headquartered. In order for dividends to flow to the hospital tax free, however, voting rights connected with the shares were transferred to a supervisory board comprised originally of seven and now nine members. Board members choose their own successors, typically including the retired chairmen of the company itself, its lead bank, other large corporations, and associated labor unions. (For U.S. tax purposes, the IRS considers the nine board members to be the ultimate holding company.) In fact, the role of the supervisory board at Bosch is limited, and the company's managers enjoy a high degree of operational autonomy as long as the overall performance of the firm is satisfactory. As the company has grown, the shareholding structure, in particular, has enabled the company to maintain stable and relatively low dividend payouts to the Bosch Foundation, while simultaneously building up substantial internal reserves. Those reserves, in turn, have enabled the company to invest continually in its technological foundations. Interview, Germany, November 11, 1993.

26. *The Economist*, December 25-January 7, 1994, p. 90; and January 8, 1994, p. 66.

27. See Jeremy Edwards and Klaus Fischer, *Banks, Finance, and Investments in Germany* (Cambridge: Cambridge University Press, 1994) chapter 6; also see Theodor Baums, "The German Banking System and its Impact on Corporate Finance and Governance," in Masahiko Aoki and Hugh Patrick, eds., *The Japanese Main Bank System* (Oxford: Oxford University Press, 1994) pp. 409–49.

28. Edwards and Fischer argue that the true motivation for banks to be involved in the reorganizations, especially of troubled large firms, has to do with the "image-effects" flowing from their shareholdings and supervisory board participations. Ibid., pp. 176–77.

29. Gerschenkron, *Economic Backwardness in Historical Perspective*. For a dissenting view, see Daniel Verdier, "Gerschenkron on His Head" (paper prepared for the 1995 annual meeting of the American Political Science Association, Chicago, Ill.).

30. Unlike the U.S. system, the depository institution of the shares (which are issued in bearer form), most often a bank, has the right to vote them

without specific authority from the actual shareholder. Formerly automatic and of indefinite duration, legal reforms now require the right of proxy voting to be reviewed by the true shareholders on a regular basis and the banks must now solicit voting instructions. In reality, the banks retain a high degree of control.

31. GAO, *Competitiveness Issues*, p. 112.

32. Edwards and Fischer, *Banks, Finance, and Investments in Germany*, p. 180.

33. GAO, *Competitiveness Issues*, p. 113.

34. Data cited in Roe, *Strong Managers, Weak Owners*, p. 173.

35. As Richard Tilly has demonstrated, deconcentration has also not been implied by the internationalization of the big German banks in the post-1970s period, for "maintaining their own market shares at home required their 'going international.' " Tilly, "The Internationalization of West German Banks, 1945–1987," in Geoffrey Jones and Harm C. Schröter, eds., *The Rise of Multinationals in Continental Europe* (Aldershot, England: Edward Elgar, 1993) p. 181.

36. Interview, Germany, November 9, 1993.

37. Giving priority to the goal of retaining control, of course, complicates the task of reshaping and reinvigorating Germany's industrial and technology base. In particular, the risk is that it will stunt the development of broad domestic capital markets and thus prevent small- and medium-size German companies from raising the kind of financing that might support new technological innovation. On the other hand, assuming that large German companies are able to regain their competitive edge (by, for example, scaling back their real wage costs and markedly increasing productivity), preserving the core of the traditional system of corporate governance could once again provide German MNCs with stabilizing financial advantages in the global marketplace.

38. *New York Times*, *Financial Times of London*, December 16, 1993. For background, see *Institutional Investor*, July 1993, pp. 81–84; November 1993, pp. 50–56; also see Gary C. Biddle and Shanrokh M. Saudagran, "Foreign Stock Listings: Benefits, Costs, and the Accounting Policy Dilemma," *Accounting Horizons* (September 1991) pp. 69–80; Frederick D. S. Choi and Richard M. Levich, "Behavioral Effects of International Accounting Diversity," *Accounting Horizons* (June 1991) pp. 1–13; and by the same authors, *The Capital Market Effects of International Accounting Diversity* (New York: Dow Jones-Irwin, 1993).

39. The practice is also common in Japan. See Howard D. Lowe, "Shortcomings of Japanese Consolidated Financial Statements," *Accounting Horizons* (September 1990) pp. 1–9. Other major areas of differences in basic accounting principles are encountered in the treatment of such items as R&D expenses, fixed assets, inventory, leases, income taxes, foreign currency translation, mergers and acquisitions, and consolidation. See Philip R. Peller and Frank J. Schwitter, "A Summary of Accounting Principle Differences Around the World," in Frederick D. S. Choi, ed., *Handbook of International Accounting* (New York: John Wiley & Sons, 1991) chapter 4.

40. In general, a lack of transparency can also have costs, especially when a firm is under pressure and needs to find new sources of financing. Here again in the German case, however, comes the backup role of the banks in mitigating this possibility. See Gordian A. Ndubizu, "Accounting Disclosure Methods and

Economic Development," *The International Journal of Accounting*, vol. 27 (1992) pp. 151–63. Note that such distinctions remain at the center of active discussions inside such bodies as the International Accounting Standards Committee and the International Organization of Securities Commissions.

41. The effect of the incremental transformations in the system that are underway will long be arguable. We are talking about relative degrees of influence, often subtle and always difficult to measure with precision. Much of the contemporary comparative business literature involves rational-choice assumptions at its core. The problem, however, is to identify what exactly is being maximized, by whom, and for what purpose. Historical trajectories and durable cultural distinctions are relevant here, but difficult to measure using standard rationalist techniques. What those techniques can suggest, however, is that by certain externally verifiable measures—such as investment and productivity levels—the German system does not necessarily perform better than other systems.

42. The strategies of the big German banks were themselves being recast somewhat more broadly. In the context of the effort to create a single European banking market, for example, the banks have been active proponents of the development of Finanzplatz Deutschland as a potential rival to capital market centers in London and elsewhere. Cross-border alliances have also begun, the most prominent including Dresdner Bank's purchase of a minority stake in Banque Nationale de Paris, and Credit Lyonnais' purchase of Bank für Gemeinwirtschaft.

43. The effort to define the precise role of government in contemporary Japan and the nature of the relationship between big business and the state has spawned an immense amount of research. In addition to encouraging cross-shareholdings and carefully shaping the institutions that would manage corporate finance, official policies have consistently ratified cautious disclosure standards, and, especially in troubled industries, sanctioned cartel-like arrangements and other business practices that have the effect of restricting market access. Certainly during the past two decades, the impact of government has been more subtle than during earlier periods. In comparative terms, however, the influence of the key ministries remains substantial, even if the relationship between big business and the ministries is more reciprocal. For related debate, see Chalmers Johnson, *MITI and the Japanese Miracle* (Stanford, Calif.: Stanford University Press, 1982); Richard Samuels, *The Business of the Japanese State* (Ithaca, N.Y.: Cornell University Press, 1987); Kent Calder, *Strategic Capitalism* (Princeton, N.J.: Princeton University Press, 1993); Jeffrey A. Hart, *Rival Capitalists* (Ithaca, N.Y.: Cornell University Press, 1992) chapter 2; Dennis J. Encarnation, *Rivals Beyond Trade* (Ithaca, N.Y.: Cornell University Press, 1992); Walter Hutch and Kozo Yamamura, *Asia in Japan's Embrace* (Cambridge: Cambridge University Press, 1996).

44. Samuels, *"Rich Nation, Strong Army"*.

45. See Kozo Kato, Tsutomo Shibata et al., *Policy-Based Finance: The Experience of Postwar Japan* (Tokyo: The Japan Development Bank, January 1993); also see World Bank, *The East Asian Miracle: Economic Growth and Public Policy* (Washington, D.C.: World Bank, 1993).

46. See Pauly, *Opening Financial Markets*, chapter 4; Frances McCall Rosenbluth, *Financial Politics in Contemporary Japan* (Ithaca, N.Y.: Cornell University Press, 1989); and J. Robert Brown, *Opening Japan's Financial Markets* (London: Routledge, 1994).

47. In some respects, however, the deregulatory legacy of the past decade appeared likely to endure. Through regulatory reinterpretation, Article 65 of Japan's Securities and Exchange Law lost its bite by the early 1990s. A few years later, the government began moving to repeal an Occupation-era ban on holding companies. The effect of these and related moves could well be to concentrate power along traditional corporate and financial lines, not to disperse it.

48. See Marco Orru, Gary G. Hamilton, and Mariko Suzuki, *Patterns of Inter-Firm Control in Japanese Business* (Papers in East Asian Business and Development, No. 7, Institute of Governmental Affairs, University of California, Davis, 1989). Also see Nigel Campbell and Fred Burton, *Japanese Multinationals: Strategies and Management in the Global Kaisha* (London: Routledge, 1994); Mark Tilton, *Restrained Trade: Cartels in Japan's Basic Materials Industry* (Ithaca, N.Y.: Cornell University Press, 1996); Robert M. Uriu, *Troubled Industries: Confronting Economic Change in Japan* (Ithaca, N.Y.: Cornell University Press, 1996).

49. For smaller Japanese companies that are not part of *keiretsu* networks, large shareholdings are more common, and they can provide the key mechanism for exerting influence over management. See Stephen D. Prowse, "The Structure of Corporate Ownership in Japan," *The Journal of Finance*, vol. 47, no. 3 (July 1992) pp. 1121–40.

50. Carl Kester, "Governance, Contracting, and Investment Time Horizons" *Working Paper* 92–003, Harvard Business School, Division of Research (1991).

51. For a straightforward defense of the system, see Yusaku Futasugi, "What Share Cross-holdings Mean for Corporate Management," *Economic Eye* (Spring 1990) pp. 17–19.

52. Kester, "Governance, Contracting, and Investment Time Horizons."

53. Michael Gerlach, *Alliance Capitalism: The Social Organization of Japanese Business* (Berkeley: University of California Press, 1992) p. 38.

54. *Keiretsu no kenkyu*, 1970, 1990, cited in Gerlach, *Alliance Capitalism*, p. 171.

55. One analysis of the issue, for example, found no evidence that the influence of financial institutions diminished during the booming 1980s. See Frank R. Lichtenberg and George M. Pushner, "Ownership Structure and Corporate Performance in Japan" (Working Paper #4092, National Bureau of Economic Research, June 1992).

56. Ibid. Also see Carl Kester, *Japanese Takeovers* (Boston: Harvard Business School Press, 1991).

57. Gerlach, *Alliance Capitalism*, p. 91. The acquisitions referred to included Merck's takeover of Banyu Pharmaceuticals and Polly Peck's purchase of Sansui Electric. To this list might be added Ford's gradually increasing stake in Mazda Motors.

58. Gerlach, *Alliance Capitalism*, p. 265. Also see James R. Lincoln, Michael L. Gerlach, and Peggy Takahashi, "*Keiretsu* Networks in the Japanese Economy: A Dyad Analysis of Intercorporate Ties," *American Sociology Review*, vol. 57, no. 5 (1992) pp. 561–85.

59. For legal analysis and debate, see John C. Coffee, "Liquidity Versus Control: The Institutional Investor as Corporate Monitor," *Columbia Law Journal*, vol. 91, no. 6 (1991) pp. 1276–1368.

60. Lorsch and MacIver, "Corporate Governance and Investment Time Horizons."

61. Porter et al., *Capital Choices*.

62. Roe, *Strong Managers, Weak Owners*, p. 173.

63. Similar structures underpin high-profile MNCs based in a number of Germany's EU partners. Nowhere is their impact clearer than in the U.S. consumer electronics market during the 1980s. Strategic mistakes by American manufacturers were the real stories behind their own eventual abandonment of the market. But quite different underlying governance structures enabled Japanese and two European firms to calculate their options in a different light. Thomson was wholly owned by the Government of France. Philips, for its part, is more widely held but a controlling block of voting rights remains vested in a foundation established by the Philips family. Combined with advantages generated by strong cash flow from other operations (notably, its lighting division), Philips had no need to fear takeover threats. For further analysis, see Alfred Chandler, "Chemicals and Electronics: Winning and Losing in Post-War American Industry" (manuscript, Harvard Business School, November 1993); and U.S. Congress, Office of Technology Assessment, *Multinationals and the U.S. Technology Base*, pp. 177–78.

64. "Wall Street: A Survey," *The Economist* (April 15, 1995).

65. Robert N. McCauley and Steven A. Zimmer, "Exchange Rates and International Differences in the Cost of Capital," *Federal Reserve Bank of New York Quarterly Review*, vol. 14 (Summer 1994) chart 7–3.

66. The traditional American distrust of financial concentration, combined with the dynamic effects of various regulatory and technological changes, created an environment conducive to the hyperactive market for corporate takeovers in the 1980s. Although some firms undoubtedly needed the shake-up, others were severely damaged. The damage was worst in sectors where core technologies were in relatively stable stages of development. But it also appears to have hurt some sectors where process technologies were rapidly changing. There is a reasonable consensus that severe damage occurred among financially weak producers of rubber products, nonelectrical machinery and machine tools, metals, and transportation equipment. In addition, a dearth of patient capital was also clearly correlated with instability in significant parts of the U.S. electronics sector. In one other high technology sector, inorganic chemicals, the high level of merger and acquisition activity of the 1980s, much of it initiated by foreign MNCs, appears to have been correlated with differences in underlying financial structure, especially between German and American firms. See Alfred Chandler, "Competitive Performance of U.S. Industrial Enterprises: A Historical Perspective." Also see U.S. Department of Commerce, *Foreign Direct Investment in the United States: An Update* (June 1993) chapter 6.

67. In addition, there appeared to be few benefits for the American economy as a whole from the excessive managerial autonomy that followed as various

states competed to provide corporations with new forms of protection from future takeovers.

68. Policy debate over how best to create and utilize venture capital crystallizes certain key issues. The American system of governance and financing, for example, has created the world's deepest pool of venture capital, but that pool is increasingly open to non-U.S.-based corporations. This is potentially very positive not only for Americans, but for the world. But serious questions remain as to whether American firms enjoy truly reciprocal access to the functional equivalents that have been developed abroad. Surely Japan's equivalent, the spinning off of new operations by established firms once they have reached competitive maturity, is not open; nor have acquisitions become easier to undertake. It is also not clear that American venture capital can easily be attracted to support the development of "boring" improvements in basic and process technologies, both of which will figure heavily in future global competition across a range of manufacturing industries. Indeed, in a number of sectors in the United States, there appears to remain a serious funding gap between the time when initial venture capital for product development runs out and the time when product commercialization attracts routine financing. In this regard, Carl Kester argues, in "Governance, Contracting, and Investment Time Horizons," that, although the German and Japanese systems may not be ideal, "they may be more efficient than the Anglo-American system in coping with hazards posed by risky investment in new environments." When corporate governance and financial market structures merely shield shoddy or overly conservative management practices, they clearly can have costly effects. But when they serve to keep corporate managers accountable to the full range of stakeholder interests, and when they provide emergency support during downturns in economic cycles, they can help build strong international competitors.

CHAPTER 4

1. T. H. Lee and P. P. Reid, eds., *National Interests in an Age of Global Technology* (Washington, D.C.: National Academy Press, 1991) p. 72. See also OECD, DSTI, *Technology and the Economy: The Key Relationships* (Paris: OECD, 1992).

2. The concept of national innovation systems has become well established in the literature on the political economy of technological change. For some of the major contributions, see: P. Patel and K. Pavitt, "National Systems of Innovation," in P. Bianci and M. Quere, eds., *Interacting Systems of Innovation: The Sources of Growth?* (London: Kluwer, forthcoming); Richard Nelson, ed., *National Innovation Systems: A Comparative Analysis* (New York: Oxford University Press, 1993); B. Lundvall, *National Systems of Innovation*; and G. Dosi et al., *Technical Change and Economic Theory* (London: Pinter Publishers, 1988).

3. For a review of relevant literature, see the special issue of *Cambridge Journal of Economics*, vol. 19 (February 1995) pp. 1–255.

4. For an account of the post–World War II origins of the U.S. R&D system, see D. C. Mowery and N. Rosenberg, *Technology and the Pursuit of Economic Growth* (New York: University of Cambridge Press, 1989). For a description of

the contemporary implications of this system, see Mowery, "The Challenges of International Trade to U.S. Technology Policy," in M. C. Harris and G. E. Moore, eds., *Linking Trade and Technology Policies: An International Comparison of the Policies of Industrialized Nations* (Washington, D.C.: National Academy Press, 1992).

5. On the distinctions between mission-oriented, diffusion-oriented, and producer-oriented technology styles, see H. Ergas, "Global Technology and National Politics" (paper prepared for the U.S. Council on Foreign Relations, Monash University, Australia, June 26, 1989); H. Ergas, "Does Technology Policy Matter?" in B. R. Guile and H. Brooks, eds., *Technology and Global Industry: Companies and Nations in the World Economy* (Washington, D.C.: National Academy Press, 1987).

6. Mowery, "The Challenges of International Trade to U.S. Technology Policy," in Harris and Moore, eds., *Linking Trade and Technology Policies,* p. 124. Both the Bush and Clinton administrations backed new policy initiatives, such as the Cooperative Research and Development Agreements and the Manufacturing Extension Partnership, which are designed to improve private access to governmental research and improve technology diffusion rates. The recent introduction of these types of programs, along with their comparatively small size and political vulnerability, reinforces the observation that U.S. government technology policies historically have favored mission-research over technology-diffusion mechanisms.

7. See J. A. Alic, "Technical Knowledge and Technology Diffusion: New Issues for U.S. Government Policy," *Technology Analysis and Strategic Management,* vol. 5, no. 4 (1993) pp. 369–83; U.S. Congress, Office of Technology Assessment, *Making Things Better: Competing in Manufacturing* (OTA-ITE-443, Washington, D.C.: U.S. Government Printing Office, February 1990).

8. The formative postwar formulation of U.S. science and technology policy was laid out by Vannevar Bush in *Science, the Endless Frontier.*

9. Mowery and Rosenberg, in Nelson, ed., *National Innovation Systems,* p. 30.

10. Over the years, numerous studies of U.S. Federal R&D funding have pointed to the need for greater administrative centralization. For the latest refrain, see National Academy of Sciences, *Allocating Federal Funds for Science and Technology* (Washington, D.C.: National Research Council, 1995).

11. For an overview of the German innovation system, see Otto Keck, "The National System for Technical Innovation in Germany," in Nelson, ed., *National Innovation Systems.* Sweden and Switzerland have innovation systems similar to Germany's.

12. Although the level in Germany is low, Japan directs the least R&D resources to the defense sector of all the advanced industrial countries. Japan's defense R&D spending is concentrated in the Technical Research and Development Institute (TRDI) of the Japan Defense Agency. The TRDI's R&D budget is quite modest relative to Japan's total R&D spending, although its programs often benefit from commercial R&D in dual-use technologies. See U.S. Congress, Office of Technology Assessment, *Global Arms Trade* (OTA-ISC-460, Washington, D.C.: U.S. Government Printing Office, 1991) pp. 116–120.

13. For a general description of Japan's innovation system, see Hiroyuki Odadiri and Akira Goto, "The Japanese System of Innovation: Past, Present, and Future," in Nelson, ed., *National Innovation Systems.*

14. See Samuels, *"Rich Nation, Strong Army."*

15. OECD, *Main Science and Technology Indicators*, 1996, no. 1, tables 17–20. Figures cited are for 1994.

16. See OECD, *National Systems for Financing Innovation* (Paris: OECD, 1995).

17. See Mowery, "The Challenges of International Trade to U.S. Technology Policy," in Harris and Moore, eds., *Linking Trade and Technology Policies.*

18. In addition, some analysts note that the cited percentage of R&D performed by higher education in Japan may be artificially high due to accounting procedures that include normal university operating expenditures in the R&D account. The OECD does use estimation techniques to try to correct for cross-national discrepancies in R&D accounting procedures.

19. On the importance of industry-university linkages in general, see David C. Mowery and Nathan Rosenberg, "The U.S. National Innovation System," in Nelson, ed., *National Innovation Systems*; National Science Board, *Science and Engineering Indicators–1993* (Washington, D.C.: U.S. Government Printing Office, 1993) pp. 116–27.

20. For an extended analysis, see J. Alic et al., *Beyond Spinoff: Military and Commercial Technologies in a Changing World* (Boston: Harvard Business School Press, 1992).

21. The data in this section have been obtained from the OECD's *Scoreboard Indicators–1996*, which compiles data from several OECD databases, including the Analytical Business Enterprise R&D (ANBERD) database. ANBERD consists of OECD estimates, based on but not necessarily equivalent to official national statistics, of the current-price value of R&D performed by all businesses. (R&D data obtained from national governments are notoriously difficult to compare, given different categorization and measurement techniques. The OECD adjusts the data to account for national variations in reporting, and in some cases, estimates data that national governments do not compile or do not provide.) The data represent R&D performed, but not necessarily financed, by businesses. For estimates of aggregate R&D financing sources, see Table 4.2. On ANBERD measures generally, see OECD, *Business Enterprise Expenditure on R&D in OECD Countries: Data at the Detailed Industry Level From 1973 to 1990* (Paris: OECD, 1992) pp. 39–41.

22. In the United States as well as other countries, manufacturing industries account for the bulk of all business R&D, and therefore remain the focus of this chapter. R&D in the service sector appears to represent a growing portion of total national R&D in some countries. However, neither the United States nor other countries have developed reliable and comparable measures of R&D in service industries. In the United States, official statistics indicate that R&D in nonmanufacturing industries (mostly but not exclusively service industries) represents approximately 25 percent of all corporate R&D expenditures. This number is somewhat unreliable, however, partly due to intrinsic measurement

difficulties and partly due to changes in NSF survey methods (which were implemented in part to better measure R&D performance in this area). Some analysts argue that R&D in the service sector historically has been underrepresented in official data, and may account for well over 25 percent of total business R&D in the United States; see J. A. Alic, "Technology in the Service Industries," *International Journal of Technology Management*, vol. 9, no. 1 (1994) pp. 1–14.

23. All data on the distribution of business R&D from OECD, *Scoreboard Indicators–1995* (Paris: OECD, 1995).

24. In 1973, the pharmaceutical industry accounted for 5 percent of industrial R&D in France and 6 percent in the United Kingdom; by 1993 it had risen to 23 percent in the United Kingdom and 9 percent in France. By contrast, the share of R&D in aerospace declined from 27 to 12 percent in the United Kingdom and from 21 to 17 percent in France. OECD, *Scoreboard Indicators–1995*.

25. The OECD distinguishes high from medium technology industries based on measures of technological intensity in each major industrial sector. According to this methodology, high technology industries comprise: drugs and medicines; office and computing machinery; electrical machinery, excluding communications equipment; radio, TV, and communication equipment; instruments; and aircraft. Medium technology industries comprise: chemicals, excluding drugs; rubber and plastic products; nonferrous metals; nonelectrical machinery; and motor vehicles.

26. The following technology groupings are based on OECD categorizations. Science-based industries involve those sectors that are based upon the rapid application of scientific advances; the category consists of pharmaceuticals, office & computing equipment, aircraft, and scientific instruments. Specialized supplier industries refer to sectors with highly differentiated products (nonelectrical machinery, electrical machinery (excluding communications equipment), and radio, TV, and communications equipment). Scale-intensive industries are self-explanatory; the category consists of paper, paper products, and printing; industrial chemicals; rubber and plastic products; iron and steel; motor vehicles; and other transport equipment. OECD, *Scoreboard Indicators–1995*.

27. For a general comparative analysis of R&D intensities, see OECD, *Scoreboard of Indicators–1995*, pp. 69–70.

28. OECD, *Scoreboard Indicators–1995*. Between 1973 and 1993, the median R&D intensity of U.S. firms in high technology industries was 10.8%; the median for U.K. firms was 7.3%, for French firms 7.4%, while it was 6.1% and 4.3% for German and Japanese firms, respectively. The magnitude of the difference in R&D intensity across firms based in each of these countries has narrowed over time.

29. The only exception to this pattern is the relatively high R&D intensity level of the United States in medium technology industries. Ibid.

30. OECD, *Scoreboard Indicators–1995*, p. 70.

31. See Daniele Archibugi and Mario Pianta, *The Technological Specialization of Advanced Countries: A Report to the EEC on International Science and Technology*

Activities (Boston: Kluwer Academic Publishers and the Commission of the European Communities, 1992).

32. The term FDI most commonly refers to "investment that is made to acquire a lasting interest in an enterprise operating in an economy other than that of the investor, the investor's purpose being to have an effective voice in the management of the enterprise." DeAnne Julius, *Global Companies and Public Policy: The Growing Challenge of Foreign Direct Investment* (London: Royal Institute of International Affairs, 1990) p. 15. FDI in the United States has a specific legal meaning. It is defined by the International Investment and Trade in Services Act as the ownership by a foreign person or corporation of 10 percent or more of the voting equity of a firm located in the United States. See U.S. Congress, Office of Technology Assessment, *Multinationals and the National Interest: Playing by Different Rules* (OTA-ITE-569, Washington, D.C.: U.S. Government Printing Office, September 1993) p. 47.

33. U.S. Department of Commerce, International Trade Administration, *International Direct Investment: Global Trends and the U.S. Role* (Washington, D.C.: U.S. Government Printing Office, 1988) table 2, p. 90; and United Nations, *World Investment Report 1993: Transnational Corporations and Integrated International Production* (New York: United Nations, 1993) table I.1, p. 14. Inward investment refers to the flows of FDI into a given country. Outward investment refers to the flows of direct investment abroad from a given country.

34. Statement by Stephen J. Canner, Treasury Official Director for International Investment, before the Defense Policy Panel and Investigations Subcommittee of the Armed Services Committee, U.S. House of Representatives, May 14, 1992; statement by Olin Wethington, Assistant Secretary for International Affairs, U.S. Department of the Treasury, at Hearing before the Subcommittee on International Finance and Monetary Policy on June 4, 1992, in *Foreign Acquisition of U.S. Owned Companies* (Washington, D.C.: U.S. Government Printing Office, 1992) pp. 5–6. For skeptical views, see Commission of the European Communities, *Report on United States Trade and Investment Barriers: Problems of Doing Business With the U.S.* (Brussels, Belgium: Commission Services, April 1993) pp. 82–90.

35. For a criticism of this stance, especially in cases where foreign government interests lie behind an investment and in cases where dual military-civilian technologies are in play, see the statement by Laura D'Andrea Tyson, at a Hearing before the Subcommittee on International Finance and Monetary Policy on June 4, 1992, in *Foreign Acquisition of U.S.-Owned Companies* (Washington, D.C.: U.S. Government Printing Office, 1992) pp. 18–19; Tyson's position is disputed in Edward M. Graham, "Foreign Direct Investment in the United States and U.S. Interests," *Science*, vol. 254 (Dec. 20, 1992) pp. 1740–45.

36. Statement by Stephen J. Canner, Treasury Official Director for International Investment, before the Defense Policy Panel and Investigations Subcommittee of the Armed Services Committee, U.S. House of Representatives, May 14, 1992.

37. Keidanren Committee on International Industrial Cooperation, "Improvement of the Investment Climate and Promotion of Foreign Direct Investment into Japan," Oct. 27, 1992.

38. From Ministry of International Trade and Industry (MITI), "Gaishi-Kei Kigyou Koudou Chousa, Houjin Kigyou Toukei," 1991, cited in House Wednesday Group, *Beyond Revisionism: Towards a New U.S.–Japan Policy for the Post–Cold War Era*, Congress of the United States, March 1993, p. 4. Also see Robert Z. Lawrence, "Japan's Low Levels of Inward Investment: The Role of Inhibitions on Acquisitions," *Transnational Corporations*, vol. 1, No. 3 (December 1992) p. 48.

39. Ibid., p. 47.

40. Office of the United States Trade Representative, *1993 National Trade Estimate Report on Foreign Trade Barriers* (Washington, D.C.: 1993) p. 143. These constraints are systematically outlined in detail in *The Second Annual Working Report of the U.S.–Japan Working Group on the Structural Impediments Initiative*, Tokyo, Japan, July 30, 1992. Also see Department of the Treasury, *Survey of G-7 Laws and Regulations on Foreign Direct Investment* (Washington, D.C.: Department of the Treasury, Dec. 7, 1988) p. 2; The House Wednesday Group, *Beyond Revisionism*, p. 6. Also see Robert J. Ballon and Iwao Tomita, *The Financial Behavior of Japanese Corporations* (Tokyo: Kodansha International, 1988) pp. 50–51; Mark Mason, *American Multinationals and Japan: The Political Economy of Japanese Capital Controls, 1899–1980* (Cambridge: Council on East Asian Studies, Harvard University, 1992) pp. 205–207.

41. C. Fred Bergsten and Marcus Noland, *Reconcilable Differences? United States–Japan Economic Conflict* (Washington, D.C.: Institute for International Economics, 1993) p. 81.

42. Lawrence, "Japan's Low Levels of Inward Investment," pp. 47, 51–52, 63.

43. For details, see Mark Mason, "United States Direct Investment in Japan: Trends and Prospects," *California Management Review*, vol. 35, no. 1 (Fall 1992) p. 108.

44. Julius, *Global Companies and Public Policy*, p. 33; The Report of the Ad-Hoc Committee on Foreign Direct Investment in Japan, Keidanren Committee on International Industrial Cooperation, Committee on Foreign Affiliated Corporations, "Improvement of the Investment Climate and Promotion of Foreign Direct Investment into Japan," p. 5.

45. Office of United States Trade Representative, *1993 National Trade Estimate Report on Foreign Trade Barriers*, p. 144. For details, see Fair Trade Commission, *Annual Report to the Committee on Competition Law and Policy, OECD, on Developments in Japan* (Tokyo: Fair Trade Commission, January-December 1990) pp. 30–31.

46. ACCJ, *The United States–Japan White Paper 1993*, p. 3.

47. Internal memorandum, Department of the Treasury, *Survey of G-7 Laws and Regulations on Foreign Direct Investment*, p. 5. For a list, see *The Second Annual Working Report of the U.S.–Japan Working Group on the Structural Impediments Initiative*, pp. 1–63.

48. Office of the United States Trade Representative, *1993 National Trade Estimate Report on Foreign Trade Barriers*, p. 161.

49. Stephen Thomsen, "Comment," in Mark Mason and Dennis Encarnation, eds., *Does Ownership Matter? Japanese Multinationals in Europe* (Oxford: Clarendon Press, 1994) p. 203.

50. For aggregate figures demonstrating the dominance of German firms in the context of the European Union, see Andrei S. Markovits and Simon Reich, *The German Predicament: Memory and Power in the New Europe* (Ithaca, N.Y.: Cornell University Press, 1997) chapter 7.

51. See Commission of the European Communities, *Panorama of EC Industry 1993* (Brussels: Office for Official Publications of the European Communities, 1993) p. 51.

52. Confidential interviews, Germany, November 1–12, 1993.

53. Geoffrey Jones and Harm G. Schröter, "Continental European Multinationals," in Geoffrey Jones and Harm G. Schröter, eds., *The Rise of Multinationals in Continental Europe* (Brookfield, Vermont: Edward Elgar, 1993) p. 8.

54. Geoffrey Jones, "The Performance of British Multinational Enterprise, 1890–1945," in Geoffrey Jones and Peter Hertner, eds., *Multinationals: Theory and History* (Aldershot, England: Edward Elgar, 1986) pp. 96–112.

55. For a comprehensive study, for example, of Ford's activities as foreign direct investors, see Mira Wilkins and Frank E. Hill, *American Business Abroad: Ford on Six Continents* (Detroit, Mich.: Wayne State University Press, 1964). For the same on Singer see Robert Bruce Davies, *Peacefully Working to Conquer the World: Singer Sewing Machines in Foreign Markets, 1854–1920* (New York: Arno Press, 1976). For more general discussions, see Mira Wilkins, *The Emergence of Multinational Enterprise* (Cambridge, Mass.: Harvard University Press, 1970); Jones and Schröter, eds., *The Rise of Multinationals in Continental Europe*.

56. Johnson, *MITI and the Japanese Miracle*; Edward Lincoln, *Japan's Unequal Trade* (Washington, D.C.: Brookings, 1990).

57. The American subsidiaries responded by attempting to merge with either Nissan or Toyota, but these moves were thwarted under the terms of the Exchange Control Law. Other measures, including those embodied in the National General Mobilization Law of 1937, essentially attempted to emulate Hitler's "New Economic Order," by fixing all prices, wages, rents and economic indices, thus eliminating the autonomous market-pricing structure, which had hitherto created potential openings for foreign firms. Phyliss Genther, *A History of Japan's Government–Business Relationship: The Passenger Car Industry* (Ann Arbor: Center for Japanese Studies, University of Michigan, 1990) pp. 48–50; Johnson, *MITI and the Japanese Miracle*, p. 139.

58. Nissan and Toyota accounted for as much as 85% of auto production from the mid-1930s until the late 1950s, while European and American firms had accounted for 95% of production in the decade preceding 1935. Ira Magaziner and Thomas Hout, *Japanese Industrial Policy* (Berkeley, Calif.: Institute of International Studies, U.C. Berkeley, 1980) p. 68; Michael Cusamano, *The Japanese Automobile Industry* (Cambridge: Council on East Asian Studies, Harvard University Press, 1985) pp. 7, 17. See also Genther, *A History of Japan's Government–Business Relationship*, pp. 48–50.

59. For a discussion of this issue, see Leon Hollerman, "International Economic Controls in Occupied Japan," *Journal of Asian Studies*, vol. 38, no. 4 (August 1979) pp. 707–19; Kozo Yamamura, *Economic Policy in Postwar Japan: Growth Versus Economic Democracy* (Berkeley: University of California Press, 1967).

60. For details concerning both the postwar development of the automobile industry and the semiconductor industry in Japan, see Simon Reich, "Ideology and Competition: The Basis of U.S. and Japanese Policies," in William Avery and David Rapkin, *National Competitiveness in a Global Economy* (Boulder, Colorado: Lynne Riener, 1995) pp. 55–102.

61. Dennis J. Encarnation and Mark Mason, "Neither MITI Nor America: The Political Economy of Capital Liberalization in Japan," *International Organization*, vol. 44, no. 1 (Winter 1990) pp. 25–54. On Japan as a trading state, see Richard Rosecrance, *The Rise of the Trading State: Commerce and Conquest in the Modern World* (New York: Basic Books, 1986).

62. For details, see Simon Reich, *The Fruits of Fascism: Postwar Prosperity in Historical Perspective* (Ithaca, N.Y.: Cornell University Press, 1990) pp. 246–61.

63. Peter J. Katzenstein, *Small States in World Markets: Industrial Policy in Europe* (Ithaca, N.Y.: Cornell University Press, 1985) p. 32.

64. For an assessment of the relative effectiveness of allied economic reforms, see Peter J. Katzenstein, *Policy and Politics in West Germany: The Growth of a Semisovereign State* (Philadelphia, Penn.: Temple University Press, 1987) p. 13.

65. Albert O. Hirschmann, *National Power and the Structure of Foreign Trade* (Berkeley: University of California Press, 1945).

66. Raymond Vernon, "International Investment and International Trade in the Product Cycle," *The Quarterly Journal of Economics*, vol. 80, no. 2 (1996) pp. 190–207.

67. For data and analysis of the direct investment account, see Fred L. Block, *The Origins of International Economic Disorder: A Study of United States International Monetary Policy from World War II to the Present* (Berkeley: University of California, 1977) pp. 151–55.

68. Simon Reich, *The Fruits of Fascism*, pp. 67–73.

69. Robert Gilpin, *U.S. Power and the Multinational Corporation*.

CHAPTER 5

1. See, for instance, Donald H. Dalton and Manuel G. Serapio, *Globalizing Industrial Research and Development* (Washington, D.C.: U.S. Department of Commerce, 1995); "Technology and Globalization," in OECD, *Technology and the Economy: The Key Relationships* (Paris: OECD, 1992) pp. 209–36. For an extended analysis with particular reference to MNCs, see O. Granstrand, L. Håkanson, and S. Sjölander, *Technology Management and International Business: Internationalization of R&D and Technology* (New York: John Wiley & Sons, 1992).

2. See David C. Mowery, *Science and Technology Policy in Interdependent Economies* (Boston: Kluwer Academic Publishers, 1994).

3. The increased frequency of offshore R&D and the increased frequency of international technology alliances have been associated with the rise of "technoglobalism" during the 1980s. See OECD, Economic Analysis and Statistics Division, *The Performance of Foreign Affiliates in OECD Countries*

(Paris: OECD, 1994) p. 49. For a broader discussion, see Sylvia Ostry and Richard Nelson, *Technonationalism and Technoglobalism* (Washington, D.C.: Brookings, 1995).

4. See, for example, Dalton and Serapio, *Globalizing Industrial Research and Development*.

5. G. Vickery, "Global Industries and National Policies," *OECD Observer*, vol. 179 (December 1992/January 1993) pp. 11–14. Smaller countries with limited domestic R&D resources (e.g., Sweden, Netherlands, and Switzerland) tend to locate even more R&D abroad, often as a means of tapping foreign technological resources.

6. J. A. Cantwell, *Technological Innovation and Multinational Corporations* (Oxford: Basil Blackwell, 1989).

7. P. Patel and K. Pavitt, "Large Firms in the Production of the World's Technology: An Important Case of 'Non-Globalization,' " *Journal of International Business Studies* (First Quarter, 1991) pp. 1–21.

8. J. H. Dunning, "Multinational Enterprises and the Globalization of Innovatory Capacity," *Research Policy*, vol. 23, no. 1 (January 1994) pp. 67–88.

9. It would be preferable to compare all the permutations of R&D conducted by U.S., European, and Japanese MNCs in each others' markets. Unfortunately, apart from the United States, there are few sources of country data that distinguish the R&D activities of foreign affiliates from those of parent firms and all domestic businesses. Consequently, the analysis of MNC R&D in this chapter is limited primarily to comparisons of foreign affiliates in the United States and U.S. affiliates in foreign markets.

10. U.S. Department of Commerce, Bureau of Economic Analysis, *U.S. Direct Investment Abroad: 1994 Benchmark Survey* (Washington, D.C., January 1997) tables II.R 1, III.I 2; U.S. Department of Commerce, Bureau of Economic Analysis, *Survey of Current Business* (Washington, D.C., June 1995) table 5, p. 36. Data expressed in billions of current dollars.

11. U.S. Department of Commerce, Bureau of Economic Analysis, *U.S. Direct Investment Abroad: 1994 Benchmark Survey* (Washington, D.C., January 1997) tables II.R 1, III.I 2. The percentage of total MNC R&D conducted by majority-owned affiliates varies somewhat by sector; in 1994 it ranged from 17 percent in food and kindred products to 6 percent in electric and electronic equipment.

12. U.S. Department of Commerce, Bureau of Economic Analysis, *U.S. Direct Investment Abroad: 1994 Benchmark Survey* (Washington, D.C., January 1997) tables II.R 1, III.I 2, II.K 1, III.E 1, III.D 6, III.G 1.

13. U.S. Congress, Office of Technology Assessment, *Multinationals and the U.S. Technology Base*, pp. 85–90.

14. This chapter uses the conventional definition of R&D intensity: the ratio of R&D expenditures to sales.

15. U.S. Department of Commerce, Bureau of Economic Analysis, *Survey of Current Business* (June 1995), table 1/p. 32; table 5/p. 36.

16. The average R&D intensity of foreign affiliates in the United States is unusually high due to the concentration of foreign direct investment in high R&D intensity sectors, principally pharmaceuticals, chemicals, and mechanical engineering. For different reasons, foreign affiliates in Ireland and Australia

also have higher average R&D intensities than domestic firms. OECD, Economic Analysis and Statistics Division, *The Performance of Foreign Affiliates in OECD Countries* (Paris: OECD, 1994) pp. 64–65.

17. U.S. Department of Commerce, Bureau of Economic Analysis, *U.S. Direct Investment Abroad: 1994 Benchmark Survey* (Washington, D.C.: January 1997) tables II.R 1, III.I 2, II.K 1, III.A 2.

18. OECD, Economic Analysis and Statistics Division, *The Performance of Foreign Affiliates in OECD Countries* (1994) pp. 61–76.

19. For data and analysis of U.S. MNCs, see U.S. Department of Commerce, Bureau of Economic Analysis, *Survey of Current Business* (June 1995) pp. 31–51. For an analysis of foreign affiliates in the United States, see U.S. Department of Commerce, *Foreign Direct Investment in the United States: An Update* (Washington, D.C.: U.S. Government Printing Office, 1995).

20. See Robert Pearce and Marina Papanastassiou, "R&D Networks and Innovation: Decentralised Product Development in Multinational Enterprises," *R&D Management*, vol. 26, no. 4 (October 1996) pp. 315–33; Donald H. Dalton and Manuel G. Serapio, *Globalizing Industrial Research and Development* (Washington, D.C.: U.S. Department of Commerce, 1995) pp. 23–26; U.S. Department of Commerce, Technology Administration, Japan Technology Program, *U.S. Research Facilities of Foreign Companies*, prepared by D. H. Dalton and M. G. Serapio, NTIS Pub. No. 93–134328 (Washington, D.C.: January 1993); U.S. Department of Commerce, Technology Administration and the Japan–U.S. Friendship Commission, *Japan–U.S. Direct R&D Investments in the Electronics Industries*, prepared by M. G. Serapio, NTIS Pub. No. 94–127974 (Washington, D.C.: 1994); OECD, Economic Analysis and Statistics Division, *Performance of Foreign Affiliates in OECD Countries* (Paris: OECD, 1994).

21. On Philips' R&D operations, see Philips Electronics NV, *Annual Report 1993* (Eindhoven, The Netherlands, 1994); Philips Electronics NV, "Electronics for People," corporate brochure (Eindhoven, The Netherlands, 1993) p. 13; Philips Research, "Philips Research: A Gateway to the Future," corporate brochure (Eindhoven, The Netherlands, 1993).

22. Presentation by Knut Merten, Siemens Inc., at the National Academy of Sciences, May 30, 1995.

23. Kevin Done, "Tomorrow, the World," *Financial Times*, Apr. 22, 1994, p. 15.

24. The relative ease of establishing R&D operations varies across industries that specialize in different scientific and technological disciplines, given variations in the degree of capital intensity and the types of linkages to production facilities characteristic of different disciplines.

25. OECD, "Globalization in the Pharmaceutical Industry," draft manuscript (March 10, 1993) table 4/p. 9, p. 42.

26. OECD, "Globalization of Industrial Activities: Sector Case Study of Globalization in the Computer Industry," draft paper (September 27, 1993) p. 11.

27. P. Patel and K. Pavitt, "Large Firms in the Production of the World's Technology: An Important Case of 'Non-Globalization'" *Journal of International Business Studies* (First Quarter, 1991) pp. 1–21; R. Miller, "Global R&D Networks and Large-Scale Innovations: The Case of the Automobile Industry,"

Research Policy, vol. 23, no. 3 (May 1993) pp. 27–46. Although the R&D intensity of the automotive industry is low relative to electronics, computers, and pharmaceuticals, it has been increasing over time and is well above the national average for manufacturing industries. OECD, "Globalization of Industrial Activities: Sector Case Study of Globalization in the Automobile Industry," (draft paper, June 16, 1993) p. 10.

28. Patent evidence also supports the conclusion that corporations retain most of their technology development functions in the home market. See P. Patel and K. Pavitt, "Large Firms in the Production of the World's Technology." Similar findings also were reached for British firms; see J. A. Cantwell and C. Hodson, "Global R&D and British Competitiveness," in M. C. Casson, ed., *Global Research Strategy and International Competitiveness* (Oxford: Basil Blackwell, 1991).

29. Data expressed in constant 1992 dollars. Data on R&D spending by foreign affiliates from U.S. Department of Commerce, Bureau of Economic Analysis, *Survey of Current Business* (May 1995) table 6/p. 62, and U.S. Department of Commerce, Bureau of Economic Analysis, *Foreign Direct Investment in the United States,* (annual surveys). Data on total U.S. industry-funded R&D from National Science Foundation, *National Patterns of R&D Resources–1995,* table B3.

30. Ibid.

31. In 1994, Swiss firms also accounted for a substantial share of R&D spending by foreign affiliates in the United States, spending $2.3 billion, or 15.4% of the total. Approximately half of Swiss affiliate R&D spending was in the pharmaceutical sector. Source: U.S. Department of Commerce, Bureau of Economic Analysis, *Foreign Direct Investment in the U.S.: Preliminary Estimates, 1994,* July 1996, table I-6. (Data expressed in constant 1992 dollars.)

32. Ibid.

33. H. Fusfeld, *Industry's Future: Changing Patterns of Industrial Research* (Washington, D.C.: Industrial Research Institute, 1994).

34. See OTA, *Multinationals and the National Interest,* figure 5–8.

35. For supporting analyses, see Dalton and Serapio, *Globalizing Industrial Research and Development;* OECD, *Performance of Foreign Affiliates,* 1994, p. 50; U.S. Department of Commerce, Bureau of Economic Analysis, *Foreign Direct Investment in the United States: An Update,* 1994, p. 70; H. Fusfeld, *Industry's Future: Changing Patterns of Industrial Research.*

36. FDI in the pharmaceutical sector increased from $2.4 billion in 1985 to $25.5 billion in 1994. In 1995, direct investment in this sector jumped another 33%, to reach $33.9 billion. U.S. Department of Commerce, Bureau of Economic Analysis, *Survey of Current Business,* September 1996, July 1995, August 1994, and July 1993.

37. Data source: U.S. Department of Commerce, Bureau of Economic Analysis, *Survey of Current Business,* September 1996, table 10.3, p. 77. See pages 116–22 in this volume for a complete analysis of national variations in the composition of direct investment.

38. Ibid.

39. U.S. Department of Commerce, Bureau of Economic Analysis, *U.S. Direct Investment Abroad,* annual series, tables III.I 3 and III.E 3; U.S. Department of

Commerce, Bureau of Economic Analysis, *Survey of Current Business,* June 1995, table 11.2, pp. 44–45. Data expressed in constant 1992 dollars. Data on overseas R&D expenditures by U.S. firms are available only since 1989.

40. U.S. Department of Commerce, Bureau of Economic Analysis, *U.S. Direct Investment Abroad: Benchmark Survey, Preliminary 1994 Estimates,* January 1997, table III.R 2; and prior annual surveys; U.S. Department of Commerce, Bureau of Economic Analysis, *Survey of Current Business,* June 1995, table 11.2, p. 45.

41. Ibid.

42. These percentages for France and the United Kingdom represent 1993 data (because of missing sectoral detail, 1994 data cannot be used).

43. There are four limitations to using royalty and license fee transactions as a proxy for technology trade. First, the available U.S. data for royalties and license fees include transactions of all forms of intellectual property, e.g., they combine industrial process technology along with other forms of intellectual property, such as copyrights, trademarks, franchises, and rights to broadcast live events. (Bureau of Economic Analysis provides data on industrial process technology only for unaffiliated or arms-length transactions; for a discussion of these transactions see the following pages.) Second, it is difficult to measure intellectual property traded between affiliated firms, since the value of affiliated transactions is not always determined on the open market. Although MNCs dispute the contention, many observers believe that both U.S. and foreign MNCs adjust intellectual property fees to shift costs from their firms in low-tax regions to those in high-tax regions, thereby lowering their net tax obligations. Third, the data do not differentiate royalty and license fees associated with new technology from those associated with old technology transactions; as a consequence, for example, a large portion of U.S. technology exports in any given year may not represent new technology leaving the country but, instead, may represent continued financial transactions from technology transferred in prior years. Fourth, technology also can be transferred through a variety of channels that are not captured by this or any other reliable measure—for instance, technology can be transferred through the exchange of technologically intensive goods, depending on how the purchaser utilizes those goods. Notwithstanding these four limitations, analysts commonly use intellectual property transactions as a proxy for technology transfer by MNCs.

44. OECD Economics Analysis and Statistics Division Database, *Main Science and Technology Indicators,* no. 1, 1995, table 82.

45. This observation holds insofar as intellectual property transactions represent technology trade per se (see endnote 43). The validity of this indicator is somewhat stronger for OECD data on technology trade than for Bureau of Economic Analysis data on intellectual property transactions, due to slight measurement differences. The available Bureau of Economic Analysis measure covers all intellectual property transactions, which includes patents for industrial process technology along with copyrights, trademarks, franchises, rights to broadcast live events, and other intangible property rights. The OECD measure is more tightly focused on technology trade per se, covering patents, licenses, trademarks, designs, know-how, and closely related technical services for industrial R&D. For the purposes of this analysis, the difference in the two

measurements is not significant. This chapter uses OECD data for broad international comparisons of technology trade, and Bureau of Economic Analysis data for more detailed analysis of technology trade patterns specific to the United States.

46. Owing to the lack of an appropriate price index for intellectual property transactions, this chapter presents the data on technology trade in current dollars.

47. See M. E. Mogee, "Inward International Licensing by U.S.-Based Firms: Trends and Implications," *The Journal of Technology Transfer*, vol. 16, no. 2 (Spring 1991) pp. 14–19.

48. U.S. Department of Commerce, Bureau of Economic Analysis, *Survey of Current Business*, September 1995, table 2, p. 76; see also tables 4.1–4.4.

49. This conclusion holds to the extent that intellectual property transactions represent technology trade; see endnote 43 regarding measurement qualifications.

50. See chapter 4 for a description of FDI trends in the United States. For data and supporting analysis of the relationship between FDI and technology trade flows, see U.S. Department of Commerce, Bureau of Economic Analysis, *Survey of Current Business*, September 1993, table 4.4, p. 132; and U.S. Department of Commerce, Bureau of Economic Analysis, "U.S. International Sales and Purchases of Private Services," *Survey of Current Business*, 1992, p. 85.

51. U.S. Department of Commerce, Bureau of Economic Analysis, *Survey of Current Business*, September 1995, p. 82.

52. Data on technology trade between Japan and Europe could provide confirming evidence of this observation. As with affiliate R&D data, however, comparable affiliate technology trade data is not available for the European-Japanese relationship.

53. Importing patterns by U.S. affiliates of foreign firms are more mixed. In 1994, 65% of total U.S. technology imports from Europe were from European MNCs to their U.S. affiliates, although there were some variations among the large European countries—78% from the United Kingdom, 70% from Germany, and just 55% from France. Of all 1994 U.S. technology imports from Japan, 73% were purchased by the U.S. affiliates of Japanese MNCs. U.S. Department of Commerce, Bureau of Economic Analysis, *Survey of Current Business*, September 1995, p. 82.

54. OECD, Economic Analysis and Statistics Division, *Performance of Foreign Affiliates in OECD Countries* (Paris: OECD, 1994). On Japan's general orientation toward a strategy of technology acquisition, see Samuels, *"Rich Nation, Strong Army."*

55. Analysts frequently use different terms to describe technological collaboration among firms. There are important distinctions in the literature between short-term tactical alliances and relatively-longer-term strategic alliances, as well as between alliances used to develop and/or diffuse technology and those used to gain market access and pursue other nontechnological goals. For simplicity, this chapter uses a single term—international technology alliances—to describe any interfirm collaboration (equity or non-equity) that includes arrangements for joint research and/or technology transfer. For more general

discussion of international alliances, see OTA, *Multinationals and the National Interest*, ch. 5.

56. In general terms, joint ventures are more common among firms seeking to improve their long-term market position, while technology alliances are more common when firms are pursuing more immediate technological achievements. See J. Hagedoorn, "Understanding the Rationale of Strategic Technology Partnering: Interorganizational Modes of Cooperation and Sectoral Differences," *Strategic Management Journal*, vol. 14 (1993) p. 371.

57. National Science Board, *Science and Engineering Indicators–1993* (Washington, D.C.: U.S. Government Printing Office, 1993) p. 122; and D. C. Mowery, "International Collaborative Ventures and U.S. Firms' Technology Strategies," in Granstrand, Håkanson, and Sjölander, *Technology Management and International Business* (New York: John Wiley, 1992) pp. 224–29.

58. See National Science Board, *Science and Engineering Indicators–1996* (Washington, D.C.: U.S. Government Printing Office, 1996) p. 43–44; and National Science Board, *Science and Engineering Indicators–1993* (Washington, D.C.: U.S. Government Printing Office, 1993) p. 123. The data cited in this source are drawn from the Maastricht Economic Research Institute's MERIT/CATI database, which covers only interfirm agreements that involve technology transfer or joint research.

59. See Hagedoorn, "Understanding the Rationale of Strategic Technology Partnering."

60. National Science Board, *Science and Engineering Indicators–1996* (Washington, D.C.: U.S. Government Printing Office, 1996) pp. 43–44; Lynn K. Mytelka and Michael Delapierre, "Strategic Partnerships, Knowledge-Based Networked Oligopolies, and the State" (manuscript, August 26, 1996).

61. National Science Board, *Science and Engineering Indicators–1996* (Washington, D.C.: U.S. Government Printing Office, 1996) appendix table 4–38. The data cited in this source are drawn from the Maastricht Economic Research Institute's MERIT/CATI database, which, although not comprehensive, is the best available source of quantitative data on interfirm technology alliances. All of the quantitative evidence cited in this section is from this data source.

62. Foreign direct investment is not easy to measure. The method most widely used is the "historical cost" approach, which calculates the value of FDI by focusing on the initial cost of any investment but largely understates its current value. It is also subject to distortion as a result of currency fluctuations. A principal alternative is the "stock" method of evaluation which calculates the value of initial investments according to their current values. Current values, however, can only be calculated in the broadest sense. A third approach adjusts for "replacement costs." This market-value method largely replicates the second method but tends to focus less on share price indices and more on price indices for investment goods. It has two major deficiencies. First, the current value of many direct investments has little to do with the replacement cost of the actual capital, much of which may be outdated. Second, the value of an investment may have less to do with the market value of the physical capital than with the value of intangible assets such as skills, knowledge, or goodwill.

Critics suggest that the historical cost approach understates European investment in the United States and overstates more recent Japanese investment. In fact, the vast majority of FDI within the Triad occurred in the 1980s. For a detailed discussion of how this influences the U.S. position, see Robert Eisner and Paul J. Pieper, "The World's Greatest Debtor Nation?," *North American Review of Economics and Finance*, vol. 1, no. 1 (1990) pp. 9–32.

63. By nature, these features resist change. Many managers of U.S.-based MNCs, for instance, contend that U.S. governmental efforts to overcome the private and public sector barriers to inward investment in Japan have achieved only limited success in making the Japanese domestic market more receptive to foreign investors. Sources: Confidential interviews with MNC executives and government officials conducted by the authors in 1993 and 1994 in Japan and the United States. See also The American Chamber of Commerce in Japan, *The United States–Japan White Paper 1993* (Tokyo: American Chamber of Commerce in Japan, 1993) pp. 30–34, 49–50, 64–68, 90–92; Office of the United States Trade Representative, *1993 National Trade Estimate Report on Foreign Trade Barriers* (Washington, D.C.: GPO, 1993) pp. 79–94, 143–170; Ad-Hoc Committee on Foreign Direct Investment in Japan, *Improvement of the Investment Climate and Promotion of Foreign Direct Investment into Japan* (Tokyo: Keidanren/Committee on International Industrial Cooperation and Committee on Foreign Affiliated Corporations, 1992); and The House Wednesday Group, *Beyond Revisionism: Towards a New U.S.–Japan Policy for the Post–Cold War Era* (Washington, D.C.: March 1993).

64. Due to accounting methods, it is difficult to identify precisely the sectoral allocation of direct investment. The BEA categorizes firms based on the sectoral location of final sales; the sector with the largest share of final sales represents the firm's entire sector of operation. In diversified affiliates, this categorization method can obscure other sectors in which the affiliate operates at a significant level. Largely for this reason, the analysis in this chapter focuses on major industrial groupings. Even at this level, however, the categorization rules can partially mischaracterize the sectoral distribution of direct investment.

65. U.S. Department of Commerce, Bureau of Economic Analysis, *U.S. Direct Investment Abroad*, annual series; U.S. Commerce Department, *Survey of Current Business*, annual series; U.S. Department of Commerce, Bureau of Economic Analysis, *Foreign Direct Investment in the United States*, annual series.

66. See U.S. Commerce Department, Bureau of Economic Analysis, *Foreign Direct Investment in the United States*, annual series; and U.S. Commerce Department, Bureau of Economic Analysis, *Survey of Current Business*, August 1987–August 1996.

67. BEA, "U.S. Intrafirm Trade in Goods," *Survey of Current Business*, February 1997, p. 23.

68. IFT data is not available for trade in services.

69. All IFT figures cited in this section were compiled from U.S. Department of Commerce, Bureau of Economic Analysis, *Foreign Direct Investment in the United States*, annual series, table G-4 (1983–1986) and table G-2 (1987–1994); U.S. Department of Commerce, Bureau of Economic Analysis, *U.S. Direct In-*

vestment Abroad: Operations of U.S. Parent Companies and their Foreign Affiliates: Preliminary 1994 Estimates, and prior annual surveys, tables 50 (1983–1988) and III.H.I (1989–1994); U.S. Department of Commerce, Bureau of Economic Analysis, *Survey of Current Business* 72(6), June 1992, table 2, pp. 88–90; 73(3), March 1993, table 2, pp. 90–91; 74(3), March 1994, table 2, pp. 68–69.

70. Undifferentiated domestic content data does not allow one to see whether the low domestic content rates are due to intermediate goods sourcing practices or to high finished goods imported through the affiliates' secondary activities in wholesale trade.

71. William J. Zeile, "Imported Inputs and the Domestic Content of Production by Foreign-Owned Manufacturing Affiliates in the United States" (unpublished paper presented at the NBER Conference on Geography and Ownership as Bases for Economic Accounting, December 6, 1995, pp. 14–15).

72. Ibid, p. 9.

73. BEA, *Survey of Current Business* (February 1994) table 9, p. 55.

74. See Edward Graham and Paul Krugman, *Foreign Direct Investment in the United States,* 3rd edition (Washington, D.C.: Institute of International Economics, 1995) pp. 35–55.

75. See OTA, *Multinationals and the U.S. Technology Base.*

76. See Nelson, ed., *National Innovation Systems;* and David C. Mowery, *Science and Technology Policy in Interdependent Economies;* and Jorge Niosi and Bertrand Bellon, "The Global Interdependence of National Innovation Systems," *Technology in Society,* vol. 16, no. 2 (1994) pp. 173–197.

77. See Lundvall, *National Systems of Innovation.*

78. Alic, "Technical Knowledge and Technology Diffusion."

79. See OECD, DSTI, "Embodied Technology Diffusion: An Empirical Analysis for 10 OECD Countries," *STI Working Papers* 1996/1 (Paris: OECD, 1996).

80. In most countries and in most sectors, the corporate research lab has been and remains the largest and most significant location of technological innovation. See Nelson, ed., *National Innovation Systems.* Of course, the innovative capabilities and activities of firms are shaped by numerous factors external to the firm, including the educational infrastructure as well as direct and indirect forms of governmental support.

81. One exception to this tendency is biotechnology, where a number of European and Japanese MNCs have close basic research contacts and often ownership arrangements with many small U.S. biotechnology firms.

82. For an analysis, see OTA, *Multinationals and the U.S. Technology Base;* see also Raymond Vernon, "International Investment and International Trade in the Product Cycle," *Quarterly Journal of Economics,* vol. 80, no. 2 (1996) pp. 190–207; J. H. Dunning, *Multinational Enterprises and the Global Economy* (Reading, Mass: Addison-Wesley, 1993); J. H. Dunning, *Japanese Participation in British Industry* (London: Croom Helm, 1986); and J. Hennert, *A Theory of Multinational Enterprise* (Ann Arbor: University of Michigan Press, 1985).

83. M. Gittelman and E. Graham, "The Performance and Structure of Japanese Affiliates in the European Community," in M. Mason and D. Encarnation, *Does Ownership Matter? Japanese Multinationals in Europe* (Oxford: Clarendon Press, 1994) pp. 154–55.

84. OECD, "Globalization in the Pharmaceutical Industry," draft paper (March 10, 1993) p. 9.

85. D. E. Westney, "Cross-Pacific Internationalization of R&D by U.S. and Japanese Firms," *R&D Management*, vol. 23, no. 2 (1993) pp. 171–81; OECD, "Globalization of Industrial Activities: Sector Case Study of Globalization in the Consumer Electronics Sector" (draft paper dated November 9, 1993) p. 17.

86. R. Miller, "Global R&D Networks and Large-Scale Innovations: The Case of the Automobile Industry," *Research Policy*, vol. 23, no. 3 (May 1993) pp. 27–46. See also P. Patel and K. Pavitt, "Large Firms in the Production of the World's Technology: An Important Case of 'Non-Globalization,' " *Journal of International Business Studies* (First Quarter, 1991) pp. 1–21.

87. The semiconductor chip development alliance between IBM, Siemens, and Toshiba is frequently cited in this regard.

88. OECD, "Globalization in the Pharmaceutical Industry," pp. 9, 39. In 1989, Japanese pharmaceutical firms commanded only 1.1% of the U.S. market, while European firms commanded 26.7% of U.S. market share. The pattern in Europe is similar: Japanese firms have a very low market presence, while U.S. pharmaceutical firms command from 18% (in Germany) to 33% (in the U.K.).

89. OECD, "Globalization of Industrial Activities: Sector Case Study of Globalization in the Consumer Electronics Sector," p. 17.

90. "Much of their activity is in component testing, procurement and process development, but more substantial product development is slowly gathering pace—the Honda Accord in the United States and the Nissan Primera in the United Kingdom had substantial local design inputs." OECD, "Globalization of Industrial Activities: Sector Case Study of Globalization in the Automobile Industry," (draft paper June 16, 1993) p. 27.

CHAPTER 6

1. On this issue, see Benjamin J. Cohen, *The Geography of Money* (Ithica, N.Y.: Cornell University Press, forthcoming); and Louis W. Pauly, *Who Elected the Bankers? Surveillance and Control in the World Economy* (Ithaca, N.Y.: Cornell University Press, 1997).

2. See Theodore J. Lowi, *The End of Liberalism: The Second Republic of the United States*, 2nd edition (New York: W. W. Norton, 1979) pp. 50–52.

3. For an example of an issue-area that further deepens this complexity by crossing the traditional military interests of states with new economic interests, see William W. Keller, *Arm in Arm: The Political Economy of the Global Arms Trade* (New York: Basic Books, 1995).

4. Paul David, "Clio and the Economics of QWERTY," *American Economic Review*, vol. 75 (1985) pp. 332–37; Paul Krugman, *Geography and Trade* (Cambridge: The MIT Press, 1991); Herman Schwartz, *States versus Markets* (New York: St. Martin's Press, 1994).

5. In the course of our fieldwork, such an idea was considered radical only in Britain and in certain quarters in the United States. In practical terms, for example, the view that the development of key technologies could ever be left to uninhibited corporate markets organized around the principle of pure na-

tional treatment typically met with derision in Germany and Japan. Outside international economic organizations, where official spokespersons often feel constrained to sing from a common hymnbook, real policy debates appear to focus not on the principle of political management but on the modalities and language of its implementation in specific national and sectoral contexts.

6. See Miles Kahler, *International Institutions and the Political Economy of Integration* (Washington, D.C.: Brookings, 1995).

7. Peter J. Katzenstein, "United Germany in an Integrating Europe," *Current History* vol. 96, no. 608 (March 1997) pp. 116–23.

SELECTED BIBLIOGRAPHY

Full references are included in the notes. We provide here a selection of accessible books for further exploration of themes highlighted in the text.

On the movement from national to multinational corporate enterprise:

Bergsten, C. Fred, Thomas Horst, and Theodore Moran. *American Multinationals and American Interests*. Washington: Brookings, 1978.

Biersteker, Thomas J. *Multinationals, the State, and Control of the Nigerian Economy*. Princeton: Princeton University Press, 1987.

Campbell, Nigel, and Fred Burton. *Japanese Multinationals*. London: Routledge, 1994.

Chandler, Alfred D. *Strategy and Structure*. Cambridge: MIT Press, 1962.

———. *Giant Enterprise*. New York: Harcourt, Brace & World, 1964.

———. *The Visible Hand*. Cambridge: Harvard University Press, 1977.

———. *Scale and Scope*. Cambridge: Belknap Press, 1990.

Dunning, John H. *American Investment in British Manufacturing*. London: Allen & Unwin, 1958.

———. *Japanese Participation in British Industry*. London: Croom Helm, 1986.

———. *The Globalization of Business*. London: Routledge, 1993.

———. *Multinational Enterprises and the Global Economy*. Reading: Addison-Wesley, 1993.

Eden, Lorraine, and Evan Potter, eds. *Multinationals in the Global Political Economy*. New York: St. Martin's, 1993.

Encarnation, Dennis J. *Dislodging the Multinationals*. Ithaca: Cornell University Press, 1989.

Evans, Peter. *Dependent Development*. Princeton: Princeton University Press, 1979.

Franko, Lawrence G. *The European Multinational*. London: Harper & Row, 1976.

Gilpin, Robert. *U.S. Power and the Multinational Corporation*. New York: Basic Books, 1975.

Hatch, Walter, and Kozo Yamamura. *Asia in Japan's Embrace*. Cambridge: Cambridge University Press, 1996.

Hymer, Stephen. *The Multinational Corporation*. New York: Cambridge University Press, 1979.

Jones, Geoffrey, and Harm G. Schröter, eds. *The Rise of Multinationals in Continental Europe*. Aldershot: Edward Elgar, 1993.

Kindleberger, Charles P., ed. *The International Corporation*. Cambridge: MIT Press, 1970.

La Palombara, Joseph, and Stephen Blank. *Multinational Corporations and Developing Countries*. New York: Conference Board, 1979.

Lall, Sanjaya, et al. *The New Multinationals*. New York: John Wiley & Sons, 1983.

Moran, Theodore, ed. *Governments and Transnational Corporations*. London: Routledge, 1993.

Reddaway, W. B., et al. *UK Investment Overseas: Volumes I and II*. Cambridge: Cambridge University Press, 1968.

Reich, Simon. *The Fruits of Fascism*. Ithaca: Cornell University Press, 1990.

Robinson, John. *Multinationals and Political Control*. New York: St. Martin's Press, 1983.

Stopford, John, and Susan Strange. *Rival States, Rival Firms*. Cambridge: Cambridge University Press, 1991.

Stopford, John, and Louis Turner. *Britain and the Multinationals*. New York: Wiley, 1985.

Thomas, Kenneth P. *Capital beyond Borders*. London: Macmillan, 1997.

Tsurumi, Yoshi. *Multinational Management: Business Strategy and Government Policy*. Cambridge: Ballinger, 1983.

Turner, Louis. *Invisible Empires*. London: Hamish Hamilton, 1970.

van Tulder, Rob, and Gerd Junne. *European Multinationals in Core Technologies*. New York: Wiley, 1988.

Vernon, Raymond. *Sovereignty at Bay*. New York: Basic Books, 1971.

———. *Storm Over the Multinationals*. Cambridge: Harvard University Press, 1977.

Wellons, Philip. *Passing the Buck*. Boston: Harvard Business School Press, 1987.

Wells, Louis. *Third World Multinationals*. Cambridge: MIT Press, 1983.

Wilkins, Mira. *The Maturing of Multinational Enterprise*. Cambridge: Harvard University Press, 1974.

On the comparative analysis of domestic political and economic structures relevant to corporate behavior:

Gourevitch, Peter. *Politics in Hard Times*. Ithaca: Cornell University Press, 1986.

Hall, Peter. *Governing the Economy*. Oxford: Oxford University Press, 1986.

Johnson, Chalmers. *MITI and the Japanese Miracle*. Stanford: Stanford University Press, 1982.

Katzenstein, Peter J. *Small States in World Markets*. Ithaca: Cornell University Press, 1984.

Katzenstein, Peter J., ed. *Between Power and Plenty*. Madison: University of Wisconsin Press, 1978.

Krasner, Stephen. *Defending the National Interest*. Princeton: Princeton University Press, 1978.

Lowi, Theodore J. *The End of Liberalism*. 2nd ed. New York: W. W. Norton, 1979.

Pauly, Louis W. *Opening Financial Markets*. Ithaca: Cornell University Press, 1988.

Porter, Michael. *The Competitive Advantage of Nations*. New York: Free Press, 1990.

Samuels, Richard J. *The Business of the Japanese State*. Ithaca: Cornell University Press 1987.

Sobel, Andrew. *Domestic Choices, International Markets*. Ann Arbor: University of Michigan Press, 1994.

Steinmo, Sven, et al. *Structuring Politics*. Cambridge: Cambridge University Press, 1992.

Vogel, David. *National Styles of Regulation*. Ithaca: Cornell University Press, 1986.

Zysman, John. *Governments, Markets and Growth*. Ithaca: Cornell University Press, 1983.

On the comparative analysis of corporate governance and control:

Adams, Walter, ed. *The Structure of American Industry*. New York: Macmillan, 1982.

Aoki, Masahiko, and Hugh Patrick, eds. *The Japanese Main Bank System*. Oxford: Oxford University Press, 1994.

Berle, Adolph, and Gardiner Means. *The Modern Corporation and Private Property*. New York: Macmillan, 1932.

Calder, Kent. *Strategic Capitalism*. Princeton: Princeton University Press, 1993.

Edwards, Jeremy, and Klaus Fischer. *Banks, Finance, and Investments in Germany*. Cambridge: Cambridge University Press, 1994.

Encarnation, Dennis J. *Rivals Beyond Trade*. Ithaca: Cornell University Press, 1992.

Fukao, Mitsuhiro. *Financial Integration, Corporate Governance, and the Performance of Multinational Companies*. Washington: Brookings, 1995.

Gerlach, Michael. *Alliance Capitalism*. Berkeley: University of California Press, 1992.

Hart, Jeffrey A. *Rival Capitalists*. Ithaca: Cornell University Press, 1992.

Hubbard, R. Glenn, ed. *Asymmetric Information, Corporate Finance, and Investment*. Chicago: University of Chicago Press, 1990.

Jacobs, Michael T. *Short-Term America*. Boston: Harvard Business School Press, 1991.

Kester, Carl. *Japanese Takeovers*. Boston: Harvard Business School Press, 1991.

Orru, Marco, Gary Hamilton, and Mariko Suzuki. *Patterns of Inter-Firm Control in Japanese Business*. Papers in East Asian Business and Development, No. 7, Institute of Governmental Affairs, University of California, Davis, 1989.

Porter, Michael, et al. *Capital Choices*. A Report to the Council on Competitiveness and co-sponsored by the Harvard Business School, June 1992.

Roe, Mark J. *Strong Managers, Weak Owners*. Princeton: Princeton University Press, 1994.

Stokeman, Fruns N. et al., eds. *Networks of Corporate Power*. Cambridge: Polity, 1985.

Tilton, Mark. *Restrained Trade*. Ithaca: Cornell University Press, 1996.

Uriu, Robert M. *Troubled Industries*. Ithaca: Cornell University Press, 1996.

Waverman, Leonard, ed. *Competition Policy in the Global Economy*. London: Routledge, 1997.

Williamson, Oliver. *The Economic Institutions of Capitalism*. New York: Free Press, 1985.

On the political economy of the deepening interdependence, especially associated with foreign direct investment:

Amin, Ash, and Nigel Thrift, eds. *Globalization, Institutions, and Regional Development in Europe*. New York: Oxford University Press, 1994.

Barnet, Richard J., and John Cavanagh. *Global Dreams*. New York: Simon & Schuster, 1994.

Berger, Suzanne, and Ronald Dore, eds. *National Diversity and Global Capitalism*. Ithaca: Cornell University Press, 1996.

Bergsten, C. Fred, and Edward M. Graham. *The Globalization of Industry and National Governments*. Washington: Institute for International Economics, 1995.

Bergsten, C. Fred, and Marcus Noland. *Reconcilable Differences?* Washington: Institute for International Economics, 1993.

Block, Fred L. *The Origins of International Economic Disorder*. Berkeley: University of California Press, 1977.

Carnoy, Martin et al. *The New Global Economy in the Information Age*. University Park: Penn State Press, 1993.

Cooper, Richard N. *The Economics of Interdependence*. New York: McGraw Hill, 1968.

Cox, Robert. *Production, Power and World Order*. New York: Columbia University Press, 1987.

de Kerckhove, Derrick. *The Skin of Culture*. Toronto: Somerville House, 1995.

Graham, Edward M. *Global Corporations and National Governments*. Washington: Institute for International Economics, 1996.

Graham, Edward M., and Paul R. Krugman. *Foreign Direct Investment in the United States*. 3rd ed. Washington: Institute for International Economics, 1995.

Greider, William. *One World, Ready or Not*. New York: Simon & Schuster, 1996.

Hirst, Paul, and Grahame Thompson. *Globalization in Question*. Cambridge: Polity, 1996.

Holm, Hans-Henrik, and Georg Sorensen. *Whose World Order?* Boulder: Westview Press, 1995.

Jones, R. J. Barry. *Globalization and Interdependence in the International Political Economy*. London: Pinter, 1995.

Julius, DeAnne. *Global Companies and Public Policy*. London: Royal Institute of International Affairs, 1990.

Keller, William W. *Arm in Arm*. New York: Basic Books, 1995.

Keohane, Robert, and Joseph Nye. *Power and Interdependence*. Boston: Little, Brown, 1977.

Keohane, Robert, and Joseph Nye, eds. *Transnational Relations and World Politics*. Cambridge: Harvard University Press, 1972.

Korten, David. C. *When Corporations Rule the World*. West Hartford, Conn.: Kumarian Press, 1995.

Lane, Christel. *Industry and Society*. Aldershot: Edward Elgar, 1995.

Lawrence, Robert Z. *Regionalism, Multilateralism and Deeper Integration*. Washington: Brookings, 1996.

Lincoln, Edward. *Japan's Unequal Trade*. Washington: Brookings, 1990.

Markovits, Andrei S., and Simon Reich. *The German Predicament*. Ithaca: Cornell University Press, 1997.

Mason, Mark. *American Multinationals and Japan*. Cambridge: Council on East Asian Studies, Harvard University, 1992.

Mason, Mark, and Dennis Encarnation, eds. *Does Ownership Matter?* Oxford: Clarendon Press, 1994.

Milner, Helen. *Resisting Protectionism*. Princeton: Princeton University Press, 1988.

Milner, Helen, and Robert Keohane, eds. *Internationalization and Domestic Politics*. Cambridge: Cambridge University Press, 1996.

Ohmae, Kenichi. *The Borderless World*. New York: Harper, 1991.

Ostry, Sylvia. *Governments and Corporations in a Shrinking World*. New York: Council on Foreign Relations Press, 1990.

Oye, Kenneth A. *Economic Discrimination and Political Exchange*. Princeton: Princeton University Press, 1993.

Pauly, Louis W. *Who Elected the Bankers?* Ithaca: Cornell University Press, 1997.

Rodrik, Dani. *Has Globalization Gone Too Far?* Washington: Institute for International Economics, 1997.

Rogowski, Ronald. *Commerce and Coalitions*. Princeton: Princeton University Press, 1989.

Ruigrok, Winfried, and Rob van Tulder. *The Logic of International Restructuring*. London: Routledge, 1995.

Sally, Razeen. *States and Firms*. London: Routledge, 1995.

Servan-Schreiber, J. J. *Le Défi Americain (The American Challenge)*. Paris: Denoël, 1967.

Spar, Debora. *The Cooperative Edge*. Ithaca: Cornell University Press. 1994.

Strange, Susan. *The Retreat of the State*. Cambridge: Cambridge University Press, 1996.

Whitley, Richard and Peer Hull, eds. *The Changing European Firm*. London: Routledge, 1995.

Wriston, Walter. *The Twilight of Sovereignty*. New York: Scribner, 1992.

Yoffie, David, ed. *Beyond Free Trade*. Boston: Harvard Business School Press, 1993.

On the comparative analysis of national innovation systems:

Archibugi, Daniele, and Mario Pianta, *The Technological Specialization of Advanced Countries*. Boston: Kluwer and the Commission of the European Communities, 1992.

Bianci, P., and M. Quere, eds. *Interacting Systems of Innovation*. London: Kluwer, forthcoming.

Dosi, Giovanni et al. *Technical Change and Economic Theory*. London: Pinter, 1988.

Harris, M. C., and G. E. Moore, eds. *Linking Trade and Technology Policies*. Washington: National Academy Press, 1992.

Lee, T. H., and P. P. Reid, eds. *National Interests in an Age of Global Technology.* Washington: National Academy Press, 1991.

Lundvall, Bengt-Åke. *National Systems of Innovation.* New York: St. Martin's Press, 1992.

Mowery, David C. *Science and Technology Policy in Interdependent Economies.* Boston: Kluwer, 1994.

Mowery, David C., and N. Rosenberg. *Technology and the Pursuit of Economic Growth.* New York: Cambridge University Press, 1989.

Nelson, Richard, ed. *National Innovation Systems.* New York: Oxford University Press, 1993.

Samuels, Richard J. *"Rich Nation, Strong Army."* Ithaca: Cornell University Press, 1994.

On corporate technological alliances:

Bleeke, Joel, and David Ernst, eds. *Collaborating to Compete.* New York: Wiley, 1993.

Cowhey, Peter F., and Jonathan D. Aronson. *Managing the World Economy.* New York: Council on Foreign Relations, 1993.

James, Harvey S., and Murray Weidenbaum. *When Businesses Cross International Borders.* New York: Praeger, 1993.

Mytelka, Lynn K. *Strategic Partnerships and the World Economy.* London: Pinter, 1991.

Waverman, Leonard, ed. *Corporate Globalization through Mergers and Acquisitions.* Calgary: University of Calgary Press, 1991.

Yoshino, Michael Y., and U. Srinivasa Rangan. *Strategic Alliances.* Boston: Harvard Business School Press, 1995.

INDEX

About the Authors

PAUL N. DOREMUS is Senior Analyst (Technology Administration) in the U.S. Department of Commerce. William W. Keller is Executive Director, Center for International Studies, Massachusetts Institute of Technology. He is the author of *The Liberals and J. Edgar Hoover: Rise and Fall of a Domestic Intelligence State* (Princeton). Louis W. Pauly is Professor of Political Science and Director, Center for International Studies, University of Toronto. He is the author of *Who Elected the Bankers? Surveillance and Control in the World Economy*. Simon Reich is Professor of Public and International Affairs, University of Pittsburgh. He is co-author of *The German Predicament: Memory and Power in the New Europe*.